COMMUNICATING THE GOSPEL

CELEBRATING 40 YEARS OF WORLD COMMUNICATIONS DAY

1967–2006

The Church in every age continues the work begun on the day of Pentecost, when the Apostles, in the power of the Holy Spirit, went forth into the streets of Jerusalem to preach the Gospel of Jesus Christ in many tongues.
(Acts 2:5-11)

COMMUNICATING THE GOSPEL

CELEBRATING 40 YEARS OF WORLD COMMUNICATIONS DAY

1967–2006

VERITAS

Published 2006 by
Veritas Publications
7/8 Lower Abbey Street
Dublin 1
Ireland
Email publications@veritas.ie
Website www.veritas.ie

ISBN 1 85390 924 6
978 1 85390 924 5 (from January 2007)

A catalogue record for this book is available from the British Library.

Designed by Colette Dower
Printed in the Republic of Ireland by Betaprint, Dublin

Veritas books are printed on paper made from the wood pulp of managed forests. For every tree felled, at least one tree is planted, thereby renewing natural resources.

CONTENTS

FOREWORD

Most Rev. Seán Brady
Archbishop of Armagh and Primate of All Ireland

Go out to the whole world and proclaim the good news! This remains the fundamental mission of the Church. Whatever the age, whatever the historical situation, in season and out of season we are called to share our joy at having discovered the way, the truth and the life of Jesus Christ.

At the Second Vatican Council the means by which the Church communicated this joy and hope to the world was considered a question of fundamental importance. Alert to the first signs of a revolution in the means of social communication, the Fathers of the Council set about preparing the Church for the challenges and opportunities that would accompany the emerging technologies of the new millennium. The speed of change in these technologies as well as their global character meant that any reflection on the Church's relationship with the means of social communication would have to be frequent and well informed. The initiation of a World Day for Communications by Pope Paul VI provided the ideal axis for such a reflection.

Some forty years later, this publication of the complete set of the messages issued on World Communications Day, is a powerful tribute to the foresight of Pope Paul VI and those who participated in the Council. Even the most cursory glance at the content of the Messages gives a sense of the rapid progress in technology which has taken place over those forty years as well as the many dramatic and historic events which dominated our newspapers and television screens. Indeed a consistent feature of these annual messages is that, true to the spirit of the Council, their reflection on the interaction between the Church and the means of social communication is set within the concrete reality of the 'joy and hope, the grief and anguish' of the people of our time.

At the beginning of a new millennium, it is this interface between social communications and the human search for meaning which continues to guide the Church's reflection on the role of modern communications media. In his first message for World Communications Day, Pope Benedict speaks of 'the idea of the media as a network facilitating communication, communion and cooperation.' (*Message for the 40th World Communications Day*, #1). Only weeks before his death, Pope John Paul II had spoken of the 'enormous potential' of the media 'for promoting peace and building bridges between peoples' and its 'unprecedented possibilities for good' (*Message for the 39th World Communications Day*, #2). What is clear is that the means of social communication will continue to provide both possibilities and challenges for the proclamation of the Gospel in the modern world.

In commending these texts to the reader, in celebration of forty years of World Communications Day, my hope is that they will continue to offer inspiration to all those who wish to see the means of social communication 'become influential and appreciated resources for building the civilisation of love for which all peoples yearn' (Pope Benedict XVI, *Message for the 40th World Communications Day*, #4).

I also thank Brenda Drumm of the Catholic Communications Office and Veritas Publications for marking the fortieth anniversary of World Communications Day with such a useful and inspiring resource.

✠ Seán Brady
Archbishop of Armagh
and Primate of All Ireland

INTRODUCTION

Brenda Drumm
Communications Officer, Catholic Communications Office

'At the dawn of a new era, a vast expansion of human communications is profoundly influencing culture everywhere. Revolutionary technological changes are only part of what is happening. Nowhere today are people untouched by the impact of media upon religious and moral attitudes, political and social systems, and education.'

The above is the opening paragraph of the Pastoral Instruction *Aetatis novae*, published by the Pontifical Council for Social Communications on 23 February 1992.

That document goes on to say that 'the first Aeropagus of the modern age is the world of communications which is unifying humanity and turning it into what is known as a "global village". The means of social communications have become so important as to be for many the chief means of information and education, of guidance and inspiration in their behaviour as individuals, families and within society at large'.

World Communications Day is the only worldwide celebration called for by the Second Vatican Council. It is marked in most countries on the recommendation of the bishops of the world on the Sunday before Pentecost. World Communications Day 2006 was celebrated on Sunday 28 May and marked the 40th anniversary of the initiative and the first World Communications Day Message from Pope Benedict XVI, on the theme: 'The Communications Media: At the Service of Understanding Among Peoples.'

In the very first message for World Communications, which was celebrated in 1957, Pope Paul VI said: 'The Church wishes to draw the attention of her children and of all people of good will to the vast and complex phenomenon of the modern means of social communications, such as the press, motion pictures, radio and television, which form one of the most characteristic notes of modern civilisation.'

The themes chosen for the messages issued each year for World Communications Day since that first message in 1957 reflect the changes and the rapid development that have taken place in the area of social communications over the past forty years, but particularly since the dawn of the 'computer age', e.g. 1990 – 'The Christian Message in a Computer Culture'; 2001 – 'Preach from the Housetops: The Gospel in the Age of Global Communications'; 2002 – 'Internet: A New Forum for Proclaiming the Gospel'.

To mark forty years of the celebration of World Communications Day, we have brought together in one volume all the messages for World Communications Day and some of the key church documents that have been issued on social communications, from *Inter mirifica* issued in 1963 to *The Rapid Development* issued by Pope John Paul II in 2005.

As we celebrate forty years of world communications day we are reminded of the ever-present challenge for the church in a rapidly developing media age to ensure that the face of Christ continues to be seen and the voice of Christ continues to be heard.

What I tell you in the dark, utter in the light
and what you hear whispered, proclaim from the housetops.
(Mt 10:27)

Brenda Drumm
Communications Officer
Catholic Communications Office

OVERVIEW

Pope Paul VI issued the World Communications Day Messages from 1967 to 1978

MESSAGES OF THE HOLY FATHER PAUL VI FOR WORLD COMMUNICATIONS DAY 1967–1978

MESSAGE OF THE HOLY FATHER PAUL VI FOR THE 1ST WORLD COMMUNICATIONS DAY

Sunday 7 May 1967

Church and Social Communication

We address you, dear brothers and sons, as World Communications Day, which will be held for the first time on Sunday, seventh of May, approaches.

The Church, realising 'that she is truly and intimately linked with mankind and its history',[1] wishes by means of this initiative, proposed by the Second Vatican Ecumenical Council, to draw the attention of her children and of all men of good will to the vast and complex phenomenon of the modern means of social communication, such as the press, motion pictures, radio and television, which form one of the most characteristic notes of modern civilization.

Thanks to these wonderful techniques, man's social life has taken on new dimensions: time and space have been conquered, and man has become as it were a citizen of the world, sharing in and witnessing the most remote events and the vicissitudes of the whole human race. As the Council has said, 'we can already speak of a true social and cultural transformation, one which has repercussions on man's religious life as well'.[2] To this transformation the means of social communication have greatly contributed, at times in a decisive manner, we are even now nearing new, amazing developments, such as that of world-wide television through artificial satellites. In all this we see the unfolding and the realisation of a wonderful plan of God's providence, which opens to man's genius ever new ways of achieving his perfection and of attaining to his final end.

One must, therefore, give full credit, at its true worth, to the contribution made by the press, motions pictures, radio and television as well as the other instruments of social communication, to the enrichment of culture, to the spread of various artistic forms, to recreation, to mutual knowledge and understanding among peoples and also towards the spread of the Gospel message.

However, while the magnitude of this phenomenon, which now embraces both individuals and the whole community of man, is reason for admiration and satisfaction, it also gives cause for reflection and concern. These instruments, as it happens, destined as they are by their very nature to spread thought, human expression, the image, information and publicity, not only act on public opinion and, consequently, on the modes of thought and action of individuals and social groups, but also bring pressure to bear upon minds, leaving their deep mark upon the mentality and the conscience of man who is being pressed and almost overpowered by a multiplicity of contradictory appeals.

One cannot ignore the danger and the damage which these means, however noble in themselves, can inflict upon individuals and society when they are not employed by man with a sense of responsibility, with an honest intent and in conformity with the objective moral order.

The greater, in fact, the power and the ambivalent efficacy of these means, the greater must be the care and the responsibility with which they are to be employed.

It is therefore with sentiments of esteem and friendship and the certainty that we are interpreting the expectations and anxieties of honest men everywhere, that we address all who are devoting their ability and their work to this sensitive and important sector of modern life. We entertain the hope that the noble service, which they are called upon to render to their brothers, may always measure up to the nobility of the mission which makes them intermediaries and, as it were, masters and guides, between the truth and the public, the reality of the exterior world and the inner reaches of conscience.

Just as they have the right not to be conditioned by undue ideological, political and economic pressures, which limit their just and responsible freedom of expression, so their speaking to the public demands a respect for the dignity of man and of society. Let every effort of theirs be directed towards spreading truth in men's minds, loyalty to what is good in their hearts and consistency in their actions. Thus they will contribute towards the uplift of humanity and will play a constructive part in the building of a new society that will be freer, more alert, more responsible, more brotherly and more noble.[3]

We have particularly in mind the younger generations. Not without difficulties and at times apparent or real lapses, these are seeking to give direction to their present and future lives. They must be able to make their choices in freedom of spirit and with a sense of responsibility. Hindering or leading astray with false perspectives their strenuous efforts would mean deceiving their just expectations, confusing their noble aspirations and killing their generous impulses.

With a fatherly heart we renew our pressing plea to the worthy members of the professional world of social communications, particularly to those among them who glory in the name of Christians, asking them to bear 'witness in the cause of the "World", that in all its temporal expressions must be a faithful echo of the eternal, uncreated Word, the Word of the Father, the Light of intellects, the Truth that so ennobles us'.[4]

It is necessary, however, that the efforts of the workers in the field of social communications be seconded by the united cooperation of all, for it is the responsibility of all that is put to the test: that of parents who are the first, irreplaceable educators of their children; that of teachers whose task it is to instruct their pupils in the knowledge and understanding of the language of modern techniques, showing them how to appreciate what is put forward, how to use these means sensibly with moderation and self-discipline. The responsibility of young people is brought into play, for they are called upon in a high degree to exploit these instruments in their own personal education as well as in the promotion of brotherhood and peace among men. The public authorities too exercise their responsibility in the furtherance and the defence of the common good with due respect for true liberty. Finally, this is the concern of all readers, spectators and hearers as they are called upon to choose carefully and wisely their daily newspapers and their periodicals, their motion pictures and their broadcasts; they are to help render communication nobler and higher, more worthy, that is, of responsible and mature human beings.

Most helpful and laudable is, therefore, every serious initiative that aims at forming the critical judgement of the reader and spectator, and at inducing him to evaluate the news, the ideas and the images that are presented to him, not only under the aesthetical and technical aspects, but also from the human, moral and religious point of view, bearing in mind the highest values of life.

The Church too wishes to make her own contribution to the orderly development of the world of social communications: a contribution of inspiration, encouragement, exhortation, guidance and cooperation.

Precisely for this reason the Second Vatican Ecumenical Council has made this a subject of study: the Conciliar Decree on the Instruments of Social Communication and the corresponding Pastoral Instruction, which is now being prepared, bear witness to the Church's motherly interest in the furtherance of human values which Christianity, as it embraces them wholeheartedly, renders more vital and nobler, Christianity directs them towards the supreme end of man, bringing it about that real, fruitful moral and spiritual progress go hand in hand with remarkable technical advance.

We therefore express the hope that this day may prove an occasion for a considered appeal aimed at an awakening of consciences and a united endeavour on the part of all in such an important cause. We exhort our sons and daughters to undertake generous action, in prayerful unity of intent with their pastors and with all who are willing to give their welcome cooperation, in order that, with God's help and the intercession of the Blessed Virgin, they might attain those results that the celebration of World Communications Day aims at achieving for the good of mankind.

These are the dearest hopes that we wish to manifest on the eve of the first World Communications Day, while we pray from our heart for abundant divine blessings on all who are listening to us, and on all who employ in this field their technical skill, their intellectual inspirations and their spiritual yearnings.

From the Vatican, 7 May 1967

PAULUS PP. VI

Notes

1. Constitutio Pastoralis de Ecclesia in mindo huius temporis prooemium.
2. Ibid, Expositio introductiva.
3. cfr. Pius XII, Discourse to the European Union Radiodiffusion; Discorsi e Radiomessaggi, vol. 17, p. 327.
4. cfr. Discourse to the National Council of the Italian Federation of the press; Oss. Rom. 24 June 1966.

MESSAGE OF THE HOLY FATHER PAUL VI FOR THE 2ND WORLD COMMUNICATIONS DAY

Sunday 26 May 1968

Social Communications and the Development of Nations

We would like to invite you all, our beloved sons and brothers, as well as all men of good will, to celebrate with us the day specially dedicated to the means of social communication. We wish to help you to consider the significance of the changes that are taking place in this field under our very eyes and to ponder the serious responsibilities that these imply for one and all.

Until recently, many did not have anything more to stimulate their reflection than vague memories of what they learned at school or in the family and what they heard in their environment. Now however, with the echos of the press, motion pictures, radio and television clamouring for attention, new horizons open wide before them and they are attuned to the throbbing life of the universe. Who will not rejoice at this progress? Do we not all see in it a road destined by providence for the advance of the whole of mankind? There is room for all hopes if man learns to master these techniques; but everything can be lost if he shirks his responsibilities.

Will the press, motion pictures, radio and television in actual fact help the development of nations? That is the question we earnestly put to you all, our Catholic sons and daughters and, no less, every human being. To begin with, what kind of progress do we have in mind? Is it economic progress? Yes, surely. Do we mean social progress? That too, undoubtedly. We have said as much in our encyclical letter *Populorum progressio*; but, as we also stress untiringly, 'progress, in order that it might be authentic, must be all-embracing, advancing all men and the whole of man' (no. 14). He will not truly feel at home with this fresh vision of the universe provided by the means of social communication, nor profit by it, unless it helps him to appreciate in their true light – without pride or awkwardness – the values as well as the shortcomings of his own way of life. This vision must also help him to discover – without complacency or bitterness – the worth of other civilizations. It will help him to take his destiny personally in hand and to achieve it in fraternal cooperation with his brethren. Lastly, it will help him to understand that there is 'no true humanism that is not open to the Absolute' (Ibid., no. 42).

Does the flood of words, of articles and of images that is poured out each day over the world favour this awareness and this broad outlook? This is a problem that we would like to put before all communicators through the press, the radio, the cinema and television, who desire to work generously in the service of their fellow men.

It is dangerous to foster in a people a spirit of self-sufficiency and narrow nationalism. On the other hand, no less is it important to aid a country to discover with legitimate pride the material, intellectual and spiritual talents with which it has been endowed by the Creator that it might bring these to full fruition for the good of the entire community of nations.

It is a mistake to foster constant dissensions and a spirit of corrosive and destructive criticism, or to nourish the illusion that violent revolution would be the universal cure for all ills and injustices. Equally is it important to enlighten responsible people about intolerable situations, to denounce crying abuses and to persuade opinion in favour of 'bold changes, radical renewals and urgent reforms that are to be undertaken without delay'.

In a world where so many people lack what is necessary – bread, knowledge and spiritual light – it would be a serious fault to use the means of social communication to encourage personal and collective selfishness, to create new and unreal needs among consumers who are already fully satisfied and tickle the taste for pleasures by multiplying empty and enervating amusements. Once this temptation is overcome, a great enterprise lies before them: they can do so much to voice the appeals of a humanity in distress, to put in bold relief the efforts at cooperation, the initiatives and strivings for peace, so as to awaken a healthy and helpful rivalry. Who does not see in this dramatic challenge that faces our world the importance of the means of social communication in encouraging 'true development which is the transition for one and all, from inhuman conditions to more human' (Ibid., no. 20)?

Christians will not forget on their part that this brotherhood that unites them to the rest of mankind has its roots in a shared divine sonship. The beginning and end of all supreme values, the living God, is also their guarantee. We ask all, our Catholic sons in particular, to leave no stone unturned in order that the means of social communication, in the midst of a world that seeks, as it were in darkness, the light that can save it, might proclaim from the roof-tops (Matt 10:27) the message of Christ, the Saviour, who is 'the Way, the Truth and the Life' (Jn 14:6).

In this way they will make their indispensable contribution to this progress of peoples that we, together with all men of good will, wish with all our heart and for which we intend to strive with all our forces. 'The future is there, in the insistent cry of peoples for greater justice, in their striving for peace, in their thirst, conscious 'or but vaguely perceived, for a nobler life, precisely that life which Christ's Church is able and willing to give' (Introduction to the Council's *Message to the World*, December 1965).

It is this future that we invite you to build generously. It is with these sentiments that we impart to you our heartfelt blessing.

From the Vatican, 26 March 1968

PAULUS PP. VI

MESSAGE OF THE HOLY FATHER PAUL VI FOR THE 3RD WORLD COMMUNICATIONS DAY

Sunday 18 May 1969

Social Communications and the Family

Beloved sons and daughters
and men of good will everywhere

The observation of the third annual 'World Communications Day' with the theme 'Social Communications and the Family' affords us an opportunity which we accept with pleasure, as we have done on previous similar occasions, of inviting all those who are interested to a positive and fruitful meditation on this subject. Indeed, who can claim today not to be affected by a phenomenon of such world-wide proportions as the ever growing expansion of the press, radio, motion pictures and television, or by their immense influence on families?

One obvious consideration comes at once to mind: the instruments of social communication have now penetrated into the very heart of the family circle. They influence people's timetables. They change established habits. They form the subject of conversation and stimulate discussions. Above all, these instruments have an impact on the psychology of those who use them. This impact, at times truly profound, is exercised over the emotions and the intellect. It extends to the moral, as well as the religious spheres. There is hardly a news item or matter of discussion, one may almost say, that is not brought within the family circle by means of the printed page, or an audiovisual means, so that it can influence the conduct of one and all, awakening the most diverse reactions.

The advantages of this new situation are undeniable. There is no doubt that the intellectual development of young people is hastened. Their cultural heritage is enriched. Their hearts and spirits are more easily alerted to the great problems of the human community, such as peace, justice and development. It is also clear, however, that the persuasive force of these new means can be utilised for good or for evil. Moreover, an abuse, even be it only quantitative, of audio-visual programmes can bring with it a deterioration of the values of family life; as a result it may well set people apart, instead of bringing them together. It is necessary then to form consciences, to use intelligently these sources of cultural enrichment. This is a new chapter added to the traditional duties of educators. It is time that the family undertake its *aggiornamento* in this area, so that with the indispensable cooperation of the school the family may progressively take care to train consciences to come of their own accord to calm and objective judgements, leading them to accept or reject the various programmes that are offered to them.

The work of education, however, does not stop here. It is necessary that a dialogue be established between the families and those who are responsible for social communications. The families are called upon not simply to make known their wishes and criticisms, but also to show understanding for those who, often at the price of strenuous effort, provide them day by day with so many elements for their culture and entertainment.

The communicators must, in their turn, know and respect the needs of the family. This presupposes at times much courage on their part and always a high sense of responsibility. It means in practice that they should exclude on the one side all that can damage the family in its existence, its stability, its order and its happiness, for every attack on the true fundamental values of the family – whether it be eroticism or violence, the defence of divorce or antisocial attitudes among young people – is an attack on genuine human welfare and the good of society. On the other hand, communicators have the difficult task of educating the public to know, appreciate and love values that are often unknown or despised but which are the strength and the glory of a given society: such as, the dedication of one's self to a great ideal, the sense of sacrifice and the hidden heroism of daily routine.

We invite all families to collaborate with those associations which by constant contact make known their yearnings and just requests to those responsible for social communications. May this World Communications Day mark the beginning of a genuinely fruitful and constructive dialogue, heralding a more tranquil future in this troubled area of modern living.

The question of the presence of Christians in the professional world of social communications now calls for close consideration. If there is a sector of present-day life where this presence is especially necessary and desirable, it is surely that of social communications. Families should not be deterred by any misgiving they might have when one of their members wishes to embark on such a career. Evil that is much more publicised than good is not bound up with one particular profession more than with another. Thank God, in the world of social communications, no less than in others, there are shining examples of moral living both in professional and in family life. There are those in the world of journalism, the theatre and the field of motion pictures who live out their faith in God in the calm and conscientious exercise of their profession. The very history of Christianity teaches us that the force of evangelical leaven increases rather than diminishes in proportion to the difficulties caused by one's environment. The evangelical leaven gathers force by vivifying and transforming an environment. Young people who have received a solid moral and religious formation and who are inspired by a genuine ideal are, therefore, to be encouraged to engage in the different activities of social communication.

A realistic appraisal of the situation leads one to see that the influence of these techniques, far from being lessened, will be on the increase in the society of the future. Nothing should be left undone in order for this influence to have a positive effect on every family.

We hope that our voice on the occasion of this World Communications Day will be heard in every country to encourage good production in the field of social communications; to enhearten those who employ these means in the service of family life and thus contribute towards a happy future for the great family of mankind.

From the Vatican, 7 April 1969

PAULUS PP. VI

MESSAGE OF THE HOLY FATHER PAUL VI FOR THE 4TH WORLD COMMUNICATIONS DAY

Sunday 10 May 1970

Social Communications and Youth

My dear sons and daughters
Men of good-will everywhere
and young people, you, in particular

The theme of World Communications Day this year touches what I am sure is one of your chief interests: 'Social Communications and Youth'. Undoubtedly, it is clear to everyone that there is an immense responsibility on the part of all, before history and God himself, to put to good account the extraordinary opportunities offered by the communications media to help young people to inform and form themselves, to bring out the real problems of the world, to seek the authentic values of life and to live up to their calling as individual persons and Christians.

It is, indeed, a burning issue for all men of good will, for private organisations both national and international, for the Church no less; all are to ask themselves: what are the young people of tomorrow going to be like as they grow up in the world being constructed today? And you, young people, what kind of society will you yourselves construct when the destiny of the world will have passed into your own hands?

Dear sons and daughters, in the full consciousness of our pastoral responsibility, we wish to say to you all: tomorrow will be precisely what we shall have made it with the grace of God.

Need we call to mind once again, now that the phenomenon is assuming ever larger proportions, that the press, motion pictures, radio and television are tending to hide, perhaps even supplant, what the traditional vehicles of culture, that is, contacts at home, at school and in the parish, as well as the teaching of educators, used to allow past generations to hand down to their heirs. These days it is the media of social communications that provide new sources of knowledge and culture, with their considerable power of moving men's feelings and minds, together with the train of ideas and stirrings of the imagination carried by the sounds and sights they transmit.

Truly they are wonderful means for broadening one's outlook, establishing contacts, communicating and sharing. Obviously however, only as long as they remain in actual fact means to an end, the one end worthy of the name: the service of the whole of mankind and of the whole man (cf. *Populorum progressio*, no. 14). Unfortunately, all too often the contrary is the case. We witness young people and children, used as easily-secured consumers by an industry that makes itself its own end, being dragged into the pit-falls of eroticism and violence or led along the perilous paths of incertitude, anxiety and anguish. It is not asking too much that all right thinking persons should unite at last to sound a cry of alarm and to put an end to enterprises that deserve to be called corrupting.

Who is unaware of the urgency of putting to good account the means of social communication with their stirring mode of address through sound, image, colour and movement, to make of them real modern instruments for communing among men, that measure up to the expectations of young people? What excellent fare they can provide, so long as it is wholesome and the organism prepared to receive it and assimilate it without being intoxicated! Undoubtedly, they have a great deal to offer to youth: choice of recreation, a wealth of information, for some the beginnings of an education before they can even read or write. We wish to stress this during this 'World Year of Education' promoted by the United Nations at the opening of the second decade of development. The communications media are capable of providing youth with access to a culture of quality as well as a taste for the authentic values of brotherhood, peace, justice and general welfare.

This is an enormous task, a truly glorious enterprise, for all who set in motion these exceptionally powerful instruments for the service of youth. All this, however, will not take us far unless parents and educators play their part in helping young people to choose, to judge and to assimilate what is presented to them, so that they too can become complete human persons and Christians. Not much can be achieved if the young people themselves remain passive as though under the spell of these powerful attractions, held captive by desire and incapable of self-control.

Finally, we ask ourselves: who is it that can bring to youth this message of true life, the sincere and courageous word that they consciously unconsciously seek? Millions of men have shared the same thrill before the images brought to them of man's first steps on the moon. Who is it that can bring them to experience together the same deep emotion before the God of love who came down to walk on our earth as a man, 'to call us all to participate as sons in the life of the Living God, Father of all men'? (cf. *Populorum progressio*, no. 21)

We lend our words of warm encouragement to the numerous pastors of souls, priests, religious and lay people who, with true zeal, endeavour to seek through the communications media a new language and find it they must, to announce to the young the good news that always remains astounding. No one will doubt that the young people of today really await this announcement. They yearn for this witness. They too know how to recognise, with profound joy, he who is the answer to their most radical and disquiting questionings, who 'for us has become wisdom, justice, sanctification and redemption' (1 Cor 1:30).

'Young people, seek Christ, in order to remain young' (St Augustine, *Ad fratres in eremo*, Sermon 44): this is our hope, this is our prayer.

With the earnest wish that parents, educators and all communicators through the media will make the best of the opportunity offered by the World Day specially dedicated to them, for beneficial reflection and fruitful resolutions for the greater advantage of youth, we address to all our affectionate and confident apostolic blessing.

From the Vatican, 6 April 1970

PAULUS PP. VI

MESSAGE OF THE HOLY FATHER PAUL VI FOR THE 5TH WORLD COMMUNICATIONS DAY

Sunday 23 May 1971

The Role of Communications Media in Promoting Unity among Men

Dear brothers and sons
and all men of good will

'The means of social communication at the service of the unity of mankind': such is the goal which the World Day of Social Communications proposes this year for your reflection, for your study, for your discussions, for your prayer and for your activity.

Who would not wish with all his heart to see the unity of the human family promoted more effectively? Have not men become aware of the solidarity that unites them in daily life as well as in exceptional moments, in the face of scientific achievements as well as in the face of world calamities. In every way, men seem determined to widen continuously the spheres where fruitful and peaceful collaboration is established at the various levels of economic, social, cultural and political life, without, for all that, losing the richness of so many multiform characteristics. Would it be utopian to imagine a universal human family in which all men would be fraternal citizens? (cf. *Populorum progressio*, no. 79)

In any case, the conviction of Christians is well assured: 'God ... has willed that all men should constitute one family and treat one another in a spirit of brotherhood. All men have been created in the image of God ... and all men are called to one and the same goal, namely, God himself.' (*Gaudium et spes*, no. 34, p. 1)

Desire for Unity

Solidarity in the vocation of the first Adam, as well as in his sin, is henceforth lived and intensified in Christ: by his cross he has broken down the wall that divided the people, reconciling them to God (c Eph 12:14), and by his resurrection he has diffused his spirit of charity into the hearts of men, these scattered children of God whom he has called to form in him one people, one single body. While the Church too experiences tensions and even divisions within her bosom, she will not rest until she realises this unity in a visible way among her children of every language and nation, in all social and professional environments. This being so, the Church is conscious of being a prophetic sign of unity and peace for the entire world (cf. Is 11:12).

Given the fact that the means of social communication have taken of such importance that they are used almost universally in modern culture, the question now arises: will the means of social communication become the privileged means of promoting this unity and brotherhood, that is to say, this mutual respect, this open dialogue and this trustful collaboration in a world where problems are becoming planetary?

Existing Tensions

We would gravely delude ourselves were we to underestimate the power of the tragic tensions that exist in the social environments, between societies and persons, between industrialised nations and nations of the third world, between adherents of ideological or political systems that are antagonistic. Conflicts which often provoke increasing repercussions all over the world continue to create dangerous rifts and translate themselves, alas, into acts of violence and warlike situations. In the face of these manifestations of tensions and discords among men and nations, we certainly cannot expect the press, the radio, the television and the cinema to minimise them or pass over them in silence. Is not their role quite the contrary, that is, to bring out all the aspects of a reality, even the most tragic ones, to approach them in an ever more profound and objective way, of a reality where misery unfortunately exists and the sin of selfishness spreads, in short, the multiple wounds that bleed in the heart of the great human family, but also of a reality where positive accomplishments appear, the signs of renewal and the reasons for hope?

Courageous Confrontation

Who would say that one is not tempted to use these powerful audiovisual means, with their profound impact, in order to aggravate tensions, discords and division, pushing them to their extreme consequences, going so far as to discourage many men of good will in their imperfect but generous attempts to promote unity and brotherhood? We must denounce this risk with force and confront it with courage. On the other hand, must we not admit that the immense possibilities of the marvellous means of social communication, still insufficiently explored, help readers, listeners and viewers become aware of the real problems of others, help men know each other better and appreciate each other more in their legitimate differences, overcome obstacles of all kinds in a spirit of understanding and love, better still, experience true solidarity in spite of so many obstacles, a solidarity that unites us one with the other and one for the other in seeking the common good of the great community of men? (cf. Allocution to the General Assembly of the UNO in New York, 4 October 1965, in *A.A.S.*, 57, 1965, pp. 879–884). The very future of man is at stake, man, 'to whom all things on earth should be related as their centre and crown' (cf. *Gaudium et spes*, no. 12).

Reflect and Pray

Artisans and beneficiaries of the means of social communication, unite your efforts that this may be so everywhere throughout the world and at all levels of participation and responsibility. Reject whatever disrupts true dialogue among men, whatever masks duties of rights of men, whatever fans misunderstandings and hatred, whatever diverts from peace and ever widening brotherhood and whatever hinders us from seeking truth in liberty. Finally, is not the following question posed to each one of us: what are you seeking? what do you want? do you wish to be a brother to your brother, yes or no? For if communication is not by itself already a communion, then it can be its privileged road.

As for you, Christian brothers and sons, we ask you especially to reflect and to pray. We also ask you to use all the means your competence and zeal suggest with boldness, discretion and courage, so that from so many threads interwoven and frequently enmeshed you may draw out the fabric and weave a world of brothers and sons of God.

'Overcoming all the destructive forces of contestation and confused talk, it is the city of men which must be built up, a city of which the sole durable cement is fraternal love between races and peoples as well as between classes and generations' (Discourse to the General Conference of the ILO, Geneva, 10 June 1969, no. 21, in *A.A.S.*, 61, 1969, p. 500).

To all those who work through means of social communication to realise this aspiration of men according to the plan of God, we impart whole heartedly our particular apostolic blessing.

From the Vatican, 25 March 1971

PAULUS PP. VI

MESSAGE OF THE HOLY FATHER PAUL VI FOR THE 6TH WORLD COMMUNICATIONS DAY

Sunday 14 May 1972

The Media of Social Communications at the Service of Truth

Venerable brothers
Beloved sons and daughters throughout the world
and men of good will everywhere

Modern man will readily agree that many of his attitudes, judgements and stances on various questions, as well as his allegiances and antagonisms, are heavily influenced and to quite a large extent even shaped by his exposure to ideas and suggestions constantly fed to him by the mass media.

In our times, both youth and adult stand in the path of a virtually ceaseless flood: of news and interpretation of the news, of image and sound, of proposal and stimulant, of suggestion, invitation and allurement. And in this kind of world a rational being will at one time or another find himself facing the disturbing question – how does one recognise the truth? How is one to isolate it, to sort it out, from this tangle of affirmation and contradiction?

1. Every fact has its own truth, but even a straight and simple fact can have many angles, so it is not always easy to grasp the truth of it in its entirety. But that is not to say that it is impossible; far from it. Given the combined diligence and the combined sincerity of the person who communicates the fact and the person to whom it is communicated, there is a very good guarantee that 'the truth, the whole truth and nothing but the truth' will be safely transmitted.

Sincerity and diligence: a little reflection on the words will reveal what a supremely honourable, what a thoroughly excellent service the truly conscientious communicator gives to mankind and to truth, whether he be reporter, editor, information officer or broadcaster. Giving information implies a great deal more than observing and reporting a passing incident. The reporter relates the incident to the context in which it happens. He searches for the causes. He examines the surrounding circumstances, tries to assess the possible effects of this happening.

The work which he does might, in a way, be compared to a piece of 'scientific research', for he must observe the facts carefully, he must check their accuracy, make a critical evaluation of the sources of his information and, finally, pass on his findings, all the time taking due care that nothing essential is overlooked or suppressed.

The burden of responsibility on the reporter is all the heavier when, as often happens, he is called upon not only to give the simple facts of a case but also to explain its implications with comment, assessment or forecast.

2. Where there is question of giving information of a religious character, or of reporting on matters which must be evaluated on religious grounds, the communicator's duty is all the more onerous, though the dignity of his labour is at the same time immeasurably enhanced.

A religious event cannot be adequately understood as long as it is considered in its merely human implications, whether psychological or sociological. For here we have something which bears on the spiritual, which touches on the relationship between man and God. The communicator is therefore faced with the task of attempting to estimate how this relationship is affected by the event which he reports, where it fits into the mystery of salvation. A daunting task indeed, but one which again highlights the nobility of his profession and underlines the truly apostolic dimension in his working day.

The task demands, of course, that he must grasp as far as possible the precisely 'religious' truth of particular happenings. He can hope to grasp it fully only on condition that he takes account of the spiritual context of the events in question and of the whole divine plan to which they must be related. This requires something beyond mere professional competence. It requires the illumination of faith which alone can offer, at least in some circumstances, a full understanding.

3. A similar respect for the truth, a corresponding diligence in the search for it, is demanded of those who have recourse to the mass media for their information. They too have need to pursue the search for truth actively and responsibly. Their consciousness of this responsibility should protect them from a merely passive and uncritical acceptance of whatever happens to be offered to them by the media.

Man, and certainly Christian man, ought never abdicate his right to make his personal contribution to the search for truth, much less allow his capacity for the search to atrophy from disuse. (We speak here not only of abstract and philosophical truth, but also of the workaday truth of concrete daily happenings.) Were he to do so he would offer an affront to his own personal dignity.

We should like therefore on the present occasion to renew our invitation to every man to exert himself in this respect; to urge an active acceptance of the consequences which follow from the possession of human dignity and human intelligence; from the gift of an independent personal judgement with the capacity to make its own decisions. Let him meet the assault of the mass media in this state of mind. Using his own judgement, exercising his right to choose, he will freely select from the many opinions presented to him only such as truly merit his assent.

4. Most people are now in daily contact with mass media in one form or another – press, radio, television, theatre, cinema or recordings. They depend on the mass media to an increasing extent for news, comment and information, but even more perhaps for entertainment and cultural enrichment. In their enjoyment of a well-produced programme, they become wrapped up in the plot as it unfolds, identifying with the various characters, involving themselves closely in the real or imaginary situations proposed to their fancy by appropriate artistic techniques. And they are inevitably exposed to the whole range of values, attitudes, sentiments and opinions implied or explicit in the presentation.

We do not intend to suggest that there is anything necessarily deplorable in this. Even fictional publications or shows aimed at giving relaxation and entertainment can help to a better understanding of our fellowmen and of the world in which we live. But it is surely evident that it would be an unhealthy thing if the listener, or reader, or viewer, were to allow his critical faculty to be lulled to sleep. The truth remains a vitally important thing, even in a recreational context, and he must remain sufficiently alert to recognise any deviation from the truth in what he reads, hears or sees.

On the other hand, due acceptance must be given to the concept of artistic freedom. To give graphic and dramatic expression to the finer things of life, to give 'life' to his creation, the artist is certainly entitled to draw on the resources of imagination. But fanciful creations, while not expected to portray concrete reality, must not, at the same time, deny this reality. Even they have an obligation of fidelity to the truth and to the values inseparable from it. True art, in fact, is one of the noblest human expressions of truth. Therefore, to give a real service to man and to be a true follower of the truth, the artist must help man in his search for truth and in his firm adhesion to it. And this will obviously exclude any exploitation – for quick profits or other unworthy ends – of either the ignorance or the human weaknesses of audiences.

5. We cannot conclude this message, beloved brothers and children of the modern world, without pointing to a yet higher way to truth, the highest truth. We are Christians, followers of Christ who is 'the way, the truth and the life' (Jn 14:6) for all men, even for those who do not know him yet.

He is the Son of God, come among men 'to give testimony to the truth' (Jn 18:37) and to assure us that only the truth can make us free (Jn 8:31-36), liberating us from all slavery (Gal 5:1).

We Christians want to be in the midst of the world, involved in the human reality of every day, giving witness, humbly but with conviction, to the truth in which we believe.

The modern instruments of social communication are the great new means available to Christians by which they may fulfil their obligation of witnessing to and serving the truth.

These instruments are especially suitable for the expression and diffusion of the word – and we have a supremely important word to say and to entrust to their powerful voice. It is the word that God speaks of himself, the absolute and definitive word that he speaks over man, continuing his saving work through the myriad events in the chronicle of each day and in the history of the ages.

We Christians know that the events which make the fabric of our personal daily lives and of the life of the world we live in are no mere accidents resulting from the whimsy of a blind destiny. They are warp and woof of a mysterious design born in the mind of the supreme artist and architect. It is not yet permitted to us to see the full glory of the tapestry, but we know that every event threaded into its pattern is God reaching out to us, touching us, inviting us into his saving company. He is urging us to a joyous acceptance of all these events and to a loving surrender to his will.

This profound vision of things is the unassailable truth, the truth of which we wish to be the followers and the witnesses – whether as communicators or as 'receivers' – and by which we will arrive, little by little, at the freedom we seek: freedom from slavery either to human passion or intellectual prejudice; freedom from fear of failure and defeat; freedom from the dominance of power structures or pressure groups striving to impose on us their interpretations of life and events with little concern for what is true; freedom, finally, from that type of opportunism which will deliberately mask or confuse the truth to avoid a personal embarrassment, to cloak something disgraceful, or to make a financial gain.

6. Brothers and beloved children, we entrust you with these considerations about the truth which ought to govern, by common consent, the use we make of the modern instruments of social communication. God, the supreme truth, is also the source of the truth of all things. The truth that came to live among men is the divinely constituted model of human conduct. If we keep in mind the ultimate purpose of things and if we continue in fidelity to the rules of Christian behaviour, we have already a guarantee that we will remain faithful to the truth in every circumstance.

We wish those priests, religious and laity who serve their brothers through the instruments of social communication to know that they have our approval and encouragement, for their efforts are guiding their fellows to an encounter with 'the true light which enlightens every man' (Jn 1:9).

In the confident hope that all, newsmen, information officers, technicians, educators, and their various audiences, will be anxious to use the occasion of this day to ponder on and profit by our reflections, we impart, from our heart and with great trust, our apostolic blessing.

From the Vatican, 21 April 1972

PAULUS PP. VI

MESSAGE OF THE HOLY FATHER
PAUL VI
FOR THE 7TH
WORLD COMMUNICATIONS DAY

Sunday 3 May 1973

The Mass Media and the
Affirmation and Promotion of Spiritual Values

Venerable brothers
Dear sons and daughters
and men of good will everywhere

Today, for the seventh time, we celebrate the annual World Communications Day. We invite all of you to reflect with us on the theme chosen for this year's celebration: 'The Mass Media and the Affirmation and Promotion of Spiritual Values.'

For centuries man has been seeking what is true and good and beautiful. Through this search he has been striving to reach the absolute and to express a relationship with his creator, often through sacrifice and prayer. He has hoped for a life beyond this life, and the hope for immortality has influenced his attitudes and behaviour in this world. With varying degrees of success his quest has likewise been for justice and freedom, for fraternal solidarity and brotherly love. Man has longed for peace within his heart, in his family and in his community. These and the other spiritual values of mankind are a heritage that is passed on by each succeeding generation, one that is the common treasure of all.

This heritage is, however, in a special way the responsibility of Christians. For the Gospel of Christ has confirmed these spiritual values and has extended their meaning and application. Christ himself, by his living, dying and rising from the dead, has given added significance to the life of every man. He has inspired men to even higher goals and made them conscious of the fact that they are called and really are the sons of God, sharing in the fellowship of his Holy Spirit (cf. 1 Jn 3:1; 2 Cor 13:14).

Indeed the Church has received the mission of affirming the spiritual values of the complete Christian message. Christ the Lord has challenged the Church to take this message to the ends of the earth (cf. Acts 1:8; Mt 28:19). His apostles were to preach the love of God and man, for giveness and reconciliation, and to proclaim a message of peace. They were to go out and be concerned about the sick and the oppressed and like their master bring the uplifting gospel to the poor (cf. Lk 4:18). Enlightened by God's guidance, and uniquely rich in human experience, the Church knows and proclaims that the true advancement of man, the true progress of peoples, can be realised only when the spiritual values which answer their highest aspirations receive due emphasis. And so the Church throughout the ages has communicated these values and promoted initiatives for the development of peoples, initiatives aimed at embracing every man and the whole man (cf. *Populorum progressio*, no. 14). The Church must then continue to affirm all the values of a truly human life, showing at the same time that our hearts are restless until they rest in God.

Christians of every age have given witness by their lives and often by their death to the spiritual values which they hold as children of God destined for eternal life. The great martyrs have found successors in every culture to testify with them to the values that make life worth living and show the true meaning of death. By a happy coincidence, this World Communications Day is also the feast of Saint Charles Lwanga and his companions. They were certain of the spiritual values in which they believed and their willingness to die for their convictions shows how deeply spiritual values can be rooted. These sons of Africa are now held in honour by the entire world precisely because they affirmed spiritual values.

Every Christian of every age, like these courageous saints, is bound to give the witness of his good example and to show reasons for the hope within him (cf. 1 Pet 3:15). It has always been thus. One of the greatest blessings of our age, however, is the advance of technology and the great progress made in social communications. Now as never before spiritual values can be affirmed and spread from one end of the earth to the other. The marvellous providence of God has reserved this wonder for our age.

Men of good will are disturbed to see how these social communications are so often used to contradict or corrupt the fundamental values of human life and produce discord and evil (*Communio et progressio*, no. 9). The abuses and the harm they cause are well known. The spread of false ideologies and excessive preoccupation with mere material progress frequently detract from concern for true wisdom and lasting values.

But what we are asking for today is positive action on the part of all Catholics and especially those engaged in the mass media to diffuse in all their fullness the values of Christ's life-giving message and to make the world ring with their conviction, with the voice of their belief and with the word of God. This is indeed an important vocation and a great service to the world. And we appeal likewise for a full measure of partnership with all brother Christians and with all men of good will in every land to affirm effectively the common principles upon which the dignity of man depends. We are asking all those engaged in social communications to tell the story of the sacrifice and dedication that exists in the world, to make known the good that abounds, and the dynamism, enthusiasm and selflessness of so many, especially among the young. We know that there are numerous 'media men' of good will who burn with the desire and determination to turn their 'lifeless instruments' (cf. *Communio et progressio*, no. 72) to the benefit of their fellowmen. We ask them all to renew their resolve to transform the mass media into burning torches and powerful beacons illuminating the path to the only true happiness. The world needs the affirmation of spiritual values as seen in their concrete expression. To reach this goal those who are able to use social communications in all their expressions must do so. The language of image and print, of light, music and sound must help to convey the message of goodness, beauty and truth. The press, the radio, television, the cinema, the theatre and advertising must be utilised to the full in this mission of conveying a meaningful message to the world.

As the mass media affirm and promote the spiritual values of an ever striving humanity, they help to prepare for the day when there will be a new creation in which the fatherhood of God will be universally acknowledged and brotherhood, justice and peace will prevail. And so with the challenge that we offer goes the expression of our gratitude to all men of good will who endeavour to make this contribution. In this regard, we wish to express our deep appreciation to all the radio and television stations as well as to the press which present the news about the Church and the Holy See and their essential mission of affirming and promoting spiritual values. In a special way we thank our own sons and daughters of the Catholic Church who through a more effective use of the mass media and through a greater dedication to this apostolate collaborate with us in spreading the gospel (cf. Phil 1:5).

For the success of the great programme based on the theme of this World Communications Day – 'the Mass Media and the Affirmation and Promotion of Spiritual Values' – we invoke the assistance of the word made flesh and in his name we impart our apostolic blessing.

From the Vatican, 1 May 1973

PAULUS PP. VI

MESSAGE OF THE HOLY FATHER PAUL VI FOR THE 8TH WORLD COMMUNICATIONS DAY

Sunday 26 May 1974

Social Communications and Evangelization in Today's World

Dear brothers and sons
and all men of goodwill

Yet once more we are pleased to address a special message to you on the occasion of World Communications Day, the celebration of which was instituted by the Second Ecumenical Vatican Council (*Inter mirifica*, no. 18).

The importance of the instruments of social communication in the structure of society today goes on steadily increasing, as likewise does their influence on the shaping of human relations. Conscious of this growing importance we reiterate our firm conviction that all men are called to offer their own contribution in the field of media, in such a way that all become involved in communication in one way or another, each according to their own particular circumstances. The manner of this involvement can take the most varied forms, ranging from direct intervention in programming and production, to the making of responsible choices concerning what one will watch or listen to. And again, each must make his own informed decision whether to accept wholly or only with some reserve each particular message which he receives from the social communications media.

We hold, too, that Christians in particular are bound to keep themselves alert always in relation to the media, ready to make fresh evaluations with each new advance in the field, quick to establish updated criteria and thus keep pace with new demands as these present themselves. This day, now being celebrated for the eight successive year, is intended to promote and to accomplish precisely this. It is a pause for reflection on the mass media, this extraordinary modern phenomenon. It is a moment for re-evaluation, for determining attitudes.

Duty to spread the Word

On this year's World Day, we invite you to reflect with us on 'Social Communications and Evangelization in Today's World', a theme which suitably coincides with the study conducted in the various countries in preparation for the coming Assembly of the Synod of Bishops.

'If the Church – we said in our encyclical letter *Ecclesiam suam* – is truly conscious of what the Lord wishes her to be, there must arise in her an overflowing fullness and a compulsion to spread, with a clear advertance to a mission which transcends her, to an announcement that she must broadcast' (*Acta Ap. Sedis*, vol. LVl, p. 639).

The fulfilment of this duty is conditioned by the particular circumstances of each period in history and thus it must in our time be carried out by means of the instruments of social communication. 'It would be difficult to suggest that Christ's command was being obeyed unless all the opportunities offered by the modern media to extend to vast numbers of people the announcement of the Good News were being used' (Pastoral Instruction *Communio et progressio*, no. 116).

Evangelization is an integral part of the mission of the Church, sent by Christ into the world to preach the gospel to every creature (Mk 16:15). The Church carries out this duty above all in her liturgical life, but she is constrained to fulfil it also in all the ways and by all the means which are available to her to use as she abides among the people of each continent.

Evangelization continues

On close reflection it will be seen that the entire life of the Christian, in so far as it conforms to the gospel, is in a permanent situation of evangelization in the midst of the world. The Christian, living as he does amongst other men, sharing their anxieties, sharing the world's suffering, engaging himself in matters of temporal development, himself always there among the currents of human search, idea, debate and exchange – he bears his evangelical witness, he makes his contribution, the contribution of a Christian leaven, a Christian influence within. And in the social communications world, this Christian influence finds a vast perspective and assumes an enormous importance.

There are many urgent necessities which vie for our attention in this context. For one, there is the need to set the contemporary vehicles of information and allied services along a line of development which will facilitate the diffusion of the good news and create a favourable climate for the strengthening of concepts such as the dignity of the human person, justice, universal brotherhood; values which make it easier for a man to understand his own true vocation and which at the same time open the way to a constructive dialogue with others and to union with God.

Then, there is the search for new and improved methods of apostolate which apply the new audiovisual and related instruments to catechesis, to educational work in many forms, to the presentation of the Church's life, of her liturgy, her aims, her difficulties, but above all to the witness of faith and charity which animates and ever renews her.

Using the Best Methods

Finally, Christians must consider how best to employ the instruments of social communication in order to reach countries, societies and persons to whom the apostolate of the word cannot be brought directly because of particular situations, or scarcity of ministers, or because the Church is unable to exercise her mission freely.

We are well aware of the efforts which are in fact being made and of the research which is being conducted – even if not yet sufficiently advanced – to find solutions to these various problems, thanks to the generous and solid work of bishops, priests, religious and of well qualified lay men and women full of high purpose. We are following with careful attention the initiative of our Commission for Social Communications, of the Episcopal Commissions in the various countries of the world, of the International Catholic Organisations for mass media and of Catholic professionals. We know very well the difficulties which they are encountering, in some cases because of local conditions, in others because of limited resources, in all to some extent because it is new ground which they are breaking.

We address to them our word of comfort and encouragement. We address it too to all men who are served by the instruments of social communication and helped towards the true advance of the human family and a better tomorrow in the world. We impart to all our special apostolic blessing.

From the Vatican, 16 May 1974

PAULUS PP. VI

MESSAGE OF THE HOLY FATHER PAUL VI FOR THE 9TH WORLD COMMUNICATIONS DAY

Sunday 11 May 1975

The Mass Media and Reconciliation

Dear sons of the Church
and all you men of good will

The Holy Year supplies us with a theme for our message on this World Day of Social Communications. The theme is 'reconciliation'.

Yes, the press and the radio, television and the cinema ought to be the servants of reconciliation among men in the world. They should be agents of unity, binding all Christians together in solid and visible charity, in the harmony of a single purpose, in a firm orientation towards goodness and towards God.

This annual day is a specially precious and privileged occasion for us all. It gives us a moment to pray together, to reflect together on one subject, to give careful thought to a matter that affects us all vitally, to a fact of our time which can have a powerful bearing on our spiritual well-being.

We pray and reflect today about the mass media. We praise God for these wonderful extensions of his creation which have been brought to such perfection in our time. We recognise the powerful influence for good which, when conscientiously and responsibly used, they can exercise on the individual man and on society. We remind ourselves also that, like so many other good things in creation, they are open to misuse; and, still all together, we consider, before God, what measures may be taken to prevent their desecration.

The communications media undoubtedly have the capacity to stimulate and support all efforts for the true liberation of mankind. They can help man enormously as he struggles to secure the realisation of his deepest hopes. But it would be senseless to conceal from ourselves that they can equally, in the hands of users who have a mind to exploit them for less worthy purposes, be employed merely to satisfy superficial needs generated by the imperative of current fashion or whimsy; or worse, to promote or support discriminatory practices in society, to create or emphasise divisions among men.

In our message of 25 March 1971 we have already drawn attention to the work mass media can do for the unity of mankind. This year we concentrate on the one essential condition which must be satisfied in social communications in order that mass media may be enabled to create a climate which is favourable to reconciliation. This condition is objectivity, respect for facts and fidelity to a genuine and reliable scale of values in presenting them. In this connection, we feel bound to express our esteem and admiration for all those craftsmen of the mass media who strive seriously, earnestly and energetically to make the truth known and to give to that which is good the prominence it deserves.

At the same time, we have to confess that there are certain situations and certain dangers which cause us concern.

Objectivity in information is something essential and irreplaceable, for each one of us requires to know the truth, in order that he may develop his personality fully according to its yardstick, as well as exercising his social responsibilities on the basis of reliable information. This is our right, and its proper exercise presupposes that facts have been honestly reported. All the better if the bare presentation of the facts is supported with well-informed comment, for this, by placing the facts in the full context in which they occur and by showing what relationship they have to human values, makes it easier to understand their meaning.

But quite evidently, such upright and honourable methods, employed sincerely for the purpose of setting the truth in relief and making it comprehensible, are not to be confused with those processes and techniques which, under the pretence of 'neutrality' and 'independence', actually set themselves to manipulate the facts and thereby to manipulate also the audiences to which they are presented. For practices of this nature there can be no commendation.

It may serve some purpose to give examples of the aberrations we have in mind, for all should be alert to recognise them for what they are. A biased concentration on human degradation is one example. Another would be working on public opinion in such a way as to create an insatiable greed for endless successions of consumer goods; an imperative craving that can never be satisfied for items that can, in fact, be easily done without. There is the presentation as desirable of manners of behaviour that are either immoral or at odds with what is actually found in real life. There is suppression of facts, distortion of facts and selective presentation of facts in reporting important happenings, and this in programmes aimed at ideological conditioning which violate man's right to information and show scant respect for his freedom. There is the fashion of urging new difficulties, sowing new doubts, thus shaking the certainty of people on ethical matters which are beyond dispute. There is the fashion of representing as art what is simple permissiveness and the corresponding fashion of putting in a bad light disciplines which are imperatively necessary if people are to live together in civilized society, by representing them as inadmissible oppression. There is the device of presenting as justice what is, in fact, violence, vengeance, or reprisal ...

That objectivity in the selection and presentation of facts which will truly promote reconciliation demands a well-developed sense of responsibility, an adequate training and a genuinely professional competence. It presupposes a renewal of attitude in cases where it may have been necessary to make one, for it implies a definite about-face from habits that have been, regretably too often, espoused in the past by the sources of information, by media professionals, and indeed, by a reading, viewing and listening public which was content to be a passive accomplice.

One thing which is very much to be desired is that, in all countries, availability of information from a variety of sources should be permitted as standard. Instead of forcing the public to rely on one official version of news and interpretation of news, an open dialogue ought to be admitted. This would not only allow the general public to compare the different versions of the news and make an intelligent judgement for themselves, but it would also ensure that a free exchange of valuable ideas could take place among the more noble minds in the community. Failing this possibility one is left with a sort of 'tyranny', a 'cultural enslavement', imposed by a faceless and quasi-anonymous authority. Paradoxically, its emissions may achieve a certain credence, for while they actually violate the religious, ethical and civic convictions of the people, they do so under the guise of promoting personal and social goods.

We would wish that our expression of concern relating to these matters might contribute positively in securing for social communications the achievements in well-doing for which they undoubtedly enjoy the capacity, and that thus they might truly and adequately fulfil their role in the promotion of human and Christian reconciliation. And we invite all the sons of the Church to assist in every way possible to bring about this happy state of affairs.

It is our best hope, in fact, that the media workers themselves may feel called upon to defend and to enlarge the freedom of expression which is their right; we mean the freedom which is based on truth, on love of the brethren and on the love of God.

We are certainly not unaware of the difficulties which confront them and of the courage demanded of them, especially when it comes to 'satisfying' a public of readers, listeners and viewers, who may seem, often enough, little concerned with the search for truth and love. But they are bound, none the less, to give due thought to the responsibility which rests upon them because of the indisputably powerful impact they exercise on information and consequently on the thinking of their audiences and on their attitudes towards life.

We address our appeal more pressingly still to those who hold political, social or economic power over the agents of social communications, urging that they should favour the progress of a sane freedom of information and of expression. Whenever the truth is stifled by unjust economic pressures, by violence on the part of those striving to disrupt civil life, or by compulsion built into the system itself, it is man who is wounded and outraged; his just aspirations are unable to gain a hearing, much less to be satisfied.

On the other hand, the freedom claimed for the mass media does not, and cannot ever, dispense these media from their obligation of fidelity to moral principles, nor from obedience to the civil laws which protect those principles; it is always conditioned, in practice, by the fact that other people have rights which must not be violated, and that life in society imposes certain requirements which must, imperatively, be met. The mass media, then, are under obligation to respect the good name of upright persons, to uphold public decency; in a word, to honour their responsibility as servants of the common good.

It should surely be evident, for example, that media coverage which makes a parade of human depravity, or deliberately provides stimulation for man's immoral inclinations, dishonours the media themselves, while at the same time blunting the moral sense of a community and corrupting its young people. Abuses of this kind cannot take shelter behind the plea of man's 'right to information', and neither can permissive legislation be advocated or justified on this plea.

In this connection, as in others, the Church claims no privileges, much less monopolies. She does no more than reaffirm the right and duty of all men to obey God's law; and the right of her members to be allowed access to the use of the instruments of communication, always showing due respect to the legitimate rights of others. Is it not a fact that all persons and all groups want to be presented fairly by the media; to be given an image that truly reflects what they are without distortion or flattery? It is the right of the Church also that public opinion should know her as she is, and that it should be given a true picture of her teaching, her aspirations and her life.

In raising these points we are indicating some of the means by which the path to reconciliation may be smoothed. For reconciliation cannot take place among men except in a climate of respect, of mutual listening, of search for the truth, of willingness to work together. We are certain that the appeal we make will find an echo in the hearts of all men of good will, sick and tired as they are of a relentless conditioning which, on the one part, tends to enslave the mind and heart, and on the other, results only in an aggravation of tensions that are already severe.

We have a special word for our brothers and sons in the faith. To them we say: work with all your energy for reconciliation within the Church, as our apostolic exhortation of last 8 December urged. Do what is in your power to ensure that the means of social communication, far from hardening antagonisms among Christians, from accentuating polarisations, from taking sides with pleasure groups, or promoting divisions, may work rather for understanding, for respect, for acceptance of others in love and forgiveness, for the building up of the one Body of Christ in truth and charity. Without these, there is no true Christianity.

Such is the renewal we implore from God in this holy year for the promoters and the beneficiaries of social communications, so that by their devoted efforts, true reconciliation may grow among the groupings of society, among the nations, among all those who believe in God, and especially among the disciples of Christ. May all those who work for these aims enjoy the blessing of the God of peace!

From the Vatican, 19 April 1975

PAULUS PP. VI

MESSAGE OF THE HOLY FATHER PAUL VI FOR THE 10TH WORLD COMMUNICATIONS DAY

Sunday 30 May 1976

Social Communications and the Fundamental Rights and Duties of Man

Beloved sons and daughters of the Catholic Church
and men of goodwill!

The annual celebration of 'World Communication Day' is undertaken in fulfilment of a directive imposed by the Second Vatican Council (cfr. Decree, *Inter mirifica,* no. 18), and it, happily, provides a suitable occasion for us to remind ourself, the people of God, and all the members of the human family, of the extraordinary possibilities and the weighty responsibilities which arise for us all in consequence of the ever-widening influence of the mass media and their continuing technical advances.

Now, for the tenth time, we contribute some thoughts intended to assist the ecclesial community as it reflects on the theme chosen for the celebration, and intended also to encourage all those who work in the field of mass media in whatever undertakings they may have in hand concerning the matter of the theme.

At the end of the holy year which was, for Christians and for all men, an invitation to reconciliation and to interior renewal, we wished to carry out a sort of search backwards, in the direction, that is, of the primary human values; and so, for this year's theme we selected the subject: 'Social communications and the fundamental rights and duties of man'. On behalf of what is ancient and permanent, then, we are appealing for support to what is new and very much of our own modern times: we would wish to mobilise, as far as this is possible to us, the press and the radio, television and the cinema, and the other vehicles created by art and science for the transmission of ideas, for united action in an enterprise that is authentically good and meritorious.

We are talking, certainly, about 'means' media, but their function is not merely to be instruments for establishing contacts and circulating messages; not merely to provide escape and entertainment; the media are also and above all instruments which are very suitable for education and training. It is well known, for instance, how effectively the media are being used in several countries in educational work, supplementing the normal methods of teaching, making a powerful contribution to literacy and to the fuller instruction of the old and new generations. It is precisely because of her recognition that the media of social communication have this educational capacity that the Church proposes, a further objective to them, one which is even more exalted and urgent. It proposes that the mass media should be actively employed in the cause of fundamental human rights and duties.

It is our observation, in fact, that in one part of the world or another, situations repeat themselves in which people require support as they strive to gain or to exercise the rights to which they are by nature entitled; and while some of these deplorable cases are brought to the notice of public opinion, others no less deplorable receive no publicity, or when they are brought to public attention it is only so that attempts may be made to justify them.

Of what rights do we speak? Is it perhaps necessary to name them once more? We will say quickly: the right to life, to study, to work; and still more fundamental: the right to be born, the right to responsible parenthood; and then, the right to peace, to freedom, to social justice; further, the right to take part in decision-making on matters which touch the life of the individual or of the people as a whole, such as the right of a man to profess and practice his religion, both as an individual and as a member of the community of those who share his faith, without danger of being discriminated against or punished.

For each of these rights, there is a corresponding duty, and we proclaim the duties with equal force and clarity; for to give the rights predominance over the duties would be to provoke an imbalance, which would be reflected in a damaging way in social life. It must be remembered that the reciprocity between rights and duties is an essential thing; the one springs from the other, and vice versa. And it is precisely in this relationship between right and duty that the social communications media will find a safe point of reference when they set themselves to reflect the human reality in their news programmes and other presentations. It is thus that they will contribute to the progress of civilization.

From a purely humanitarian point of view, there is already sufficient reason for us to re-emphasise these principles; but our faith supplies still more compelling reasons for doing so. In the mystery of the Word Incarnate we recognise the criterion on which the estimate of man's supreme value is based, and throughout the entire gospel we find the most authoritative declaration of his rights and duties. Since the word was made flesh and dwelt amongst us (Jn 1:14), and since he left us as a new commandment an obligation of mutual love on the model of his own (cfr. Jn 15:12), the Church knows, and is in duty bound to remind all, that every outrage against man's rights and each failure in the corresponding duties is also a violation of this supreme law.

In every human being who suffers whether because his rights are trampled upon or because he has not been educated to a sense of his own duties, we discover the passion of Christ continuing through our times; and a Christian professional in social communications would do well not to lose sight of this, for it is part of the matter of his own faith, too.

Certainly, there is nothing new about the Church's concern for human rights or for the observance of the consequent duties; we give testimony to it frequently in our teaching, as our predecessors have done before us. But it is the particular tasks of the instruments of social communication in relation to man's fundamental rights and duties that we would like to point up in this message.

Among these tasks – and here is something which modern civilization brings into sharp relief – there is one which, it could be said, rests almost completely on the communications media: it is the task of supplying the correct and complete information which men have a right to. We should say even that it depends, in great part, on the informative-educational activity of the social communications media whether men will or will not have a healthy awareness of their own rights and duties. It is easy, then, to appreciate the weight of responsibility which rests on all those who work in this sensitive field.

In this connection, we feel obliged to call attention to a menacing phenomenon which nowadays renews itself with menacing frequency in different parts of the world: fundamental rights of man are denied, not only as an arbitrary exercise of violence, but also as desires artificially provoked in public opinion, so that what in reality is a flagrant violation of rights appears as a vindication of rights.

We do not wish to affirm by this that the social communications media are solely responsible for such distortions; but neither can it be denied that they can have a considerable influence in 'manipulating' ideas, principles, values and interpretations, in diminishing the critical capacity of large sections of the population, in exercising what might be called a sort of cultural oppression, by proposing or exciting only those hopes to which it is intended to respond.

We think that all this, whenever it happens, constitutes a serious affront to any human being, for he is a free creature, made in the image of God. No communicated message may ignore the humanity of the person to whom it is addressed, or impose on him a manner of thinking or of living which is in contrast to the dignity that is proper to him; neither should it seek to dissuade him from developing to the utmost the potential which he carries in himself, nor discourage him from affirming his authentic rights, nor impede him from the fulfilment of the duties consequent on those rights. Prior to achieving dominance over his environment, man needs first to master himself, to conduct himself responsibly; this is one of his deeply felt aspirations. And this spiritual need of his should be respected – even more, it should be assisted – by a correct use of the media of social communication.

In the name of this service to mankind, which is an essential part of the mission entrusted to us by Christ, we address our paternal exhortation to the media, urging that they should truly be the servants and the defenders of man's fundamental rights and man's fundamental duties.

From the public authorities we ask that they should favour the promotion of culture through the communications media; we ask respect for facts and opinions; we ask a genuine search for the truth, which allows man to see what he really is before his fellows and before God; we ask that the findings of this search may be reflected in an attitude of enlightened deference towards the supreme values of the person.

We would wish to ask of the mass media workers, firstly, sincerity; a true consistency between what they believe and what they transmit in their programmes of news or interpretation of the news; that they should express without equivocation by what ideal of life they are inspired, disdaining to be part of any plan or policy which would seek to 'manipulate' their audiences; that they should put the love and service of men before the desire for popularity and before any consideration of economic advantage.

Of the readers and audiences who enjoy the service of the communications media, we ask that they should train themselves to be watchfully critical of what they read and hear, for in this way they will put themselves in a position where they can encourage and support, both morally and materially, the people who write or produce those publications, broadcasts and films which defend man's rights and educate him in his duties; and they will provide themselves, at the same time, with a defence against aggressions or enticements which are contrary to truth and to human dignity.

We ask them to make a well-judged estimate of the matter which the media present to them and to qualify themselves to intervene, individually collectively, as the occasion permits, in order to secure improvements in the services of information. Readers, viewers and listeners will always have the deciding word on the future of the communications media, for it is they who decide whether to accept or reject what is offered to them. This gives them a responsibility which they too often ignore.

The Church, on its part, does not claim any special privilege in the field of mass media, but it reaffirms its right and duty to be present in it, enriching its products from the storehouse of its long and universal tradition, a historical and cultural tradition and, above all, one which is religious and educative. This applies whether the media are under public or private management.

Where necessary, the Church will maintain its own social communications establishments, not only to enable it to carry out its primary duty of evangelization, but also so that it may be in a position to continue, as in the past, in its role as promoter of integral human development, to affirm man's rights. And, in fact, that primary duty of the Church to preach the gospel to every creature (Mk 16, 15), with the conjoint mission to be an architect of civilization, places on it an obligation to take its proper place in every modern form of communication among men.

With the hope that the media of social communication may offer their positive support in the promotion of man's rights and also in alerting him to his duties, we impart our apostolic blessing from the heart to all who will lend their help towards this noble and difficult achievement, which will so greatly improve the lot of the human family, as it makes its way towards the year 2000.

From the Vatican, 11 April 1976

PAULUS PP. VI

MESSAGE OF THE HOLY FATHER PAUL VI FOR THE 11TH WORLD COMMUNICATIONS DAY

Sunday 27 May 1977

Advertising in the Mass Media: Benefits, Dangers, Responsibilities

Venerable brothers
and beloved children of the Church
and all you men of good will

The dioceses of the Catholic Church, in response to the invitation of the Second Ecumenical Vatican Council (cfr. *Decree Inter mirifica*, no. 18), again this year celebrate the World Day of Social Communications, in order to help, through reflection, through prayer, by their interest and concern and by moral and material support, the press the, radio, the television, the cinema and the other modern instruments of social communication in the discharge of their important function in information, education and, where the specific responsibility of Christians is concerned, evangelization of the world.

This day, now being celebrated for the eleventh time, has happily become in many countries an occasion for direct contact between the local Churches and the professionals of the mass media and an opportunity for the growth of better understanding between them. By means of appropriate liturgical and cultural events, it goes some way towards alerting the conscience of the person who uses social communications – whether he be reader, listener, viewer, or cinema spectator – to the necessity of being selective in what he reads, views and listens to; a selectivity that often effectively influences those responsible on the production end as regards the type of matter they will offer for his consumption. But still more, it stimulates him to make a mature evaluation of the content of the communications which he receives.

For such is the complexity of the communications phenomenon today that it requires not only that society and the individuals who comprise it shall be constantly reminded of their respective duties and continually refined by being brought face to face with the true values of human life, but also that everyone who exercises influence on the communications process shall do his part.

For this reason, the Church, as well as dedicating the annual day to a study of all the pastoral questions which arise in the sector of communications, has been careful to call the attention of Christians and men of good will to particular aspects of this very wide subject. The Church hopes, by these means, to help each man to find his direction and keep his balance in the midst of the many-sided reality which is the 'mass media'. She hopes also to contribute, as the nature of her mission demands, to the common good. This brings us to the theme chosen for this year, 'Advertising in the mass media: benefits, dangers, responsibilities', which is intended to focus our reflection on one powerful factor of the present social organisation.

It may be asked why advertising and its bearing upon the instruments of social communication should be of interest to the Church. The answer is that advertising is quite an important element in the common life of man because it conditions his integral development and, directly or indirectly, has an influence upon his cultural life. No one now can escape the influence of advertising, and, even apart from the actual content of its messages, it presents, at least suggests, particular visions of the world, which inevitably pull at the Christian, affect his judgement and influence his manner of acting. Advertising, moreover, takes on an ever growing importance, because in large part it finances the development of the communications media and uses them for its own purposes, directly and sometimes dangerously influencing their orientation and their freedom.

The Church looks with favour on the growth of man's productive capacity and also on the ever widening network of relationships and exchanges between persons and social groups; they are for her a reason, a sign and an anticipation of an ever greater brotherhood and from this point of view she encourages advertising, which can become a wholesome and efficacious instrument for reciprocal help among men. Another fundamental aspect which the Church recognises in advertising is its informative aspect, with all the weight and the obligations deriving from it. It has to be truthful, prudent, respectful of man and of his essential values, careful in its choice of the circumstances in which it addresses him and of the manner in which it makes its presentation.

Advertising is, then, a promotional tool of particular interests which, even if legitimate, must take the common good into account, keep in mind the equally legitimate interests of others and especially have due regard for the concrete circumstances of the integral development affecting the people to whom it addresses itself, for their cultural and economic environment and for the level of education they have attained. As is well known, the advertising message is, naturally, designed to convince people, makes use of techniques based on precise psychological and social knowledge, and is constantly researching the ways and means of persuasion. It is here, above all that there is imposed on it and, therefore, on those within the advertising profession, the imperative requirement to respect the human person, his right-duty to make a responsible choice, his interior freedom; all these goods would be violated if man's lower inclinations were to be exploited, or his capacity to reflect and decide compromised.

The vast advertising phenomenon, with its moral and religious implications, involves first of all the instruments of social communication, which often themselves become agents of publicity, but which more usually serve as vehicles for messages coming from other economic agents and maintain themselves partially or entirely on the revenues eamed by carrying the advertising. It can be said, therefore, that all the communicative activity of these instruments is closely linked to the modern phenomenon of advertising and this connection permits the factors of economic life to help the socially necessary development; but there ought not to be any imposition of conditions which limit the freedom of the media or inhibit the exchange of cultural or religious values (cfr. Pastoral Instruction *Communio et progessio*, no. 62)

It is our belief that these guidelines could serve to bring about an advertising respectful of the fundamental rights and duties of man and deserving of the support of the Christian conscience, if the various categories of professionals concerned were to unite their efforts in collaboration to this end. It is up to the advertising agencies, to the publicity workers and to the directors and managers of the media which carry advertising, to make known to the public, to subscribe to and to apply the codes of professional ethics which already have been opportunely established so as to have the cooperation of the public in making these codes still better and in enforcing their observance.

All this touches, very often, on delicate moral questions, such as, for instance, the education of youth, respect for woman, the safeguarding of the family and the protection of the rights of the human person (cfr. our *Discourse of the European Association of Advertising Agencies*, in the audience of 28 April 1976), and it therefore justifies the interest of the Church and, sometimes, her well-founded concern.

How could she remain silent when offence is caused to certain ethical principles? And how could we ourself neglect to utter a strong protest, in which we know we are joined by all men of good will, concerning the widespread display of certain types of cinema publicity which do no honour to our civilization, but which gravely offend the dignity of man, disturb the peace of consciences, and promote disharmony among men? It is for this reason that we ask the bishops, priests and laity engaged in pastoral activity to enter into a healthy and open dialogue with the directors of the publicity process, in respect of reciprocal interests and in common acknowledgment of the good of human society.

At the same time, we invite the promoters of the Catholic press, those in charge of Catholic transmissions on radio and television, and those who are engaged in any way in any form of social communication, to give the example of their religious conviction and of their ideal of life precisely by the advertising they choose and by the excellence of their own performance in respect of advertising practice. We request, meanwhile, of the distributors of advertising, that they shall not neglect those channels of communication which give a guarantee to promote and protect moral principles and which truly favour the development of the person and of his spiritual and human values.

It is our wish also that the Catholic institutions, in their various kinds and according to their specific character, will follow with constant attention the development of the modern techniques of advertising and will know how to make opportune use of them in order to spread the gospel message in a manner which answers the expectations and needs of contemporary man.

With these wishes, we willingly impart our apostolic blessing on all those who take part in the celebration of the forthcoming day of Social Communications and offer the contribution of their mature human experience and of their attentive Christian sensibility to the reflection on this important matter.

From the Vatican, 12 May 1977

PAULUS PP. VI

MESSAGE OF THE HOLY FATHER PAUL VI FOR THE 12TH WORLD COMMUNICATIONS DAY

Sunday 7 May 1978

The Receiver in Social Communications: His Expectations, his Rights, his Duties

Venerable brothers and beloved children

For the people of God, the annual Social Communications Day is an important occasion. This day, as you well know, is set aside for deliberate reflection on the instruments of social communication, on the manner in which they operate and on the use we make of them. The fathers of Vatican Council II had no hesitation in calling these instruments 'marvellous'. Every remotest corner is within their reach, every day they become technically more efficient, the time alloted to their use is constantly increasing. Who, then, could measure the influence they are in a position to exercise on public opinion, or estimate the precise effect of them in terms of value formation or in the determination of the choices people will make?

It should not cause any great surprise, then, that the Church follows the development of a cultural phenomenon of such vast implications with closer and closer attention, or that she never tires of reminding the media directors and their associates of the special responsibilities that go with their office. Moved by the same pastoral concern we have chosen as the theme of this message an examination of the expectations, the rights and the duties of the 'recipients', of the person, that is, to whom social communications are directed. Obviously, we look at the recipient from the point of view which is proper to us, that of a Christian estimate of the person as a living image of God (cfr. Gen 1, 26) and, as such, providentially designed for a transcendent destiny.

The first expectation of 'recipients' which should be looked at and evaluated is the possibility for two-way exchange (cfr. Encyclical Letter *Ecclesiam suam*, A.A.S. 56, 1964, p. 659). The space allotted by newspapers and radio and television stations for correspondence with their readers, listeners or viewers only partly answers this legitimate desire, for it affects always only isolated cases, while all 'recipients' feel the need to be able to express in some way their own opinion and to offer their own personal ideas and proposals. Now, in order to ensure such a dialogue, to promote a two-way exchange and to focus it on the more important problems, the 'communicators' will need to establish a continuous and stimulating contact with society and to bring the 'recipients' to the point where they are active participants.

The next requirement is for the truth. To be given the truth is a fundamental right of the person, rooted in human nature itself, and closely connected with that right to belong and participate, which present day evolution tends to guarantee to every member of society. This aspiration, this demand for the truth, has a direct bearing on the media of information, from which the recipients have a right to expect up-to-date briefing, honesty, objective research and presentation, respect for the hierarchy of values and, where stage and screen are concerned, a truthful image of man, whether as an individual or as a part of a determined social context.

Nor should the desire of modern man for recreation and rest be lost sight of or undervalued, for he needs to recoup his forces and his psychic equilibrium, so sorely tested by the not infrequently exhausting conditions which life and work today impose upon him. It is a legitimate desire and it has spiritual implications, for with recreation religious and moral questions can arise. Christians are aware that the resolution of these questions, with the guidance of the Holy Spirit, brings man to the fullness of his own high destiny.

To satisfy these aspirations, responsible collaboration is required from the 'recipient' himself, who ought to take an active part in the formative process of communication. This is not to advocate the creation of pressure groups, which would merely aggravate the tensions and confrontations of the present time. But it could happen that, instead of a 'round table of society' to which all would have access by right according to their individual competence and to the importance of the subjects under discussion, use of the media might be restricted to suit the purposes of non-representative groups who would thus impose only a point of view favourable to their own vested interest. This must not be allowed to happen and it is for the 'recipient' to see to it that it does not happen. It is, on the contrary, to be urged that, between 'communicators' and 'recipients', a genuine and authentic dialogue and exchange shall be instituted (cfr. Pastoral Instruction *Communio et progressio*, in A.A.S. LXIII/1971, no. 81, p. 623).

This means that it is you, dear readers, listeners, viewers who must learn the language of the social communications media, however difficult that may be, so that you may be in a position to intervene with effect. You must know how to make a good choice when deciding what newspaper or book to buy, what film you will see, what programmes you will listen to on radio, or view on television; all the time conscious that the choice you make is a vote cast for the encouragement and support (even actual economic support) of the publication or programme you favour, and at the same time a vote to reject and discourage those which meet with your disfavour (cfr. Ibid., no. 82, p. 624).

It is necessary, further, to bear in mind what a complex thing is modern communications in which, by their nature – and often enough indeed by intent – truth can appear to be falsehood and good, evil. There is, in fact, no truth, no sacred thing, no moral principle, that cannot be directly or indirectly corroded or contested in the wide-ranging discourse of those communications. You must, for this reason, exercise discernment, measuring what you receive from the communications media with the yardstick of genuine ethico-religious values, prizing and accepting the positive elements and excluding those which are negative.

This triple capacity which the 'recipient' needs to acquire today in order to be a mature and responsible citizen – the capacity, that is, to understand the language of the mass media, to make opportune choices and to make sensible assessments – fits the 'recipient' for dialogue with the 'communicator'. Then, when circumstances arise which require the 'recipient's' intervent the intervention should be made in correct and proper form, and while it should be frank and decisive, it should always be courteous.

We are very well aware of the difficulty which, in the concrete circumstances of the contemporary world, is encountered by every 'recipient', beginning with those who are Christian, when he sets out to equip himself with the know-how which he requires in order to exercise his rights and duties and fulfil his just aspirations. But if it is true that the future of the human family depends largely on its manner of using the communications media, then it is necessary that training of 'recipients' should be regarded as a priority both in the sphere of pastoral ministry and in educational work, generally.

The first steps in media education ought to be taken within the family; in the field of a total education for life, place must be given to teaching the children to understand the communications media, how to choose among their programmes and how to assess their content. And the duty rests on parents of helping their own children to make a choice, to work out considered judgements and to dialogue with the 'communicators'.

This training, then, should continue in the schools. The Second Ecumenical Vatican Council imposed this as a specific obligation on Catholic schools of all grades (cfr. *Decree Inter mirifica*, no. 16) and on associations of Christian inspiration engaged in education. The Decree added the following: 'To bring this about more promptly and effectively, Catholic teachings and policies regarding media are to be presented and explained in catechetical manuals' (Ibid.). Teachers must remember that they are working in a context in which their pupils are exposed daily to ever so many programmes and transmissions touching in one way or another on faith and moral principles, and that they need therefore to have constant clarifications or corrections made for them.

Local communities of believers, finally, must help their membership in choosing, understanding and assessing. We make an appeal to the Catholic press, to the other media which are available to dioceses, parishes and religious families, to give their space generously to information on social communications programmes, recommending or advising against them, as the case may be, and explaining the reasons why they are doing so, and thus assisting the faithful to shape their attitude to media programmes in full conformity with the teaching of the gospel.

Christians, and particularly young people, must bear in mind that to use the communications media wisely is, in the last analysis, a matter of personal responsibility, and that from the choice they make, the holiness of their lives will depend, as also the integrity of their faith and the riches of their culture. And the value of their contribution to the general development of society is also at stake here. Yes, the Church must instruct them and give them every help, but it cannot supply any substitute for their personal consistent decision.

The task, as is easily seen, is complex and extremely demanding. Nothing but generous collaboration on the part of all concerned can bring it about that the social communications media not only will abandon expressions and attitudes, unfortunately prevalent enough, which lean to violence, eroticism, vulgarity and egoism and are dictated unjustifiably by particular vested interests, but will reach the point where they offer information which is abundant, carefully checked and truthful, and programmes and shows that are culturally and spiritually wholesome. This would be a notable contribution to that all-embracing humanism which is so close to the Church's heart (Encyclical Letter *Populorum progressio*, A.A.S. 59/1967; no. 42; also see no. 14, p. 264).

Whilst encouraging the efforts of those who give this special service a place of priority in their lifework, we invoke on them and on all who take part in the celebration of the twelfth World Communications Day and abundance of the gifts of the Holy Spirit, and from our heart we impart to them the apostolic blessing.

From the Vatican, 28 April 1978

PAULUS PP. VI

MESSAGES OF THE HOLY FATHER JOHN PAUL II FOR WORLD COMMUNICATIONS DAY 1979–2005

MESSAGE OF THE HOLY FATHER JOHN PAUL II FOR THE 13TH WORLD COMMUNICATIONS DAY

Sunday 23 May 1979

Social Communications: Protecting the Child and Promoting his Best Interest in the Family and in Society

Dearest brothers and children of the Holy Church

With the same sentiments of sincere trust and living hope which have marked my pastoral service in the Chair of Peter from its beginning, I turn to you, especially to those among you who are engaged in social communications, on the day which is consecrated to this important subject by the wish of the Second Vatican Council (cfr. *Decree Inter mirifica*, 18).

The theme for which I wish to claim your attention contains, in fact, an implicit invitation to trust and hope because it deals with childhood, and I discuss it all the more willingly because it was already selected by my beloved predecessor Paul VI. It is opportune to reflect, in this year declared by the United Nations Organisation the 'Year of the Child', on the particular needs of this vast band of 'receivers' – the children – and on the consequent responsibilities of the adults, particularly those who work in communications and who can and do exercise such great influence on the formation – or unfortunately the malformation – of the young generations. Here is contained the seriousness and the complexity of the subject: 'Social Communications: Protecting the Child and Promoting his best interests in the Family and in Society.'

Without making any pretense of examining the subject, or much less, of exhausting the various aspects of it, I wish simply to recall briefly what children have a right to expect and to obtain from the communications media. Enchanted by the instruments of social communication and defenseless against the world and adult persons, they are naturally ready to accept whatever is offered to them, whether good or bad. You, communications professionals, and particularly those of you who work with the audiovisual media, are well aware of this. They are attracted by the 'small screen' and by the 'large screen', they follow every gesture represented on them, and they perceive, quicker and better than anyone else, the emotions and sentiments which result.

Like soft wax on which every tiniest pressure leaves a mark, so the child is responsive to every stimulus that plays upon his imagination, his emotions, his instincts and his ideas. Yet the impressions received at this age are the ones which are destined to penetrate most deeply into the psychology of the human being and to condition, often in a lasting way, the successive relationship with himself, with others and with his environment. It was precisely out of an intuition regarding the extreme delicacy of this phase of life that pagan wisdom enunciated the well-known pedagogical guideline which direct that 'maxima debetur puero reverentia'; and it is in this same light that we must regard Christ's warning, with its reasoned severity: 'Whoever causes one of these little ones who believe in me to sin, it would be better for him to have a great millstone fastened round his neck and to be drowned in the depth of the sea' (Mt 18:6). And certainly among the 'little ones' meant by the gospel, the children especially are included.

For the believer who intends to base the conduct of his own life on the gospel, the example of Christ has to be the norm. Now, it is as one who lovingly welcomes little children that Christ presents himself (cfr. Mk 10:16), as one who defends them in their spontaneous desire to come close to him (cfr. Mk 10:14), who praises their typical and trusting simplicity, as being worthy of the kingdom (cfr. Mt 18:3-4), and who draws our attention to their interior transparency which disposes them so easily to experience God (cfr. Mt 18:10). He does not hesitate to set down a surprising equation: 'Whoever receives one such child in my name receives me' (Mt 18:5). As I had occasion to write recently, 'The Lord identifies himself with the world of young children ... Jesus does not condition children, he does not use children. He calls them, and brings them into his plan for the salvation of the world' (cfr.

Message to the President of the Pontifical Society of Missionary Childhood in *L'Osservatore Romano*, 21 April 1979).

What then shall be the attitude of responsible Christians and especially of parents and mass media workers conscious of their duties in regard to children? They ought, before all else, to take charge of the human growth of the child; any pretence of maintaining a 'neutral' position in his regard and of letting him grow up in his own way merely disguises a dangerous lack of interest under the appearance of respect for the child's personality.

No such disengagement in relation to children can be accepted; for children really have a need for help in their development toward maturity. To be sure, there is a great richness and vitality in a child's heart; however, he is not capable, all by himself, of resolving the diverse mysteries and longings that assail him from within. It is on the adults that the duty falls – on the parents, the educators, the communications workers – and it is they also who have the capability of enabling the child to sort things out and find himself. Does not every child in some way resemble the boy Samuel, of whom the sacred scripture speaks? Unable to interpret the call of God, he sought help from his master, who at first replied to him: 'No, I did not call you; go back to sleep' (1 Sm 3:5-6). Now, shall we adopt this kind of attitude and smother the inspirations that impel the child to higher things? Shall we not rather help him to understand and respond, as the priest Eli eventually did with Samuel: 'If he calls you again, you shall say: Speak Lord, for your servant is listening' (Ibid. 3:9).

There are enormous possibilities and means at the disposal of you adults in this connection. You are in a position to arouse the spirit of the children so that they will listen, or to lull it to sleep and – God forbid! – poison it irremediably. What is required is that you should take such action as will cause the child to avail to the fullest of all the possibilities for personal realisation and thus insert himself creatively into the stream of life in the world; and this thanks to the pains you take to give him an education which dulls none of his promise or talent but brings out the best in him. You especially who are engaged in the mass media, stand by his side and help him in his search for knowledge, giving him cultural and recreational programmes in which he may find an answer to his quest for his identity and for his gradual 'entry' into the human community. Then, in your actual programmes, it is important that the child actors should not appear merely in walk-on parts, a diversion to relieve the tired eyes or disenchanted ears of apathetic viewers or listeners, but that they should be allowed to represent characters that can serve as valid models for the younger generation.

I am well aware that in begging you to make this kind of human and 'poetic' effort (I use 'poetic' in its true meaning as the creative capacity proper to art), I am implicitly asking you to relinquish to some extent your adherence to programme-planning geared to instant success and closely tied to maximum audience 'ratings.' Is not the true work of art, perhaps, that which is born not from ambition to succeed, but from genuine ability and sure professional maturity? Do not exclude from your productions – I ask this of you as a brother – the opportunity to offer the heart of the children a spiritual and religious invitation; and you may take this as a trusting appeal for your collaboration in the spiritual task of the Church.

Similarly I turn to you, parents and educators, and to you, catechists and officials of the various ecclesial associations, and I urge you to give very serious thought to the problem of the use of the social communications media by and for children, as a matter of capital importance; not only for their enlightened training which, as well as developing their critical sense and teaching them – as you might say – self-discipline in choosing their programmes, helps them along on the human plane, but also for the evolution of the whole society along the lines of uprightness, of truth and of brotherhood.

Dearest brothers and children, childhood is not just any period of human life which can be isolated from the whole artificially; as a child is flesh of the flesh of his parents, so are all the children a living part of society. It is for this reason that what is at stake in childhood is the fate of the whole of life, of the child's life and of ours, that is, of the life of all. Let us therefore serve childhood, valuing life and choosing 'for' life at every level, and let us help childhood, presenting before the eyes and to the vulnerable and sensitive hearts of the little ones the noblest and highest things in life.

Raising the eyes to this ideal, to me it seems that I meet the gaze of the most sweet Mother of Jesus who, totally given to the service of her divine little Son, 'kept all these things in her heart' (Lk 2:51). In the light of her example, I pay honour to the teaching mission which belongs to all of you and, in the confidence that you will carry it out with a love commensurate with its dignity, I bless you from my heart.

From the Vatican, 23 May 1979

IOANNES PAULUS PP. II

MESSAGE OF THE HOLY FATHER JOHN PAUL II FOR THE 14TH WORLD COMMUNICATIONS DAY

Sunday 18 May 1980

Social Communications and Family

Beloved brothers and sisters in Christ

It is in obedience to a direction of the Second Vatican Council that the Catholic Church celebrates (on 18 May) the World Day of Social Communications. In one of its first documents, the Council ordered that a day should be set aside each year in all the dioceses of the world, and that on that special day the faithful should pray for a particular intention, namely, that the Church's work in the field of communications might be effective. In addition, each one was to reflect on his own duties regarding the communications media and to make a contribution for the support of the Church's social communications establishments and undertakings.

In the years since the Council's Decree on the Social Communications Media, the World Day has come to be an increasingly important event in the Church's life. In many countries, Catholics have been joined by the members of other Christian communities in the celebration; a practical manifestation of solidarity admirably in keeping with the ecumenical principle 'not to do separately what we can do together'. Let us thank God for it.

This year, in harmony with the theme of the coming Synod of Bishops, which will be considering the problems confronting the family in the changed circumstances of modern times, we are invited to focus our reflection on the relationship between the mass media and the family. One circumstance which intimately affects all families today is the prevalence of the social communications media: the press, the cinema, the radio and television. It is a rare home indeed to which entry has not been gained by one or other of these. Where once, not very long ago, the family consisted of parents and children with the addition, perhaps, of a relative or two or a servant, now the circle is, in a sense, extended to admit the more or less permanent 'company' of announcers, newsreaders, entertainers, commentators on sport and current affairs, with frequent visits as well from famous and influential people of every nationality, persuasion and profession.

It is a state of affairs with very great potential for good, but also with built-in risks that may not be disregarded. The family of today suffers its share of the strong tensions and of the growing disorientation which is affecting modern social life in general. Certain of the stabilising factors which in the past helped to ensure its solid internal cohesion have now been diminished or have altogether disappeared. Formerly, there were compelling reciprocal interests and the demands of tasks in which every member had to take part, to keep the family together in almost uninterrupted community throughout the working hours, thus permitting it to play a decisive part in the training and education of the children. In today's altered working conditions, however, the members of the family are often widely separated from each other for the greater part of the day.

The obvious difficulties of this situation can be seriously aggravated by the communications media. If media programmes frequently present a distorted picture of what a family is, or caricature family life, or if they misrepresent or play down the family's function as an educator, members of the family, accepting these distortions passively and uncritically, may quite easily begin to imitate the conduct and adopt the attitudes presented to them notwithstanding its deficiencies or superficiality. It may not occur to them to question the values implied, nor may they have the opportunity or the capacity, even if they do, to challenge the producers or to engage in constructive dialogue with them on the issues. There is the further risk – it is real and great – that the family may abdicate the responsibility which rightly belongs to it of shaping the children's attitudes to life and training their sense of values, and may cede it unwittingly to the media.

In this connection, it is wise to be alert to the growing influence which the mass media, and especially television, are exercising on the developing minds of the young, particularly as regards their vision of man, of the world and of relationships with others; for the vision furnished them by the media often differs profoundly from that which the family would wish to transmit to them. Parents, in many cases, do not show sufficient concern about this. Generally, they pay vigilant attention to the type of friends with whom their children associate, but do not exercise a similar vigilance regarding the ideas which the radio, the television, records, papers and comics carry into the 'protected' and 'safe' intimacy of their homes. And so the mass media often enter the lives of the youngest members of the family with no possibility of the necessary explanations or corrections from parents or other educators which could neutralise any harmful elements and which could equally, employ the many valuable aspects to assist in the process by which children are gradually transformed into well-adjusted men and women.

It is undoubtedly true, on the other hand, that the social communications media can be a most valuable source of cultural enrichment for the family and for each of its members. Well-ordered reading, listening and viewing can contribute greatly to the stimulation of dialogue and interchange within the little community and can create a broadening of interests which will involve the family in the activities of the larger human family outside. Through the media, a certain participation is also frequently made possible in religious events occurring in distant places, something which is a special comfort to the sick and the housebound in particular. The family's consciousness of the universality of the Church and its awareness of the problems of all races and peoples becomes more vivid. Thus the media can greatly assist in drawing the hearts of mankind closer together in sympathy, understanding and brotherhood, and the family can acquire a deep and loving 'family feeling' for the whole human race. Benefits, these, which should not be underestimated.

But in order that the family may really draw such benefits from its use of the media and at the same time protect itself from any harmful effects, it is necessary that its members, particularly the parents, shall make more active use of their critical faculty. They must take a more searching look at the content of the programmes offered to them. They must exercise judgement on the messages which the media are transmitting to them. Further, the family needs to take a deliberate decision regarding the amount of time it can responsibly afford to spend with the media, taking account of the various other activities and tasks which it must attend to.

In short: it is the duty of parents to educate themselves, and to educate their children, to appreciate the value of communication, to make an intelligent choice between the programmes available to them, and then, having made that choice, to make a reasonable and conscious judgement as to whether the message coming from the programme merits to be accepted or rejected. In families where this kind of control is exercised, the media will be less a danger to the wellbeing and proper functioning of the home, but will, on the contrary, be a valuable aid in preparing the gradually maturing younger members to take their place in society.

It is evident that the family needs to be able to count on the good will and integrity, as also on the sense of responsibility, of the media professionals, the publishers, editors, writers, the producers and directors of the broadcasting media, the dramatists, commentators, entertainers, newsmen and women. All these are categories in which the laity are predominant. To all of them men and women, I want to repeat something which I said last year in one of my journeys abroad: 'The great forces which shape the world – politics, the mass media, science, technology, culture, education, industry and work – are precisely the areas where lay people are specially competent to exercise their mission' (Limerick, 1 October 1979). Undoubtedly, mass media is one of the great forces which is shaping the world at this moment, and it is in the field of mass media that increasing numbers of talented and highly trained people are finding their lifework and vocation. The Church thinks of them today with love and concern and earnestly prays for them all. There are few vocations which make such demands on the energy, the dedication, the integrity and the conscience of a man or woman as are made by a profession in the media. At the same time, and let this not be forgotten, the truly dedicated professional communicator of today can be a force for good in the world which has few parallels.

I earnestly invite all media workets, therefore, to join us in the Church's day of reflection and prayer. We beg the Almighty together to deepen their consciousness of the tremendous opportunity which is theirs to serve mankind and shape the world towards good. We ask him to endow them with the understanding, wisdom and courage which they will always need in bearing their awesome responsibility. We beg him to keep them always intensely mindful of their audiences, which for the most part are families like their own, with overworked parents often too tired to be alert, and with children who are trusting, impressionable, vulnerable, easily led. For remembering this, they will keep in mind also the enormous consequences which their work may have for good or ill and will not easily be false to themselves or to the principles of their noble calling.

My special apostolic blessing goes today to all mass media workers, to all families, and to all those who search through prayer, reflection and consultation to put the communications media to the best use for the service of man and the greater glory of God.

From the Vatican, 1 May 1980

IOANNES PAULUS PP. II

MESSAGE OF THE HOLY FATHER JOHN PAUL II FOR THE 15TH WORLD COMMUNICATIONS DAY

Sunday 31 May 1981

Social Communications and Responsible Human Freeedom

Beloved brothers and sisters

The XV World Communications Day has as its theme: 'Social communications in the service of responsible human freedom'. Though this important subject I intend to devote this message, which I address lovingly to the sons of the Catholic Church and to all men of good will.

1. In the continual expansion and progress of the mass media we can discern a sign of the times, which constitutes an immense potential for universal understanding and a strengthening of the grounds for peace and brotherhood among the nations.

Pius XII, of venerable memory, very rightly spoke, in the encyclical *Miranda prorsus* of 8 September 1957, of these media, classifying them as 'wonderful inventions of which our age is proud', and seeing in them a gift of God. The *Decree lnter Mirifica* of the Second Vatican Ecumenical Council, confirming this view, stressed the possibilities of these media, which 'by their very nature are able to reach and move not only individuals, but even multitudes and the whole of human society'.

The Church, taking note of the enormous possibilities of the mass media, has always added to this positive evaluation, an appeal to considerations that go beyond enthusiasm, and asks people to reflect and consider what powers of suggestion these media have and will continue to have in their various kinds of influences on man. Of these we must always take full account. Man, even in the presence of the mass media, is called to be himself: that is, free and responsible, a user and not an object, critical and not passive.

2. Repeatedly, in the course of my pastoral ministry, I have spoken of that vision of man as a free person, which is based on divine revelation, and confirmed and demanded as a vital necessity by that same human nature. It is a vision more deeply felt at this time, perhaps as a reaction to the dangers and threats to which men are subjected and respond to with fear.

At the beginning of this year of 1981, in the message for the World Day of Peace, I wished to call attention to freedom as a necessary condition for the pursuit of peace – freedom of individuals, of groups, of families, of peoples, of ethnic, language, or religious minorities.

In truth, it is in freedom that a man becomes his true self. Towards this achievement he must grow, never halting for verbal or rhetorical distractions, as too often happens; nor distorting the meaning of freedom, nor forming a habit perversely as a license for doing whatever pleases him, even if it is evil (cf. *Gaudium et spes,* 17). No, he must see and strictly apply himself, in thought and in action, to the freedom that is his because of his dignity as the creature made in the image of God. This dignity demands that a man make choices informed and free, moved and persuaded by personal conviction and not by blind interior impulse or by mere external pressure (*Gaudium et spes*, 1.c.). Even a psychological suggestion – apparently harmless – can, when skillfully handled with the tools of persuasion, make a man a target and endanger his freedom. This is the sense in which I mean to speak of social communications as the servant of responsible human freedom. Man is created free. But he is of the kind that must grow and develop by overcoming the self. Freedom has to be won. So a man must free himself from everything that might disqualify him from winning freedom.

3. Now the mass media are here to offer themselves as agents who have a special role in this endeavour to achieve responsible human freedom. It is a context ever present in the mind of the Church. And the question has to be put to the media – can you show that there is a road from your great potential to the

achievement of your purpose? Can the mass media, in truth, meet the expectations laid upon them as factors in the achievement among men of responsible freedom?

How do these media support and promote the struggle for human freedom? In fact, they present as reality their own terms of expression. And often this amounts to an imposition of the media view on the man of today, who cannot detach himself or free himself from contacts he feels he needs.

Often, the media are instruments of power that can become oppressive, especially where pluralism is not admitted. This can come about not only where freedom does not exist, as under a dictatorship of whatever brand, but also where freedom is to a degree preserved, but large vested interests bring constant pressure to bear on the media.

This is particularly true of the violation of the right of religious freedom. But it also holds in other situations, where oppression consists of exploiting people.

The responsible freedom of the communicators, who have the power of choosing what they communicate, must take account of the users of their production, who are also free and responsible.

To remind the communicators that their employment demands from them love, justice, truth, as well as freedom – this is a duty of my pastoral ministry. Truth must never be distorted, justice neglected, love forgotten, if one is to observe ethical standards. To forget or lose sight of these is to produce bias, scandal, submission to the powerful, compliance with 'reasons of state'. The Church will not be the one to suggest adulterating or concealing truth, even a hard truth. The Church, precisely because she is experienced in human nature, does not indulge in an immature optimism; she preaches hope and does not approve of causing scandal.

4. Still: one notes a certain aggressiveness in the information and images of the 'mass media': from the field of entertainment to political speeches, from prefabricated and guided 'cultural discoveries' which are nothing but 'indoctrination', to the very field of advertising.

In our world, it is difficult to hypothesise regarding those mass media professionals who have been withdrawn from their own cultural matrix; this, however, must not cause anyone to impose his personal ideology on outside parties. The communicator has to fulfil his task with the maximum objectivity and not turn himself into a 'hidden persuader' out of personal interest, for reasons of conformism, or for financial gain.

There is then the danger to the responsible freedom of those who use the means of social communications, a danger which takes the form of a serious attack and is marked by the use of sex to the point where there is an outbreak of pornography: in the spoken or written word, in pictures and even so-called 'artistic' posters. At times this is tantamount to pandering, the result of which is both destructive and perverting. The denunciation of this state of affairs does not mean displaying what is so often described as 'reactionary mentality' or censorship of free-will: the denunciation is done in the very name of freedom, which demands and necessitates that one does not suffer the imposition of those who seek to transform sexuality into an end in itself. This action would be not only anti-Christian but anti-human, with the consequent transition to drugs, perversion and degeneration.

The intrinsic capacity of the means of social communication offers enormous possibilities. Among these there is the possibility to extol violence through the description and representation of that already appearing in daily newspapers along with consenting words and pictures, which perhaps even pretend to be condemning it! Too often it is something like a 'search' tending to excite violent emotions to stimulate the attention, which is often slack.

5. One cannot fail to speak of the effect and influence all this exercises, especially on the imagination of the young and of children, unthinking and open to messages and sensations, and great enjoyers of the mass media.

Here is a subject which is still undergoing formation. Its maturation must therefore be aided without artificial traumatisation. In this as in other areas, the Church requests responsibility not only from the communicators themselves, but also and in a special way, from the family.

The life style – especially in the more industrialised nations – all too often causes families to abandon their responsibility to educate their children. Evasion of this duty is made easy by the presence of television and of printed materials in the home. These occupy the time for children and young people. No one can deny the justification for this when the means are lacking, to develop and use to advantage the free time of the young and to direct their energies.

The result is that these young people are in most need of help in developing their responsible freedom. There is the duty – especially for believers, for men and women who love freedom – to protect the young from the aggressions they are subjected to by the media. May no one shirk from this duty by using the excuse that he or she is not involved.

6. It must be asked, especially on this day, if pastoral action has achieved all that was asked of it in the uses of mass media!

In fact, it must be remembered that, beyond the document *Communio et progressio* – whose tenth anniversary it is – much was said at the Synod of Bishops in 1977 and ratified in the Apostolic Constitution *Catechesi tradendae*. And still more emerged at the Synod of Bishops on the problems of the family, which ended in October 1980.

Theology and pastoral practice, catechetical organisation, the schools – especially the Catholic schools, the Catholic associations and groups – what have they done, concretely, on this specific, central matter? Direct action must be intensified in the creation of a critical conscience that will affect the attitudes and behaviour not only of Catholics and brother Christians, but of all men and women, adults and young people, to the point where they will truly know, as free and responsible people, how to see, judge and act in the production as well as the choices which the media of social communication make.

The pastoral ministry vested in me, the conciliar outlook I have so often spoken about and encouraged; my personal experience and convictions about humanity, about Christianity and about the role of bishop, all lead me to emphasise the possibilities for good, the richness, the timeliness of the media. I can add that the part of the media work which is labelled artistic does not escape me, but exalts me. But all this cannot hide the fact that in their use, or abuse, there are those who have the profit, the industry, the means of power.

There are so many aspects to consider in a global evaluation of the media. May they become ever less the instruments of manipulating people. May they become, more and more, promoters of freedom, media of influence, of growth, of maturing the freedom of man.

With these wishes, I am happy to invoke upon all who read these words and seek to understand and share my pastoral care, the fullest heavenly grace, of which my apostolic blessing is a pledge.

From the Vatican, 10 May 1981

IOANNES PAULUS PP. II

MESSAGE OF THE HOLY FATHER JOHN PAUL II FOR THE 16TH WORLD COMMUNICATIONS DAY

Sunday 23 May 1982

Social Communications and the Problems of the Elderly

Dearest brothers and sisters in Christ

For sixteen years now the Church has been holding this 'day' celebration in which the faithful are invited, in response to a specific direction of the conciliar *Decree Inter mirifica*, to engage in prayerful reflection concerning their personal obligations in the important matter of social communications (cf. *Inter mirifica*, no. 18). It has been the practice to focus attention on a particular theme for each celebration, while inviting the prayers and offerings of the faithful (Ibid.). In line with this tradition, it has been my wish that the day should this year be devoted to the elderly, gladly adopting the theme on which the United Nations Organisation has chosen to concentrate in 1982.

1. The problems of the elderly today differ considerably from those with which they had to contend in the past. There is, firstly, the fact that the numbers of old people have been steadily increasing; in countries with a high standard of living the increase is accounted for by the improvement in health services and medical care, by better working conditions and general welfare.

Then there are certain factors proper to the modern industrial society, the principal being the alteration in the pattern of the family, which is now generally reduced to a small nucleus, whereas in a peasant society it was a patriarchal grouping. Further, it is often isolated and unstable, sometimes even broken up. Various things have contributed to bring this about, such as the flight from the land and the rush to the cities; and to these may be added in our times the (sometimes immoderate) search for comforts and tendency towards consumerism. In this kind of context, the elderly, often enough, finish by becoming an encumbrance.

And so there come about those conditions that far too often make the lives of the elderly a misery: abject poverty, especially in countries where there are no social security provisions for the old; forced inaction for the pensioners, particularly those who have worked in industry, or who are now very old; desolate loneliness for those deprived of the affection of family or the company of friends. Then, as the years pass and their strength fails and illness comes to debilitate them further, they are made to feel increasingly conscious of their physical fragility and, above all, of the burden of life.

Concern of Humanity

2. There can be no adequate solution to these problems unless they are taken to heart by everybody and accepted as a matter with which the whole of humanity must concern itself; for all humanity is called upon to support and care for the elderly, because of the dignity of each and every human being and because of the significance of human life, which 'is a gift, always'.

The sacred scripture, which speaks frequently about the old, considers old age as a gift which renews itself and which ought to be lived each day in openness to God and to the neighbour.

In the Old Testament, the old person is regarded as a master of life: 'How attractive is wisdom in the aged! Rich experience is the crown of the aged, and their boast is the fear of the Lord' (Sir 25:5-6). What is more, the old have another important task: to pass on the word of God to the new generations: 'We have heard with our ears, O God, our fathers have told us, what deeds thou didst perform in their days' (Ps 44:1). Announcing to the young their own faith in God, they preserve a fecundity of the spirit which suffers no decline with the weakening of their physical powers: 'They still bring forth fruit in old age, they are ever full of sap and green, to show that the Lord is upright' (Ps 92:1-15). For these tasks of the aged there are corresponding duties for the young. They must listen to them: 'Do not disregard the discourse of the aged' (Sir 8:9), 'ask your father, and he will show you; your elders, and they will tell you' (Deut 32:7); and they must assist them: 'Help your father in his old age, and do not grieve him as long as he lives; even if he is lacking in understanding, show forbearance; in all your strength do not despise him' (Sir 3:12-13).

No less rich is the teaching of the New Testament, where St Paul gives 'evangelical' counsels for an ideal of life in old age, prescribing sobriety, dignity, judiciousness, soundness in the faith, in love and patience (cf Tit 2:2). A very striking example is given by the old man Simeon, who lived in the hope and expectation of meeting the Messiah, and for whom the Christ became the fullness of life and the hope of the future. Having prepared himself in faith and humility, he was able to recognise the Lord, and joyfully sang, not a farewell to life, but a hymn of thanks to the Saviour of the world, on the threshold of eternity (cf. Lk 2:25-32).

Dispensers of Wisdom and Hope

3. Precisely because old age is a time of life which needs to fulfil itself in active and loving engagement, adequate prominence and help should be given to all those 'movements' which assist the elderly to emerge from an attitude of mistrust, solitude and resignation, and to become rather dispensers of wisdom, witnesses of hope and workers of charity.

It is within the family that the elderly ought to find their first field of action. Their wisdom and experience are a treasure for the young married folk who, in the difficulties of early married life, can find in aged parents agreeable counsellors and confidants, while the children will find in the example and affectionate care of their grandparents something which will compensate for the absences of the parents, which, for various reasons, are so frequent today.

And this is not all: in the civil society itself, which has always entrusted the stable organisation of its social arrangements, as well as the progress of necessary reforms, to mature persons, the elderly can still provide a stabilising factor in working out the kind of co-existence that achieves renewal and advance, not by means of ruinous experiences, but by prudent and gradual development.

Mass Media can form Attitudes

4. Workers in the social communications profession have a mission to fulfil in favour of the elderly which is ever so important; I should say, in fact, there is nothing else which can substitute for it. The media instruments in their hands, with their worldwide range of action and with their immediacy in getting messages across, can quickly and eloquently concentrate general attention and excite general reflection on the elderly and on their conditions of life. It is only when it is jerked into awareness, given a salutary shock, and then mobilised into taking appropriate action, that society can go about seeking ways and means to give effective solutions to the new needs.

Another contribution from the communications fraternity will be to correct among the young certain modes of thinking regarding the old, restoring to those of mature years and to the old a confidence of their own usefulness and re-modelling the attitudes of society so that it will see the elderly at their true value. It is also in their power to give opportune reminders to public opinion that, alongside the problem of a 'just wage', there also exists the problem of a 'just pension' which equally requires attention as a demand of 'social justice'.

The fact is that modern cultural patterns, in which an unbalanced emphasis is often given to economic productivity, efficiency, physical strength and beauty, personal comfort, can have the effect of making the elderly seem burdensome, superfluous and useless and of isolating them from family and social life. A careful examination reveals that part of the responsibility for this situation may be attributed to certain attitudes of the mass media: if it is true that the media reflect the society in which they operate, it is no less true that they contribute to making it the sort of society which it is, and therefore, cannot be exempted from taking their share of the responsibility.

Media people are particularly well qualified to communicate widely a vision of the old, as outlined above, which is genuinely human and therefore also Christian: a vision of old age as a gift of God to the individual, to the family and to society. Authors, writers, producers, actors, can succeed, through the wonderful ways of the arts, in making such a vision understandable and attractive. All of us know the success they have achieved in other campaigns, conducted with finesse and perseverance.

Culture and Prayer

5. These human and Christian attitudes, broadcast widely by the mass media, will help the elderly to look upon this period of their life with serenity and acceptance, and to employ their intellectual, moral and physical energies, to whatever extent is possible, for the benefit of others, giving what help they can in projects of a humanitarian, educational, social or religious character; also to fill their long silences by means of culture and prayer. Their children will be persuaded that the ideal dwelling place for the elderly is within the family, or at least a place where they can be surrounded by the affection of its members, and made to feel sincerely accepted and loved and cared for.

The civil society, meanwhile, will be stimulated to adopt adequate systems of social security and assistance, which will take account not only of physical and material needs but also of those which are psychological and spiritual, so as to integrate the elderly once and for all into the community's benefits and allow them a full life. Generous persons will feel themselves called upon to give their time and energies to this cause, having recognised Christ himself in their needy brother.

Beyond this work of animation the media workers, well aware that the elderly form a large and stable proportion of their public, especially as readers and users of radio and television, will take care to see that there are programmes and publications suitable for them, thus offering them not only recreational material, but also an assistance in their continuing education, a thing that is required at every age. Communicators will merit the special gratitude of the housebound and the sick for making it possible for them to participate with the people of God in liturgical services and other Church events.

In such transmissions it will naturally be necessary to keep in mind the needs and special sensibilities of the old, avoiding novelties which may upset them and showing respect for the sense of the sacred which old people possess in large measure and which constitutes in the Church a good which is worth preserving intact.

Serving a Noble Cause

6. Let the elderly themselves be the first, on this World Communications Day specially devoted to their problems, to offer their prayers and sacrifices to the Lord that the Christian vision of old age may grow in the world.

As for those who are still in their childhood, those still in the vigour, may they look upon their elders with loving respect and gratitude.

May the communications people find joy and happiness in serving this noble and deserving cause with their wonderful talents and resources.

And may the Lord bless and sustain them all in their resolve.

With this wish, I gladly give my apostolic blessing to all those who work in the field of social communications, to all those who are responsible beneficiaries of their services, and especially to the elderly. May it bring them copious gifts of tranquil joy and spiritual progress.

From the Vatican, 10 May 1982

IOANNES PAULUS PP. II

MESSAGE OF THE HOLY FATHER JOHN PAUL II FOR THE 17TH WORLD COMMUNICATIONS DAY

Sunday 15 May 1983

Social Communications and the Promotion of Peace

Dearest brothers and sisters in Christ

1. The promotion of peace: this is the theme proposed for your reflection on the World Day of social communications in the present year. A theme of extreme importance and of vibrating topicality.

In a world whose various elements have become ever more interdependent, thanks to the spectacular progress and rapid expansion of the mass media, communication and information today represent a force which can very powerfully serve the great and noble cause of peace, but which can equally aggravate tensions and favour new forms of injustice and of violations of human rights.

Fully conscious of the role of those engaged in social communications, I believed it to be necessary, in my recent message for the World Day of Peace (1 January 1983) which was on the theme: 'The dialogue for peace, a challenge for our time', to address a special appeal to all who work in the mass media encouraging them to weigh well their responsibility and to put forward with fullest objectivity the rights, problems and mentalities of the two sides, so as to promote understanding and dialogue between groups, countries and civilizations (cfr. no. II).

In what way can social communication promote peace?

2. First of all, through the establishment on the institutional plane of an order of communication that guarantees a correct, just and constructive use of information, free from oppression, abuses and

discriminations based on political, economic or ideological power. It is not the intention here in the first place to think of new technical applications, but rather to re-think the fundamental principles and the aims which must be given precedence in social communication, in a world which has become like a single family and where a legitimate pluralism ought to be assured on a common basis of consensus about the essential values of human coexistence. To achieve this, an erudite maturing of conscience is required on the part of both the communications workers and their audiences, and enlightened, upright and courageous choices have to be made by public authorities, by society at large and by the international institutions. A right order of social communication and an equal participation in its benefits, in full respect for the rights of all, create an environment and conditions favourable for a mutually enriching dialogue between citizens, peoples and the different cultures, while injustices and disorders in this area favour situations of conflict. Thus, one-way information imposed arbitrarily from on high, or from the laws of the market and of advertising, concentration in monopolies, manipulation of whatever kind; not only are such things attacks upon the right order of social communication, but they also finish by injuring the rights to responsible information and by endangering peace.

3. Secondly, communication promotes peace when in its content it educates constructively in the spirit of peace. Closely considered, information is not ever neutral; it corresponds always, at least implicity and in its intentions, to chosen stances. Communication and education to values are intimately linked. Cleverly placed emphasis, slanted interpretation, even loaded silences, are devices which can profoundly alter the significance of what is being communicated. So, the form and manner in which situations and problems are presented – such matters as development, human rights, relations between peoples, ideological conflicts, social and political differences, national claims, the arms race, to give but a few instances – directly or indirectly influence the formation of public opinion and create mentalities which are either inclined towards peace or, on the contrary, towards seeking solutions through the use of force.

If it is to be an instrument of peace, social communication will have to rise above unilateral and partisan considerations, shake itself free from prejudices and create instead a spirit of understanding and reciprocal solidarity. The faithful acceptance of the logic of peaceful co-existence among diverse elements requires the constant application of the method of dialogue which, while recognising the right to existence and to expression of all the parties concerned, affirms also the obligation which each has to integrate itself with all the others, in order to achieve that higher good, which is peace; and to peace there is opposed today, as a dramatic alternative, the threat of the atomic destruction of human civilization.

Consequently, it becomes today all the more necessary and all the more urgent to put forward the values of a total humanism, founded on recognition of the true dignity and of the rights of man, open to cultural solidarity, as well as to social and economic solidarity among persons, groups and nations, in the consciousness that all humanity has the same vocation in common.

4. Social communication, finally, promotes peace if the professionals of information are workers for peace.

The peculiar responsibility and unavoidable task which falls to the lot of communicators in regard to peace can be deduced from a consideration of the capacity and power which are theirs to influence, sometimes in a decisive way, both public opinion and the attitudes of those in government.

To the communications operatives, there should certainly be accorded, for the exercise of their important functions, fundamental rights, such as access to the sources of information and freedom to present the facts objectively.

But, on the other hand, it is also necessary that the communications workers should rise above the demands of an ethic which is conceived merely as relating to the individual and that, above all, they should not let themselves be enslaved to power groups, whether these are clearly recognisable as such, or in disguise. They ought instead to keep in mind that, above and beyond their contractual obligations to the organs of information, and their legal responsibilities, they also have precise duties regarding the truth towards the public and relating to the common good of society.

If in the exercise of their task, which is truly a mission, the social communicators contrive to promote calm and impartial information, to favour understanding and dialogue, to strengthen comprehension and solidarity, they will have made a magnificent contribution to the cause of peace.

I confide to you, dearest brothers and sisters, these considerations of mine, now, exactly at the beginning of the extraordinary Holy Year, with which we intend to celebrate the 1950th anniversary of the Redemption of mankind, achieved by Jesus Christ, 'the Prince of Peace' (cfr. Is 9:6), who is 'our peace' and who is come 'to announce peace' (cfr. Eph 2:14; 17).

While I invoke on you and on the workers in social communications the divine gift of peace, which is a 'fruit of the Spirit' (cfr. Gal 5:22), I give you from my heart my apostolic blessing.

From the Vatican, 25 March 1983

IOANNES PAULUS PP. II

MESSAGE OF THE HOLY FATHER JOHN PAUL II FOR THE 18TH WORLD COMMUNICATIONS DAY

Sunday 24 May 1984

Social Communication:
Instruments of Encounter between Faith and Culture

Beloved brothers and sisters in Christ

1. Desired by the Second Vatican Council to 'make the Church's multiple apostolate in the field of social communication more effective' (*Decree Inter mirifica*, no. 18), this annual day, which is being celebrated for the eighteenth time, has the scope of ever better educating the faithful in their duties in such an important sector. On this occasion, in the first place I wish to exhort each of you to join me in prayer that the world of social communication, with its operators and multitude of receivers, may faithfully carry out its function in the service of truth, freedom and the promotion of the whole man in all people.

The theme chosen for this eighteenth day is of great importance: Social communications: instrument of encounter between faith and culture. Culture, faith and communication are three realities among which a relationship is established on which depend the present and the future of our civilization, which is called to express itself ever more fully in its planetary dimension.

2. Culture, as I had the opportunity to say earlier (cf. *Discourse to UNESCO*, 2 June 1980), is a specific dimension of the existence and being of man. It creates among the persons within each community a complex of bonds, determining the interpersonal and social character of human existence. Man is both subject and creator of culture in which he expresses himself and finds his equilibrium.

Faith is the meeting between God and man: to God, who in history reveals and realises his plan of salvation, man responds through faith, receiving and making his own this plan, directing his life to this message (cf. Rm 10:9, 2 Cor 4:13). Faith is a gift from God to which man's resolve must correspond.

But if culture is the specifically human way to approach ever more to being and if, on the other hand, in faith man opens himself to knowledge of the supreme being in whose image and likeness he was created (cf. Gen 1:26), there is no one who does not see what a profound relationship there is between one and the other human experience. One understands, then, why the Second Vatican Council wanted to emphasise the 'outstanding incentives and encouragements' which the mystery of Christian faith offers to man that he may fulfil with greater commitment the task of building up a more human world, that is, one corresponding to his 'total vocation' (cf. *Gaudium et spes*, no. 57).

And further: culture in itself is communication: communication not only and not so much of man with the environment that he is called to dominate (cf. Gn 2:19-20, 1:28) as of man with other men. Indeed, culture is a relational and social dimension of human existence. Enlightened by faith, it expresses also man's full communication with God in Christ and, upon contact with the truths revealed by God, more easily finds the foundation of the human truths which foster the common good.

3. Faith and culture, therefore, are called to meet and to interact precisely in the sphere of communications: the effective achievement of the meeting and interaction, as well as their intensity and effectiveness, in large measure depends on the suitability of the media through which communication takes place. The press, cinema, the theatre, radio, television, with the evolution which each of these media has undergone during the course of history, have proved to be not always adequate to the encounter between faith and culture. The culture of our time particularly seems to be dominated and shaped by the newest and most powerful among the means of communication – radio and, above all, television – so much so that at times they seem to assert themselves as ends and not as simple means, also because of the characteristics of organisation and structure which they require.

Nevertheless, this aspect of modern mass media must not

make us forget that it is a question always, of means of communication and that this, by its nature, is always the communication of something. The content of the communication is therefore always determinant, and such, indeed, as to qualify the communication itself. Hence, with regard to the contents, the sense of responsibility of the communicators as well as the critical sense of the receivers must always be stressed.

4. Certain disappointing aspects of the use of the modern mass media must not make us forget that with their contents they can become marvellous instruments for the spread of the Gospel, suitable to the times, capable of reaching the remotest corners of the earth. In particular, they can be of great help in catechesis, as I pointed out in the apostolic exhortation *Catechesi tradendae* (no. 46).

May those who use the means of social communication for the purposes of evangelization – contributing also to building up in this way a cultural fabric in which man, aware of his relationship with God, becomes more man – be therefore aware of their lofty mission. May they have the necessary professional competence and may they feel the responsibility of transmitting the gospel message in its purity and totalily, without confusing the divine doctrine with men's opinions. Indeed, the mass media, whether they deal with news or concern themselves with precisly cultural topics, or whether they are used for the purpose of artistic expression and entertainment, always return to a particular concept of man; and it is precisely on the basis of the exactness and completeness of this concept that they will be judged.

At this point my appeal becomes stronger and is addressed to all workers in the field of social communications, in whatever location and of whatever religion:

- Operators of communications, do not give an incomplete, distorted picture of man, one closed to authentic human values!
- Give space to the transcendent, which makes man more man!
- Do not deride religious values, do not ignore them, do not interpret them according to ideological schemes!

- May your information be always inspired by criteria of truth and justice; may you feel the duty to rectify and remedy when you happen to make an error.
- Do not corrupt society, and in particular youth, by the approving and insistent depiction of evil, of violence, of moral abjection, carrying out a work of ideological manipulation, sowing discord!
- All you who work in the mass media, know that your messages reach a mass that is such because of the number of its members, each of whom, however, is man, a person concrete and unique, who must be recognised and respected as such. Woe to anyone who will have given scandal, especially to the little ones! (cf. Mt 18:6).
- In short, commit yourselves to fostering a culture which is truly to man's standard, aware that by doing this you will facilitate the encounter with faith, which no one must fear.

5. Unfortunately, a realistic examination leads us to recognise that in our time the immense potentials of the mass media are very often used against man, and that the prevailing culture disregards the encounter with faith, both in countries in which the free circulation of ideas is permitted and also in places where freedom of expression is confused with irresponsible license. It is the task of everyone to improve the field of social communication and to lead it back to its noble aims. May communicators adhere to the rules of a correct professional ethic. May critics carry out their useful clarifying action, fostering the formation of the critical awareness of the receivers. May the receivers themselves know how to choose with prudent care books, newspapers, films, plays and television programmes in order to derive from them occasions of growth and not corruption. Furthermore, also through suitable associated forms, may they make their voice heard by the operators of the communication that it may always be respectful of man's dignity and his inalienable rights. And, with the words of the Second Vatican Council, I point out that the 'civil authorities, which rightly regard the well-being of the citizens as their concern, are also bound to ensure, equitably and vigilantly, that public morality and social progress are not gravely endangered through the misuse of these media' (*Inter mirifica*, no. 12).

6. Indeed, since at the beginning of communication there is a man-communicator and, at its end, there is a man-receiver, the media of social communication will facilitate the encounter between faith and culture the more they foster the encounter of persons among themselves, so that a mass of isolated individuals will not be formed, each one of whom may be in dialogue with the written page, or the stage, or the small or large screen, but a community of persons aware of the importance of the meeting with faith and with culture and determined to achieve it through personal contact, in the family, in the place of employment, in social relations. May culture and faith, which find useful and often indispensable direct or indirect aids in the mass media, circulate in the dialogue between parents and children, become enriched through the work of teachers and educators, develop through direct pastoral action, up to the personal encounter with Christ present in the Church and in his sacraments.

With the intercession of Mary Most Holy, I invoke on the workers in the field of communications and on the vast community of receivers the heavenly favours of which my apostolic blessing is pledge, that each one in his own role may commit himself to ensure that social communications be an ever more effective means of encounter between faith and culture.

From the Vatican, 24 May 1984

IOANNES PAULUS PP. II

MESSAGE OF THE HOLY FATHER JOHN PAUL II FOR THE 19TH WORLD COMMUNICATIONS DAY

Sunday 19 May 1985

Social Communications for a Christian Promotion of Youth

My dearest brothers and sisters in Christ, men and women who have at heart the dignity of the human person, and, above all, you young people of the whole world, who have to write a new page of history for the year 2000!

1. The Church is getting ready, as it does every year, to celebrate World Communications Day. An occasion of prayers and reflection, in which the whole Church community, called to announce and witness to the Gospel (Mk 16:15), ought to feel involved, so that the mass media, through the cooperation of all persons of good will, may truly contribute to 'the realisation of justice, of peace, of freedom and of human progress' (*Communio et progressio*, 100).

The theme of the world day – 'Social communications for a Christian Promotion of Youth' – echoes the initiative of the United Nations, which has proclaimed 1985 as the 'Intemational Year of Youth'. The instruments of social communication, which are 'capable of extending almost infinitely the area over which it is possible to make the word of God heard' (*Evangelii nuntiandi*, 45), can effectively contribute towards young people's realisation of their personal vocation as persons and as Christians, through a free and responsible choice, thus preparing them to be the builders and leaders of tomorrow's society.

Instruments for the Service of Humanity

2. The Church, in its teaching of the Second Vatican Council – the twentieth anniversary of its closing is celebrated this year – and in

its subsequent teaching, has clearly acknowledged the great importance of the mass media in the development of the human person: from the point of view of information, of education and training, of cultural maturation, as well as of leisure time, occupation and entertainment. The Church has also, however, pointed out that the media are instruments for the service of humanity and of the common good; means, that is, not ends.

The world of social communications is engaged today in a development which is dizzying in its extreme complexity, a development whose ultimate unfolding cannot be foreseen (we talk nowadays of a technotronic age, to indicate the growing interaction between technology and electronics); and in this complex world we encounter not a few problems, connected with the elaboration of a new world order of information and communication, in interplay with the prospects opened up by the employment of satellites and the conquest of space.

We are speaking of a revolution which not only implies a change in the systems and techniques of communication, but involves the whole cultural, social and spiritual universe of the human person. In consequence, it cannot respond simply to its own internal norms, but must draw its own basic criteria from the truth of and about the human person, formed in the image of God.

According to the right to information which every person has, communication must always respond in its content to the truth, and out of respect for justice and charity it ought to be complete. With all the greater reason, this hold true when the communication is addressed to young people, who are in the position of opening themselves to the experiences of life. Above all in this case, information cannot remain indifferent to values which touch human existence down to the roots, such as the primacy of life from the moment of its conception, the moral and spiritual dimension, peace, and justice. Information cannot be neutral in the face of problems and situations which on the national and international levels damage the connective fabric of society, such as war, violation of human rights, poverty, violence, drugs.

Challenges to Social Communications

3. For all time, the destiny of man has been decided in the confrontation of the truth, in the choice which he, in virtue of the freedom conferred on him by his Creator, makes between good and evil between the light and the darkness. But it is a striking and painful thing to see today an ever growing number of men blocked from the free exercise of this choice: because they are subjugated by authoritarian regimes, suffocated by ideological systems, manipulated by a totalitarian science and technique, conditioned by the mechanism of a society which generates ever increasing depersonalisation.

Liberty seems the great challenge which social communication must confront, to achieve the conquest of enough space for sufficient autonomy, right there where it must at present submit to the censorship of totalitarian regimes, or to the impositions of powerful cultural economic or political pressure groups.

The mass media, as elements of unity and advancement, must overcome ideological and political barriers, walking with humanity in its march towards peace, and assisting the process of integration and fraternal solidarity among peoples, in two directions, east-west and north-south. As vehicles of education and culture, the mass media must contribute to the renewal of society and, in particular, to the human and moral development of young people, focusing their awareness on the historic tasks which await them on the threshold of the third millennium. With this end in mind, the mass media ought to open to youth new horizons, educating them to a sense of duty, to honesty, to respect for their peers, to a sense of justice, to friendship, to study, to work.

Immense Potential for Good

4. These considerations bring into clear relief the immense potential for good which the instruments of social communication have in their power to set free. But at the same time they leave us to imagine the grave threats which the mass media can hold over society – if bent to the purposes of power or self-interest, or if used with the intention of distortion, against the truth, against the dignity of the human person or his freedom and, worst of all, against the weakest and most defenseless.

The newspaper, the book, the record, the film, the radio, and the television in particular, and the ever more sophisticated computer, these already represent an important point of contact, even if not the only one, between the young person and the external reality within which his daily life is lived. And the young person has recourse to the mass media with increasing frequency, either because he now has more spare time, or because the frantic rush of modern life causes him to seek more frequent escape in recreation. Then, the absence of both parents, when the mother as well as the father has to work outside the home, occasions a slackening in the traditional control over the use which is made of the media.

Young people, therefore, are the first and most immediate receivers of the mass media, but they are also the most exposed to the flood of information and images which arrive in the house by means of the media. Furthermore, it is not possible to ignore the danger of certain messages, transmitted even during the hours when youth listening and viewing is at its peak, slipped in under cover of ever more explicit and aggressive advertising, or introduced in shows which give the impression that the life of man is regulated only by the laws of sex and violence.

The term 'videodependence' is already in common use to describe the ever mightier influence that the instruments of social communication, with their capacity for suggestion and modernity, have upon the young people. There is need to examine this phenomenon very thoroughly, to verify its real consequences on receivers who have not yet developed a suffciently mature critical sense. It is not merely a question of conditioning free time, that is, of limiting the amount of time available each day for other intellectual and recreational activities, but there is also question of the effects upon the very psychology, the culture, the behaviour of youth.

The education imparted by the traditional teachers, particularly the parents, was achieved by a fundamental interpersonal relationship which permitted the two-way flow of dialogue; this tends now to be replaced by a one-way education. In place of a culture laid down upon a value-content framework, on the quality of the information, there thus enters a culture of the temporary which favours the rejection of long term commitments, with a culture so overpowering that it induces a flight from the making of free personal choices. For a training directed towards encouraging the growth of a sense of responsibility, individual and collective, there is substituted an attitude of passive acceptance towards the fashions and the needs imposed by a materialism which, while stimulating consumption of goods, empties the conscience. The imagination, which is the very property of our early years, the expression of youth's creativity, of its impulsive generosity, dries up in the glut of images absorbed so effortlessly, and a habit of indolence is formed which quences stimuli and desires and smothers any impulse to undertake new tasks or projects.

Demanding Task

5. It is a situation which, if it is not to become more widespread, must surely persuade those who work in social communications to reflect very seriously and very deeply. They have an uplifting task, but one which is at the same time tremendously demanding: the use which they make of their resources of talent and expertise depend in large measure on the training and education of the people who, tomorrow, must achieve the betterment of this society of ours, impoverished in its human and spiritual values and threatened with self-destruction.

Parents and educators have an even more demanding task. The witness they give, supported by conduct which is culturally and morally consistent, may in fact very well be the most efficacious and credible teaching the young can receive. Dialogue, critical discernment, vigilance; these are the conditions which are indispensable when educating the young person to behave responsibly in the use of mass media, re-establishing in him or her the right balance whenever there has been a negative impact from these instruments.

The International Year of Youth, even in this area, makes demands upon the world of adults. It is a duty upon all to help the young enter society as responsible citizens, well-rounded people, conscious of their own dignity.

Church's Mission

6. It is here precisely that the 19th World Communications Day takes on its full significance. The theme of this forthcoming

celebration goes right to the heart of the Church's mission, for the Church must bring salvation to all men, preaching the Gospel 'from the housetops' (Mt 10:27; Lk 12:3). Great possibilities are offered today to social communications, in which the Church recognises the sign of God's creative and redemptive work, the work which man must continue. These instruments can therefore become powerful channels for the transmission of the Gospel, on the level of pre-evangelization, and on that of the deepening of faith, to favour the human and Christian promotion of youth.

This evidently calls for:

- profound educational activity, in the family, in the school, in the parish, through the catechism, to instruct and guide the young to a balanced and disciplined use of the mass media, helping them to form a critical judgement, illumined by faith, on what they see, hear and read (*Inter mirifica* 10, 16; *Communio et progressio* 67-70, 107);
- careful and specific practical and theoretical training in the seminaries, in apostolic associations of laity, in the new ecclesial movements, especially youth movements, not only to secure an adequate acquaintance with the instruments of social communication, but also to realise their undoubted potential for strengthening dialogue in charity and reinforcing the bonds of unity (*CP* 108, 110, 115-117);
- the active and coherent presence of Christians in all the sectors of social communication, bringing not only the contribution of their cultural and professional expertise, but also the living witness of their faith (*CP*, 103);
- the engagement of the Catholic community, so that, when the need arises, it will denounce shows and programmes which assault the moral good of the young, state its claim for more truthful information about the Church, and demand transmissions more positively inspired by the authentic values of life (*IM* 14);
- the presentation of the gospel message in its integrity: taking trouble not to betray it, not to trivialise it, not to reduce it, with intent, to a merely socio-political vision; but also, after the example of Christ the perfect communicator, adapting it to the receivers, to the mentality of young people, to their

manner of speaking, to their state and condition (*Catechesi tradendae*, 35, 39, 40).

Especially Youth

7. And it is to the youth in particular that I wish to address myself at the conclusion of this message: to the young people who have already encountered Christ, to those who have come to Rome at the beginning of Holy Week, in spiritual unity with millions of their age group, to proclaim with the Pope that 'Christ is our peace' but also to all young people who, even in a confused way, amid uncertainties, anguish and mistakes, aspire to encounter this 'Jesus who is called Christ' (Mt 1:16), to give a meaning and a purpose to their life.

Dearest young people! Up to now, I have addressed myself to the world of adults. But in reality, it is to you in particular that I wish to send this message. The importance and the ultimate meaning of the instruments of social communication depend, definitively, on the use which human freedom makes of them. It will, therefore, depend on you, on the use you make of them, on the critical judgement with which you know how to use them, whether these instruments are going to serve your human and Christian formation, whether, on the contrary, they are going to be turned against you, suffocating your liberty and putting an end to your thirst for authenticity.

It will depend on you, young people, for to you it falls to construct the society of tommorow, in which the intensified flow of information and of communications will multiply the forms of association among men, and technological development will hammer on the barriers that separate men and nations. It will depend on you whether the new society is going to be one sole human family, where men and peoples can live in closest collaboration, fully integrated, or whether in the society of the future the conflicts and divisions which afflict the world today are simply going to be more bitter.

In the words of the apostle Peter, I repeat the wish which was expressed in my letter to the young men and women of the world: that you may 'always have your answer ready for people who ask you the reason for the hope that you all have' (1 Pet 3:15).

'Yes, you your very selves, for on you depends the future, on you depends what are left of the thousand years now ending and the quality of the opening years of the new millennium. Therefore, don't be passive; take over your responsibilities in every field open to you in our world'! (no. 16).

Search for Truth

Dearest young people! The invitation I offer you to responsibility, to engagement, is first of all an invitation to search for 'the truth that will make you free' (Jn 8:32), and the truth is Christ (cf. Jn 14:6). And so it is an invitation to place the truth of Christ at the centre of your life to give witness to this truth in the story of your daily life, in the decisive choices you have to make, in order to help humanity set its feet firmly on the path of peace and of justice.

With these sentiments I impart to all my apostolic blessing, praying that you may be enlightened from heaven.

From the Vatican, 15 April 1985

IOANNES PAULUS PP. II

MESSAGE OF THE HOLY FATHER JOHN PAUL II FOR THE 20TH WORLD COMMUNICATIONS DAY

Sunday 11 May 1986

Social Communications and the Christian Formation of Public Opinion

Dear brothers and sisters

1. The recent Extraordinary Synod of Bishops, on the occasion of the twentieth anniversary of the conclusion of the Second Vatican Council, did not set out merely to be a solemn commemoration of that event, which was destined to mark so deeply the life of the Church in this century; more importantly, it brought the Council's spirit to life again and recalled anew its teachings and decisions. Thus, the Synod took the Second Vatican Council and relaunched it into the Church's life.

Among the initiatives given birth by a directive of the Council there is one which is worthy of special mention. It is the annual World Communications Day, established in the first place 'to strengthen more effectively the various forms of the Church's apostolate in the field of communications in all the dioceses of the world' (*Inter mirifica*, 18). The decision to establish it, which shows what great importance the Council Fathers attributed to social communications, is seen to have even greater relevance today, with the ever growing influence of the communications media.

The Church which, this year for the twentieth time, in faithful obedience to the Council, celebrates World Communications Day, has been accustomed to assign a particular theme to each successive celebration. This year, the day is to be dedicated to considering, in depth, what contribution social communications can make to the Christian formation of public opinion.

This is not the first time that the Church has turned its attention to this theme. 'The Church does not speak and listen to her own members alone', said the Pastoral Instruction *Communio et progressio*, in 1971; 'her dialogue is with the whole world. By virtue of a divine command and by the right to knowledge possessed by the people whose lot she shares on earth, the Church is in duty bound publicity to communicate her belief and her way of life' (no. 122).

Morally Healthy Public Opinion

2. Paul Vl, in his turn, wrote in the Apostolic Exhortation *Evangelii nuntiandi*: 'In our age which is characterised by the mass media, we must not fail to avail ourselves of the media for the first proclamation of the message, for catechetical instruction and for a deeper study of the faith. These, when they are employed in the sevice of the gospel, can disseminate the word of God over a vast area and carry the message of salvation to millions of men. The Church would feel herself guilty before God if she did not avail herself of those powerful instruments which human skill is constantly developing and perfecting. With their aid she may preach 'upon the housetops' the message which has been entrusted to her. In them she finds in a new and more effective form a platform or pulpit from which she may address the multitudes' (no. 45).

'Public opinion' consists in the common and collective way of thinking and feeling which is found in a fairly large social group at a particular time in a particular place. It is the indicator regarding what the body of the people think about a subject, or a fact, or a problem of some importance. Public opinion is formed by the fact that a large number of people do, because it seems to them right and proper, just what some persons or groups who have a certain cultural, scientific, or moral authority, think and say. This shows the grave responsibility borne by people who, because of their education or prestige, form public opinion or influence its formation in some measure. People, in fact, have a right to think and feel in conformity with what is true and right, because from their way of thinking and feeling depends their moral performance. lt will be right if their way of thinking conforms to the truth.

It needs to be underlined, in this connection, that public opinion has a great influence on the modes of thinking, feeling and behaving of those who, either because of their youth or their lack of education, are not capable of making critical judgements. Thus, there are many who think and act according to what is commonly thought in the community, without being in a position to resist the pressure it imposes on them. It must also be emphasised that public opinion exercises a powerful influence on the formation of laws. In fact, there is no doubt that the introduction in some countries of unjust laws, such as, for instance, legalised abortion, must be attributed to the pressure exercised by a public opinion which was favourable to the measure.

3. From this arises the importance of forming a morally healthy public opinion on matters which more closely affect the well-being of humanity in our time. Among these we would place the values of life, of the family, of peace, of justice and of solidarity among peoples.

It is necessary that a public opinion should be formed which is sensitive to the absolute value of human life, so that it shall be recognised in all its stages, from conception to death, and in all its forms, even those marked by sickness or disability, physical or spiritual, as having this value. A materialistic and hedonistic mentality is in fact spreading, according to which life is worth living only when it is healthy, young and beautiful.

It is necessary that a correct public opinion should be formed on the family, a public opinion which will help to overcome some ways of thinking and of feeling which are not in conformity with the plan of God who has established the family indissoluble and productive. Unfortunately, a public opinion is becoming widespread favouring free love, divorce and the drastic reduction of births, by any and every means; this needs to be rectified because it is injurious to the true good of humanity, which will enjoy true happiness to the exact extent that the family is united and in a healthy state.

Then, it is necessary to create a public opinion of constantly growing strength in favour of peace, and of what serves to bring it about and preserve it, such as reciprocal appreciation and mutual agreement among peoples; the rejection of every form of racial discrimination and exaggerated nationalism; the recognitions of the rights and just aspirations of peoples; disarmament, first of the spirit and then of the instruments of destruction; the effort to achieve the peaceful resolution of conflicts. It is clear that only a strong public opinion favourable to peace can put a stop to such as are tempted to see in war the way to resolve tensions and conflicts.

'State leaders rely to a large extent,' states the pastoral constitution *Gaudium et spes*, 'on public opinion and public attitudes. Their peace-making efforts will be in vain, as long as men are divided and warring among themselves through hostility, contempt and distrust, as well as through racial hatred and uncompromising hostilities. Hence, there is a very urgent need of re-education and a new orientation of public opinion' (n. 82).

Finally, there is need for the formation of a strong public opinion in favour of the solution of the very distressing problems of social justice, of hunger and underdevelopment. What is required, in fact, is that these problems should be better known today in their tremendous reality and gravity, so that a strong and very widespread public opinion in favour of finding solutions to them shall be created. It is only under the vigorous and unrelenting pressure of such public opinion that the responsible politicians and economists of the rich countries will be induced to help the developing countries.

4. It is specially urgent that a healthy public opinion shall be formed in the area of morality and religion. To block the wider spread of a mentality favourable to moral permissiveness and religious indifference, there is need to form a public opinion which respects and appreciates moral and religious values for the reason that they make a person fully 'human' and give life its full meaning. The danger of nihilism, that is, of the loss of the values which are most properly human, moral and religious, hangs over humanity today like a grave threat.

A correct public opinion, then, ought to be formed regarding the nature, mission and work of the Church, which is seen by many today as a simply human structure, and not as what it really is, a mysterious reality that incarnates the love of God in history and brings the love and the grace of Christ to humanity.

Communications Serve Humanity

5. In the world of today as it is, the instruments of social communications in their many forms – press, cinema, radio, television – are the principal makers of public opinion. Great, then, is the moral responsibility of all those who have these instruments in their employ, or who are the guiding forces behind them. The media of social communications ought to be put at the service of humanity, and therefore of truth and goodness which constitute humanity's most important and necessary values. Those, therefore, who work professionally in the field of social communications should feel themselves under obligation to form and to make widespread a public opinion which conforms with truth and goodness.

In this task Christians are expected to distinguish themselves, knowing well that in contributing to the formation of a public opinion favourable to justice, peace, fraternity, and religious and moral values, they are contributing in no small way to the growth of God's kingdom, which is a kingdom of justice, of truth and of peace. From the Christian message which is directed to the well-being and the salvation of humanity, they can draw inspiration to assist their brothers in forming opinions that are right and sound, because they are in conformity with the plan of love and salvation for humankind which God has revealed and put into action in Jesus Christ. In fact, the Christian faith and teaching of the Church, precisely because they are founded on Christ, the way, the truth and the life, are light and strength for humanity in his passage through history.

I conclude this message with a special blessing for all those who work in social communications with a Christian spirit of service to the truth and promotion of moral and religious values. I assure them of my prayers, and I wish to encourage them in this work, which calls for courage and consistency and which is a service to truth and to freedom. It is, in fact, the truth that makes people free (cf. Jn 8:32). And therefore, to work for the formation of a public opinion which is in conformity with the truth is to work for the growth of freedom.

From the Vatican,
24 January 1986, the Feast of Saint Francis de Sales

IOANNES PAULUS PP. II

MESSAGE OF THE HOLY FATHER JOHN PAUL II FOR THE 21ST WORLD COMMUNICATIONS DAY

Sunday 31 May 1987

Social Communications at the Service of Justice and Peace

Beloved brothers and sisters in Christ

Social communications constitutes a platform of exchange and dialogue which responds to a particular concern of my pontificate, and that of my predecessor, Paul Vl (cf. *Message to the Special Session of the United Nations on Disarmament*, 24 May 1978, 5): to contribute, in the promotion of peace through justice, to the passage from a balance of terror to a strategy of trust. With some urgency, therefore, I proposed as the theme for World Social Communications Day 1987: 'Social Communications at the Service of Justice and Peace.' This I have repeated often, but I emphasise it today adding the following: trust cannot be the work simply of those involved in politics, but it must come from the conscience of peoples. Having already dealt with the problem of peace (*World Day of Peace* 1983), this year I would like to continue this brief reflection on the work of justice which brings about peace, the strategy of trust as the fulfilment of justice in view of peace.

I know that for you, workers in the field of social communications, the masses are not an anonymous multitude. They represent a continuous challenge to reach each and everyone in their particular context, at their own level of understanding and sensibility, thanks to the ever-more advanced technologies and ever-more effective means of communication. This appeal might resound in your conscience: transmit the strategy of trust through the means of communication, at the service of justice and peace!

To a large extent, your strategy of communication is a plan of information with the aim of contributing to the building up of this society with the knowledge of what we are doing, no matter what might happen. Allow me to recall what I have already said in this respect: peace in the world depends on a better knowledge of men and communities; the qualified information of public opinion has a direct influence on the promotion of justice and peace (cf. *Message for World Peace Day* 1982, no. 6 and 8). Your task seems to go beyond human possibilities: informing in order to form, while the stream of news carries you to the four corners of the earth, sometimes in a dangerous manner, and without giving you the time to ponder over each case or each event. And therefore, the users of social communications depend on you for understanding the harm of terror and the hopes of trust.

Peace is not possible without dialogue (cf. *Message for World Peace Day* 1986, no. 4-5), but true dialogue cannot be established without being well-informed, in the east and in the west, in the south and in the north. Furthermore, your dialogue wishes to be 'total dialogue', that is, a dialogue established in the context of a global strategy of communications: information, certainly, but also entertainment, publicity, artistic creation, education, sensitivity to cultural values. It is through this strategy of communications that the strategy of trust should be realised. From the balance of apprehension, to that of fear, and finally to that of terror, springs a 'cold peace' – as Pius XII said – which is not true peace. Only communication can, through true dialogue, bring about a desire and expectancy of a warm peace, seen as a necessity, in the hearts of peoples. And, it could be added, a 'cold justice' is not true justice. Justice cannot live if not in trust, otherwise it is simply a 'justice against' and not for 'justice for' and 'justice with' each human person.

How can we link the strategy of trust and the strategy of communication? I would like to develop this theme for reflection. I know that mass communication is programmed and carefully organised. It is, therefore, important to bring to mind what could be a strategy of trust transmitted by the media. It seems to me that this could comprise seven fundamental aspects: making people aware, denouncing, renouncing, overcoming, contributing, spreading and affirming.

In the first place, it is necessary to make people aware, or, in other words, to carry out a work of intelligence. Did not Paul VI say that peace is a work of intelligence? It will be necessary, therefore, through the various programmes, to make people aware that every war can lose everything, and that nothing can be lost with peace. For this, the strategy of communications can, better than any other means, make the cause of war understood: the innumerable injustices which stimulate violence. Every injustice can lead to war.

Violence is in us; we must free ourselves of it to discover peace. Such is the work of justice which is carried out as a fruit of intelligence. Intelligence, according to the teaching of the Second Vatican Council (cf. *Gaudium et spes,* no. 82–91), expresses itself above all through the positive choices suggested by questions of justice and peace, in the face of injustice and war. And it is precisely here that your role becomes interesting, due to the spirit of initiative which it bears.

Communicating the constructive choices of justice and peace goes hand in hand with your duty to denounce all causes of violence and conflict: generalised armaments, commerce of arms, oppression and torture, terrorism of every kind, over-militarisation and an exaggerated concern for national security, North-South tension, and all forms of domination, occupation, repression, exploitation and discrimination.

To denounce in a coherent way, you must renounce yourself the roots of violence and injustice. One of the images most firmly integrated into the production of means of communication seems to be the 'ideal of the strongest, this desire for supremacy which does nothing but increase mutual fear. Along the lines of what John XXIII affirmed, it is necessary to arrive, in your production, at a 'disarmament of spirits' (Cf. *Address to Journalists at the Council*, 13 October 1962). What could be the progress of exchanges in communication, if the market was amply supplied with programmes which present things entirely different from this will for domination which is the inspiration for so many works in circulation at the moment! And what improvement in quality could be obtained if the users, through their requests, could renounce the idea of the strongest! To act in a spirit of justice, it is not enough to 'act against' in the name of a hardened force.

Rather it is necessary to 'act through and with' others, or, in the world of the media, to communicate through and with each one.

The strategy of trust also signifies overcoming all the obstacles to the 'works of justice' in view of peace. In the first place, it is necessary to overcome the barriers of mistrust. What better than social communications can overcome all the barriers of race, class and culture which confront each other? Mistrust can be born from all forms of partiality and social, political or religious intolerance. Mistrust feeds on the discouragement which becomes defeatism. Trust, on the other hand, is the fruit of a more rigorous ethical attitude at all levels of daily life. Pope John XXIII recalled that it was necessary at all costs to overcome the imbalance between the technical possibilities and ethical commitment of the human community.

And you, both workers and users of social communications, you know well that the world of communications is an exploding world of technological progress. Even in this advanced sector of human experience, the ethical need is the most urgent at all levels.

Your role, furthermore, is that of contributing to making peace possible through justice. Information is the way of awareness, of verification, of controlling the reality of facts on the paths of peace. This contribution can be deepened by debates and public discussions within the media. It is perhaps at this level that your imagination will be put to its hardest test. And it is precisely here that the users' answer is most necessary.

We must not then forget the task of spreading with some insistence all that can help to make peace and justice understood and lived, right from the most humble initiatives at the service of peace and justice up to the efforts of international meetings. Among these initiatives, the role of a new world information and communications order, at the service of peace and justice, and with the guarantee of widespread information in favour of all, certainly occupies an important place, as I have already mentioned on the occasion of one of the congresses of the International Union of the Catholic Press (cf. *Address to the UCIP*, 25 September 1980). Your role as those responsible for social communications is one of continual education. As users of social communications, your duty is one of continual research for access to all data which can form your opinions and make you ever-more aware of your responsibilities. We are all responsible for the destiny of justice and peace.

In the midst of all the initiatives which you must spread, allow me to ask you with some insistence not to ignore the presentation of the Christian idea of peace and justice, the Christian message of peace and justice, without forgetting exhortations to commitment, but also to prayer for peace: irreplaceable dimensions of the ecclesial contributions to peace initiatives and in favour of efforts to live in justice.

These things you already know, as suggested by the presentation, through the means of social communication, of the true and complete image of the human person, foundation of every reference to justice and peace. Anything that wounds the person is already 'an act of war' in its beginning. Therefore, what incalculable consequences each of these communications' initiatives, of which you are the animators, will have!

In spreading these things, it is necessary finally to affirm all preliminary conditions in view of justice and peace: the inalienable rights of the human person, equal fundamental liberties in view of the participation of all in the common good, respect for legitimate sovereignty, the duties of indemnity and aid ... But above all, we must shed light on the values of life: existence no longer seen as relentlessly engaged in a 'struggle for life', but life lived with the intelligence of wisdom, in goodness, or again, love as a source and ideal of life. Only love, re-discovering fraternity every day, can definitively defeat terror. May love, inspired by the gift of God, act on these 'marvellous techniques' of communication, which are also 'gifts of God' (cf. *Miranda prorsus*)!

In the hope that these words will help you never to lose sight of justice and peace, as you, workers in social communications, begin to carry out your programmes, and as you, the users, listen and respond, I give you all my trust and ask you all to work for trust at the service of the whole of humanity. In this spirit, I impart to you with joy my apostolic blessing.

From the Vatican,
24 January 1987, the Feast of Saint Francis de Sales

IOANNES PAULUS PP. II

MESSAGE OF THE HOLY FATHER JOHN PAUL II FOR THE 22ND WORLD COMMUNICATIONS DAY

Sunday 15 May 1988

Social Communications and the Promotion of Solidarity and Fraternity between Peoples and Nations

Brothers and sisters
My dear friends, the communicators

If one day it can be truly said that 'to communicate' is the same as 'to fraternise', that 'communication' signifies human 'solidarity', will not this be the most beautiful result of 'mass communications'? It is on this theme that I would propose to you that we reflect on the 22nd World Communications Day.

In speaking of fraternity, I use the term in its strict meaning. It is Christ, in effect, 'the first-born among many brethren' (Rom 8:29), who makes us discover in every human person, friend or even enemy, a brother or a sister. Christ who came 'not to condemn the world but to save it' (cf. John 3:17), calls all humanity to unity. The spirit of love which he gives to the world is also a spirit of unity: St Paul shows us the same spirit who grants a variety of gifts, who acts in the different members of the same Body: there are 'varieties of gifts ... but it is the same God who inspires them all in every one' (1 Cor 12:4-6).

If I mention first the spiritual basis of fraternity and solidarity, it is because this Christian meaning is not at all unrelated to the human reality which the words primarily signify. The Church does not consider fraternity and solidarity to be values in any way reserved to itself. On the contrary, we remind ourselves always how Jesus praised the Good Samaritan who recognised a brother in the man who was wounded, in contrast to the priest and the Levite (cf. Luke 10:29-37). In like manner, the apostle Paul invites us not to despise the gifts of others, but to rejoice in the Spirit's workings in each of our brothers (1 Cor 12:14-30).

Fraternity and solidarity are basic and urgent things: they ought to be, in our times, distinguishing marks of peoples and cultures. The joyous unveiling of their happy, friendly, helpful relationships with one another: ought this not be the most beautiful 'festival' offered by mass communications, their most successful 'show', in the best sense of these terms?

In this period of spectacular development in mass communications, the bonds which they weave between peoples and cultures represent the most precious and valuable support that they offer to humanity. I know, at the same time, that you communicators are aware of perverse effects as well, which threaten distortion and disfigurement to these relations between peoples and cultures. Exaltation of the self, contempt for and rejection of those who are different, can aggravate tensions and divisions. From such attitudes spring violence, mistaken directions, destruction of true communication; for they render impossible all brotherly relationship.

In order that the very existence of brotherhood and human solidarity may be made possible, and still more so that their Christian dimension may be more intensely developed, the elementary values which underlie them have to be given recognition. Permit me here to recall certain of these: respect for others, a willingness to dialogue, justice, healthy ethics in personal and community living, freedom, equality, peace in unity, promotion of the dignity of the human person, the capacity to share and to divine with others. Brotherhood and solidarity rise above all clannish and corporation spirit, all nationalism, all racism, every abuse of power, every individual fanaticism, be it cultural religious.

It is for the agents of mass communication to use the techniques and media at their disposal always with a conscientious regard for these primary values. Here I suggest only some of the possible applications:

- Let the information agencies and the whole ensemble of the press demonstrate their respect for others by giving complete and balanced information;

- the radiophonic diffusion of the word will the better attain its purpose in the measure in which the possibility of reciprocal exchange is offered to all;
- media which are the mouthpiece of particular groups contribute to the operation of justice in giving a voice also to the voiceless;
- television programmes touch on almost all aspects of life and the networks have countless possible applications and interconnections: considering their great influence, there must rest on those responsible for them an ethical imperative, obliging them to offer to persons and communities images which favour the mutual penetration of cultures, without intolerance and without violence, in the service of unity;
- the possibility of personal communications by telephone, their extension by teletext, their wider and wider spread by satellite: all this suggests that we should have a care for equality among persons and facilitate access to these media to a greater number, so as to permit really meaningful exchanges;
- information increasingly concerns economic or cultural activities, data banks bring together a quantity of diverse information which was unimaginable in earlier times: it is known that this could be used in such a way as to bring all sorts of pressure to bear on private community life; and the wise management of these media thus becomes a veritable precondition of peace;
- to create the 'shows' which sustain the various audiovisual media implies an obligation to respect the consciences of the countless 'spectators' in the audiences;
- advertising publicity awakens or increases desires and also creates needs: those who commission it or bring it to realisation have to keep in mind the disavantaged for whom the benefits advertised are out of reach.

Whatever the exact mode by which they intervene, it is necessary that the communicators observe a code of honour, that they have a care for the sharing out of the truth among and about humankind, and that they shall contribute to a new world order of information and of communication.

In the midst of the ever more concentrated and active network of social communications spanning the world, the Church binds itself simply to keep on ceaselessly recalling, as 'an expert in humanity', the values which constitute the grandeur of the human being. But she is at the same time convinced that these cannot be assimilated and put into action in the concrete, if the spiritual life of the human being is forgotten. For Christians, the revelation of God in Christ is an illumination on man and woman, on humanity itself. Faith in the message of salvation constitutes the most deeply felt motivation for serving the human race. The gifts of the Spirit engage us in the service of others in a brotherly solidarity.

The question may be asked of us: are we not perhaps too trusting in our openness to this kind of thinking? Do the tendencies which are apparent in the field of mass communication really permit us to entertain such hopes?

To hearts which are troubled by the risks of the new technologies of communication, I would reply: 'Fear not'! Far from ignoring the reality in which we live, we read it more profoundly. We distinguish, in the light of faith, the authentic signs of the times. The Church, full of care for man and woman, is aware of the deep aspiration of the human race for fraternity and solidarity – an inspiration often disowned or disfigured, but indestructible because it is sculpted in the human heart by the same God who has created in it the need for communication and the capacity to develop it on a planetary scale.

On the threshold of the third millennium, the Church reminds men and women that fraternity and solidarity cannot be regarded merely as conditions for survival; they are essentials of their vocation, a vocation which the exercise of social communication permits them to realise freely.

Permit me then to say to you all, especially in this Marian Year, 'Do not be afraid!' Was not Mary herself frightened at the announcement which contained the sign of salvation offered to the whole of humanity?

'Blessed is she who believed', as Elizabeth testified (Lk 1:45). It is thanks to her faith that the Virgin Mary accepts God's plan, enters into the mystery of trinitarian communion, and, becoming the Mother of Christ, inaugurates in history a new fraternity.

Blessed are those who believe, those whom the faith liberates from fear and opens to hope and leads to the construction of a world where, in fraternity and solidarity, there is place for the communication of joy!

Animated by this profound joy for the gifts of communication received for the building-up of all, in this solid fraternity, I invoke on each one of you the blessing of the most high.

From the Vatican,
24 January 1988, the Feast of Saint Francis de Sales

IOANNES PAULUS PP. II

MESSAGE OF THE HOLY FATHER JOHN PAUL II FOR THE 23RD WORLD COMMUNICATIONS DAY

Sunday 27 May 1989

Religion in the Mass Media

Brothers and sisters
My dear friends, the communicators

1. The theme of the World Day of Social Communications this year, 'Religion in the media', underlines the special importance of the Church's presence and of the part it plays in public dialogue. In our days, in fact, religious messages, as well as cultural messages, gain an increased impact from the intervention of the social communications media. The reflection which I would like to share with you on this occasion will illustrate a concern that has been constantly with me throughout my pontificate: what place can religion have in the life of society and, more exactly, what place can religion have in the media?

2. In the course of its pastoral activity, the Church naturally asks itself questions regarding the media's attitude to 'religion'. The fact is that at the very time the media and the techniques of communication are enjoying such developments, the industrial world which has assisted their extraordinary growth itself shows a 'secularism' which is apparently bent on hastening the disappearance of any sense of religion among the people of our day.

3. Meanwhile, it is plain to see that religious information is tending to get more attention in the media, by reason of the increased interest which is now generally taken in the religious dimension of human realities, whether of the individual or of

society. To analyse this phenomenon, one should question the readers of newspapers and the people who watch television or listen to the radio, because it is not a matter of the media imposing religion upon them unasked; it is rather that those responsible for mass communication are simply responding to specific requests they have been receiving to give more space to information and commentary on religious affairs. Throughout the entire world there are millions of persons who turn to religion in order to make sense of their lives; millions of people for whom relationship vith God, their creator and father, is the happiest reality of human existence. The communications professionals are well aware of this, and act accordingly. And even if this interaction between those in the communications media and the public is marked by incompleteness and partiality, there is this positive fact: religion is there today in the mainstream of media information.

4. By a happy blend of circumstances, World Communications Day in 1989 coincides with the twenty-fifth anniversary of the foundation of the Pontifical Commission for social communications, which from now on will be a 'Pontifical Council'. What has it achieved in its twenty-five years of service in the apostolate of communications? Assuredly, the Church itself has learnt to discern more clearly the 'signs of the times', and the phenomenon of communication is very much one ot them. My predecessor Pius XII had already invited it to look upon the media not as a threat, but as a 'gift' (cfr. *Miranda prorsus*, 1957). The Second Vatican Council in its turn solemnly confirmed this positive attitude (cfr. *Decree Inter mirifica*, 1963). The Pontifical Commission which was then born and which today exists as the Pontifical Council has given itself fully and perseveringly to the promotion within the Church of an attitude of participation and of creativity in this sector, or, better, in the new style of life and sharing of humanity.

5. The question confronting the Church today in not any longer whether the man in the street can grasp a religious message, but how to employ the communications media so as to let him have the full impact of the gospel message. The Lord encourages us

very directly and very simply to take the broader view in our witness and our communication: Do not be afraid ... what you hear in whispers, proclaim from the housetops (Mt 10:26-27). To what is he referring? The evangelist throws light upon it: Christ wishes us to declare ourselves for him before men (cfr. Mt 10:32). So here it is then, the daring, humble and serene at the same time, which inspires the Christian presence in the middle of the public media debate! St Paul says to us: 'Preaching the gospel is not a thing I boast about, since it is a duty which has been laid on me' (1 Cor 9:16). Throughout the scriptures the same fidelity is spoken of: 'I have made no secret of your love and faithfulness in the Great Assembly' (Ps 40(39):10), and 'All men will tell what God has wrought' (Ps 64(63):9).

Communicators and public of the media, you must both question yourselves about the constantly changing demands of this 'religion pure and undefiled' which invites us to keep ourselves unstained from the world (Jas 1:27). Even these pieces of wisdom from the Bible make you understand immediately that the great challenge of religious witness for those who are in the midst of the public debate is to keep the messages and exchanges authentic and to maintain high standards of quality in the programmes and productions.

6. In the name of the whole Church, I wish to thank the world of communication for the place which it offers religion in the media. I am certain that I am interpreting correctly the feeling of all people of good will when I express this gratitude, even if it does often seem to us that there is room for improvement in the possibilities permitted for a Christian presence in the public debate. I am happy to join in expressing thanks to the media for giving prominence to religious information, documentation, dialogue and data gathering.

I would also like to ask of all communicators that they show themselves, by their careful adherence to the highest standards of professional ethics and practice, worthy of the opportunity given them to present the message of hope and reconciliation with God in media of every kind and discipline. The 'gifts of God' (cfr. Pius XII, encyclical *Miranda prorsus*): do we not have here a mysterious encounter between the technological possibilities of the language of communication and the openness of the human spirit to the splendid message of the Lord and his witnesses? It is at this level that the quality of our ecclesial presence in the public debate is in play. More than ever, the holiness of the apostle supposes a 'divinization' (to use an expression of the Church Fathers) of the entirety of human ingenuity. It is for this reason also that the liturgical celebration of the mysteries of faith cannot be left out in this vast movement of presence to the world of today through the mass media.

7. Thinking about all this, I make with simplicity and confidence a request for something very close to my heart. It comes out of the same feeling of friendship as that which made Paul say to Philemon: 'I write with full confidence ... knowing that you will do even more than I ask' (Phil 1:21). Here is my request: give to religion all the space possible in mass communications. 'Open the gates, let the upright nation come in; she, the faithful one ... who keeps the peace' (cfr. Is 26:2a, 3a). It is this that I ask in favour of religion. You will see, dear friends, that these religious themes will have the power to inspire in the measure in which they are competently presented by professionals, themselves deeply convinced of them in their own souls. Once the communicator is open to the religious message, his own message gains in quality and interest. To Church media workers I repeat: equally in your case 'you have received the spirit of adoption of sons, which makes you cry out: Abba! Father!' (cfr. Rom 8:15).

The message and the initiatives of religion can be present in all types of media: in the press, in written and audio-visual information programmes, in cinematographic creations, in data banks and telematic exchanges, in theatrical communication and stage shows and high level cultural presentations, in public opinion debate and in commentaries on the news, in services which educate public thinking, in all the productions of group media, through animated drawings and quality cartoon strips, in all the varied forms in which written literature is distributed, in audio- and video-recordings, in the moments of relaxation with music on local or network radio! It is my very ardent wish that the Catholic and Christian networks may be able to collaborate constructively with cultural communications networks of every kind, overcoming a preoccupation with competition in view of the ultimate good which comes from the message of religion. The Church itself, on this occasion of World Communications Day, invites all concerned to take under serious consideration the demand for ecumenical and inter-religious cooperation in the media.

8. Concluding this message, I certainly must not fail to encourage all those who have at heart the apostolate of communication to give themselves with ardour and energy, and with due respect for every person, to the great work of evangelization in which each is challenged to take part: 'But as for you, go and proclaim the kingdom of God' (Lk 9:60). And there is something I must add: it is in proclaiming and in living the word that we ourselves will come to grasp the unsuspected depths of the gift of God.

Welcoming God's will and with confidence, I declare to all of you, media workers and public, my joy at finding you linked together today across such mighty distances in a common reflection designed to find and deepen that 'religion pure and undefiled' which we will all then take our part in proclaiming 'from the housetops'; and I invoke on you all the blessing of the Lord.

From the Vatican,
24 January 1989, the Feast of Saint Francis de Sales

IOANNES PAULUS PP. II

MESSAGE OF THE HOLY FATHER JOHN PAUL II FOR THE 24TH WORLD COMMUNICATIONS DAY

Sunday 27 May 1990

The Christian Message in a Computer Culture

Brothers and sisters
Dear friends

In one of her eucharistic prayers, the Church addresses God in these words: 'You formed man in your own likeness and set him over the whole world, to serve you, his creator, and to rule over all creatures' (*Eucharistic Prayer IV*).

For man and woman thus created and commissioned by God, the ordinary working day has great and wonderful significance. People's ideas, activities and undertakings – however commonplace they may be – are used by the Creator to renew the world, to lead it to salvation, to make it a more perfect instrument of divine glory.

Almost twenty-five years ago, the Fathers of the Second Vatican Council, reflecting on the Church in the modern world, declared that men and women, serving their families and the community in their ordinary occupations, were entitled to look upon their work as 'a prolongation of the work of the Creator ... and as their personal contribution to the fulfilment in history of the divine plan' (*Gaudium et spes*, 34).

As the Council Fathers looked to the future and tried to discern the context in which the Church would be called upon to carry out her mission, they could clearly see that the progress of technology was already 'transforming the face of the earth' and even reaching out to conquer space (cf. *Gaudium et spes*, 5). They recognised that developments in communications technology, in particular, were likely to set off chain reactions with unforeseen consequences.

Far from suggesting that the Church should stand aloof or try to isolate herself from the mainstream of these events, the Council Fathers saw the Church as being in the very midst of human progress, sharing the experiences of the rest of humanity, seeking to understand them and to interpret them in the light of faith. It was for God's faithful people to make creative use of the new discoveries and technologies for the benefit of humanity and the fulfilment of God's plan for the world.

This recognition of rapid change and this openness to new developments have proved timely in the years that followed, for the pace of change and development has continued to accelerate. Today, for example, one no longer thinks or speaks of social communications as mere instruments or technologies. Rather they are now seen as part of a still unfolding culture whose full implications are as yet imperfectly understood and whose potentialities remain for the moment only partly exploited.

Here we find the basis for our reflections on this twenty-fourth World Communications Day. With each day that passes the vision of earlier years becomes ever more a reality. It was a vision which foresaw the possibility of real dialogue between widely-separated peoples, of a worldwide sharing of ideas and aspirations, of growth in mutual knowledge and understanding, of a strengthening of brotherhood across many hitherto insurmountable barriers (cf. *Communio et progressio*, 181, 182).

With the advent of computer telecommunications and what are known as computer participation systems, the Church is offered further means for fulfilling her mission. Methods of facilitating communication and dialogue among her own members can strengthen the bonds of unity between them. Immediate access to information makes it possible for her to deepen her dialogue with the contemporary world. In the new 'computer culture' the Church can more readily inform the world of her beliefs and explain the reasons for her stance on any given issue or event. She can hear more clearly the voice of public opinion, and enter into a continuous discussion with the world around her, thus involving herself more immediately in the common search for solutions to humanity's many pressing problems (cf. *Communio et progressio*, 114 ff.).

It is clear that the Church must also avail herself of the new resources provided by human exploration in computer and satellite technology for her ever pressing task of evangelization. Her most vital and urgent message has to do with knowledge of Christ and the way of salvation which he offers. This is something she must put before the people of every age, inviting them to embrace the Gospel out of love, ever mindful that 'truth cannot impose itself except by virtue of its own truth, which wins over the mind with both gentleness and power' (*Dignitatis humanae*, 1).

As the wisdom and insights of past years teach us: 'God has spoken to humanity according to the culture proper to each age. Similarly the Church, which in the course of time has existed in varying circumstances, has utilised the resources of different cultures in her preaching to spread and explain the message of Christ' (*Gaudium et spes*, 58). 'The first proclamation, catechesis or the further deepening of faith cannot do without the (means of social communication) ... The Church would feel guilty before the Lord if she did not utilise these powerful means that human skill is daily rendering more perfect. It is through them that she proclaims 'from the housetops' the message of which she is the depositary' (*Evangelii nuntiandi*, 45).

Surely we must be grateful for the new technology which enables us to store information in vast man-made artificial memories, thus providing wide and instant access to the knowledge which is our human heritage to the Church's teaching and tradition, the words of sacred scripture, the counsels of the great masters of spirituality, the history and traditions of the local Churches, of religious orders and lay institutes, and to the ideas and experiences of initiators and innovators whose insights bear constant witness to the faithful presence in our midst of a loving Father who brings out of his treasure new things and old (cf. Mt 13:52).

Young people especially are readily adapting to the computer culture and its 'language'. This is surely a cause for satisfaction. Let us 'trust the young' (*Communio et progressio*, 70). They have had the advantage of growing up with the new developments and it will be their duty to employ these new instruments for a wider and more intense dialogue among all the diverse races and classes who share this 'shrinking globe'. It falls to them to search out ways in which the new systems of data conservation and exchange can be used to assist in promoting greater universal justice, greater respect for human rights, a healthy development for all individuals and peoples and the freedoms essential for a fully human life.

Whether we are young or old, let us rise to the challenge of new discoveries and technologies by bringing to them a moral vision rooted in our religious faith, in our respect for the human person, and our commitment to transform the world in accordance with God's plan. On this World Communications Day, let us pray for wisdom in using the potential of the 'computer age' to serve man's human and transcendent calling, and thus to give glory to the Father from whom all good things come.

From the Vatican,
24 January 1990, the Feast of Saint Francis de Sales

IOANNES PAULUS PP. II

MESSAGE OF THE HOLY FATHER JOHN PAUL II FOR THE 25TH WORLD COMMUNICATIONS DAY

Sunday 12 May 1991

The Communications Media and the Unity and Progress of the Human Family

Dear brothers and sisters

For the celebration of this World Communications Day, we return to the theme which formed the central message of the Pastoral Instruction *Communio et progressio*, approved by Pope Paul VI in 1971, regarding the application of the Decree of the Second Vatican Council on the Means of Social Communication. Prepared in obedience to the Council Fathers wishes, that instruction saw the chief aims of social communication and all the means it uses as the unity and progress of the human family. On the twentieth anniversary of this important document, I wish to return to that basic consideration in order to invite the members of the Church to reflect once more on the serious problems and rich new opportunities occasioned by continuing developments in the communications media, especially in relation to the unity and progress of peoples everywhere.

The Church has long held the conviction that the media (press, radio, television, film and cinema) are to be regarded as 'gifts of God' (cf. Pius XII, Encyclical Letter *Miranda prorsus, AAS*, 24, 1957, p. 765). The list of the 'gifts' which comprise the communications media has continued to lengthen since the pastoral instruction was published. Such contemporary items as satellites, computers, home video recorders and ever improving methods for the transmission of information are now at the disposal of the human family. The purpose of these new gifts is the same as that of the more traditional communications media: to draw us closer together in brotherhood and mutual understanding, and to help us to go forward in the pursuit of our human destiny as God's beloved sons and daughters.

The link between this general consideration and the reflection I wish to offer on this occasion is clear and direct: such powerful means placed at man's disposal demand in their use a lofty sense of responsibility on the part of all involved. In the words of the 1971 pastoral instruction, the communications media are 'lifeless instruments'. Whether or not they fulfil the purpose for which they were given to us greatly depends on the wisdom and sense of responsibility with which they are used.

In the Christian view, the communications media are wonderful instruments at man's disposal, under God's providence, for building closer and more enlightened relationships between individuals and throughout the human family. Indeed, as they develop, the media are capable of fashioning a new language which enables people to know and understand one another more easily, and therefore to work together more readily for the common good (cf. *Communio et progressio*, 12). If, however, they are to be effective means of fellowship and genuine human advancement, the media must be a channel and expression of truth, justice and peace, good will and active charity, mutual help, love and communion (cf. ibid., 12, 13). Whether the media serve to enrich or impoverish man's nature depends on the moral vision and ethical responsibility of those involved in the communications process and of the recipients of the media's message.

Every member of the human family, whether the humblest consumer or the most powerful producer of media programmes, has an individual responsibility in this respect. I therefore appeal to the pastors of the Church and to the Catholic faithful who are engaged in the world of communications to refresh their knowledge of the principles and guidelines which were so clearly set out in *Communio et progressio*. May all better understand where their duties lie and may they be encouraged to carry out these duties as a fundamental service to the unity and progress of the human family.

It is my hope that this twenty-fifth World Communications Day will be an occasion of renewed attention on the part of parishes and local communities to the realities of the media and their influence on society, on the family, and on individuals, especially children and young people. Twenty years after *Communio et progressio* it is possible to subscribe fully to that. Document's warning and expectation about developments in communications: 'Suddenly ... the responsibilities of the people of God will enormously increase. Never before will they have been offered such opportunities. It will be possible to ensure that the media promote the advance of the whole human race ... It will be possible to strengthen the brotherhood of man. And then the good news can be given everywhere, bearing witness to Christ the Saviour' (no. 182). I earnestly ask God to guide and support you in the realisation of that great hope and task!

From the Vatican,
24 January 1991, the Feast of Saint Francis de Sales

IOANNES PAULUS PP. II

MESSAGE OF THE HOLY FATHER JOHN PAUL II FOR THE 26TH WORLD COMMUNICATIONS DAY

Sunday 31 May 1992

The Proclamation of Christ's Message in the Communications Media

Dear brothers and sisters

For the twenty-sixth successive year, in response to a directive given by the Second Vatican Council, the Church celebrates a World Day dedicated to social communications.

What is it that this day celebrates? It is a way of acknowledging with gratitude a specific gift of God, a gift which has enormous significance for the period of human history in which we are living, the gift of all those technical means which facilitate, enhance and enrich communications between human beings.

On this day, we celebrate the blessings of speech, of hearing and of sight, which enable us to emerge from our isolation and loneliness in order to exchange with those around us the thoughts and sentiments which arise in our hearts. We celebrate the gifts of writing and reading by which the wisdom of our ancestors is placed at our disposal and our own experience and reflection are passed on to the generations that follow us. Then, as if these wonders were of small account, we recognise the value of 'marvels' even more wonderful: 'the marvels of technology which God has destined human genius to discover' (*Inter mirifica*, 1), inventions which in our time have immeasurably increased and extended the range over which our communications may carry and have amplified the volume of our voice so that it can simultaneously come to the ears of multitudes beyond counting.

The communications media – and we exclude none of them from our celebration – are the admission ticket of every man and woman to the modern marketplace where thoughts are given public utterance, where idea are exchanged, news is passed around, and information of all kind is transmitted and received (cf. *Redemptoris missio*, 37). For all of this we praise our Heavenly Father from whom comes 'every good endowment and every perfect gift' (Jas 1:17).

Our celebration, while essentially one of gladness and thanksgiving, is of necessity tempered with sadness and regret. By the very media we are celebrating we receive constant reminders of the limitations of our human condition, of the presence of evil in individuals and in society, of the senseless violence and injustice human beings wreak upon one another under so many pretexts. Through the media we often find ourselves in the position of helpless spectators assisting at atrocities committed all over the globe, whether the reason for them be historical rivalries, or racial prejudices, a desire for vengeance, a lust for power, greed for possessions, selfishness, or a lack of respect for human life and human rights. Christians deplore these happenings and motivations. But they are called to do much more; they must endeavour to overcome evil with good (cf. Rom 12:21).

The Christian response to evil is, above all, to harken to the good news and to make God's message of salvation in Jesus Christ ever more present. Christians have a 'good news' to tell. We have Christ's message – and it is our joy to share it with every man and woman of good will who is prepared to listen.

We tell it first by the witness of our lives, for, as Pope Paul VI wisely said, 'modern man listens more willingly to witnesses than to teachers, and if he does listen to teachers, it is because they are witnesses' (*Evangelii nuntiandi*, 41). We are expected to be like a city on a hill, like a lamp on a lampstand, visible to all, our light shining like a beacon signalling the safe channel to a peaceful haven (cf. Mt 5:13-14).

When our individual and community lives exemplify the beliefs and values we profess as Christians, this fact cannot fail to be brought to the attention of the world by all communications media that truly reflect the reality of things. Such a proclamation of Christ's message can already accomplish great good. How effective would be such a universal witness on the part of the members of the Church!

But, a still more explicit proclamation is also expected of Christ's followers. We are obliged to proclaim our beliefs 'in the light of day' and 'from the housetops' (Mt 10:27; Lk 12:3), without fear or compromise, adapting the divine message, naturally, 'to people's way of talking and their patterns of thought' (*Communio et progressio*, 11), and always with a sensitivity towards their actual beliefs and convictions equal to the sensitivity which we expect from them in regard to our own. Our proclamation must invariably be made with that twofold respect which the Church insists on: respect for all human beings without exception in their quest for answers to the deepest questions of their lives, and respect for the action of the Spirit, already mysteriously present in every human heart (cf. *Redemptoris missio*, 29).

Christ, we remember, forced his teaching on no one. He presented it to all without exclusion, but left each one free to respond to his invitation. This is the pattern which we, his disciples, follow. We claim that all men and women have the right to hear the saving message which he left with us; and we claim for them the right to embrace it if it convinces them. Far from feeling any obligation to apologise for putting Christ's message at the disposal of all, we claim with full conviction that it is our right and obligation to do no less.

There exists a corresponding right and obligation to use for this purpose all the new media of communication which distinguish our times. Indeed 'the Church would feel herself guilty before God if she did not avail herself of those powerful instruments which human skill is constantly developing and perfecting' (*Evangelii nuntiandi*, 45).

It is clearly realised that these 'powerful instruments' require specific skills and disciplines on the part of those who use them, and that to communicate intelligibly in these 'new languages' there is a need for both special aptitudes and appropriate training.

It is in this connection that on World Communications Day I recall the activities of Catholics, individually and in a myriad of institutions and organisations, in this field. In particular I mention the three great Catholic Media Organisations: the International Catholic Office for Film and Cinema (OCIC), The International Catholic Press Union (UCIP) and the International

Catholic Association for Radio and Television (Unda). It is to them in particular and to the vast resources of professional knowledge, skill and zeal among their extensive international membership that the Church hopefully and confidently turns as she seeks to proclaim Christ's message in a form adapted to the instruments now at her disposal and in language intelligible to the worldwide media-conditioned culture to which it must be addressed.

The great body of Catholic media professionals, lay men and women for the most part, must be reminded on this special day of the awesome responsibility which rests upon them, but they must also be made to feel that they enjoy the spiritual support and firm solidarity of the whole body of the faithful. I wish to encourage them to even greater and more urgent efforts, both to communicate the message through the media and to train others to do so. I appeal to all Catholic organisations, to religious congregations and ecclesial movements, but in a special way to episcopal conferences, both national and regional, to foster the Church's presence in the media and to work for greater coordination among the Catholic agencies involved. In fulfilling her mission, the Church needs to be able to count on a far-reaching and more effective use of the means of social communication.

May God be the strength and support of all Catholics involved in the world of communications as they re-dedicate themselves to the work which he so clearly requires of them. As a token of his divine presence and of his all-empowering help for their efforts, I gladly impart to them my apostolic blessing.

From the Vatican,
24 January 1992, the Feast of Saint Francis de Sales

IOANNES PAULUS PP. II

MESSAGE OF THE HOLY FATHER JOHN PAUL II FOR THE 27TH WORLD COMMUNICATIONS DAY

Sunday 23 May 1993

Videocassettes and Audiocassettes in the Formation of Culture and of Conscience

My dear brothers and sisters

More than a full year after the publication of the Church's latest pastoral instruction on communications media, *Aetatis novae*, we are still reflecting on the vision of the modern world which it presented, and still trying to grasp the practical implications of the media situation it described. This is precisely what the Church would wish us to do. The entire family of the Church must involve itself prayerfully in the search for understanding and awareness in the unprecedented situations so often nowadays cast up by the world's headlong progress in discovery and development. Each individual must add his voice to the Church's unceasing petition for wisdom, for we greatly need divine guidance in order to grasp each opportunity that offers to serve God and his people, while at the same time taking the measures necessary to fend off whatever evil may threaten them.

The pastoral instruction *Aetatis novae*, we should notice, uses the word 'new' even in its own title. 'At the dawn of a new era,' it says, 'a vast expansion of human communications is profoundly influencing culture everywhere', and it goes on to claim that everybody is affected. The instruction uses the word 'new' again and again: 'new media', 'new languages', 'new opportunities', in its anxiety to illustrate that the world in the eighties and nineties is no longer the same as it was in previous decades and generations. The argument is that the world in which God's people are on pilgrimage is quite largely a changed place and that 'new media' are quite largely responsible for changing it.

The pilgrim people, however, must adapt to what is changed, must find ways to cope with it, must search to turn it to God's glory and the service of all his creation.

In my message for World Communications Day last year, I mentioned that among the things we always celebrate on this annual occasion are the gifts of speech, of hearing and of sight, which God has given us in order to make communication possible between us. This year the theme of the day focuses on two specific 'new' media which serve these very senses in a quite remarkable way, namely, audiocassettes and videocassettes.

These are truly remarkable gifts of God to our times, making it possible for us to conserve and easily transport, so that we may hear and view them over and over again, by ourselves or in the company of others, in our homes or elsewhere, as we choose, unlimited numbers of programmes in voice or vision, or both, whether for instruction or entertainment, for more complete understanding of news and information, or solely, perhaps, for artistic enjoyment.

Let me say again, and with emphasis, that the audiocassette and the videscassette are gifts of God, gifts, we may say, kept in his treasury through all the ages until our time, kept – for us. We must clearly understand that he did not give them to us for our harm. 'All things you love,' says wisdom, 'nor hold any of your creatures in abhorrence; hate and create you could not, nor does aught abide save at your will, whose summoning word hold them in being. They are yours, and you spare them, ... you the master of them all' (Wisdom 11:24-25).

It is not by accident that we find ourselves exactly where we are in this passing world and at this passing moment, never to be repeated, in the history of the human race. This has come about by a special disposition of God's providence. He wills us to be here, now and at no other time, with opportunities to serve our contemporaries by means never before available or even imagined, and thus to render glory to his majesty in ways never previously possible.

For those engaged professionally in the production of audio or video programmes in cassette or other forms, there will often be opportunities to integrate the Christian message in one way or another, explicitly or implicitly, 'into the 'new culture' created by modern communications' (*Aetatis novae,* 11). This is something which should be expected to happen as a natural consequence of 'the Church's active, sympathetic presence within the world of communications' (Ibid.).

The professional who rates at its true value the impact and influence of the media productions he creates, will take particular care to make them of such high moral quality that their effect upon the formation of the culture of his generation will be invariably a positive one. To be true to himself, to his craft and to his faith, he must evidently resist the ever-present blandishments of easy profit and firmly refuse to take part in any production which exploits human weakness, offends human conscience, or affronts human dignity.

The role of the non-specialist, or 'ordinary christian/citizen', in relation to media such as the audio- or video-cassette, must not be seen as that of a consumer merely. Each individual, simply by making his reactions to the media offerings placed before him known to those who produce and market them, will exercise a definite effect on the subject matter and moral tone of future offerings. The consumer must take very seriously his responsibility to make this active contribution to the protection and improvement of the media environment in which he and his dependents must exist.

To all the media professionals, men and women, who strive to serve their fellows in the various branches of the social communications industry, to all the beloved members of the International Catholic Organisations for Media active and at their posts throughout the world, and to the vast body of media consumers who are their audience and very weighty responsibility, I send, with affection and warmest fellow-feelings, on this World Communications Day, my apostolic blessing.

From the Vatican,
24 January 1993, the Feast of Saint Francis de Sales

IOANNES PAULUS PP. II

MESSAGE OF THE HOLY FATHER JOHN PAUL II FOR THE 28TH WORLD COMMUNICATIONS DAY

Sunday 15 May 1994

Television and Family: Guidelines for Good Viewing

Dear brothers and sisters

In recent decades, television has spearheaded a communications revolution which has profoundly affected family life. Today television is a primary source of news, information and entertainment for countless families, shaping their attitudes and opinions, their values and patterns of behaviour.

Television can enrich family life. It can draw family members closer together and foster their solidarity with other families and with the community at large. It can increase not only their general knowledge but also their religious knowledge, making it possible for them to hear God's word, to strengthen their religious identity and to nurture their moral and spiritual life.

Television can also harm family life: by propagating degrading values and models of behaviour; by broadcasting pornography and graphic depictions of brutal violence; by inculcating moral relativism and religious scepticism; by spreading distorted, manipulative accounts of news events and current issues; by carrying exploitative advertising that appeals to base instincts and by glorifying false visions of life that obstruct the realisation of mutual respect, of justice and of peace.

Even when television programmes themselves are not morally objectionable, television can still have negative effects on the family. It can isolate family members in their private worlds, cutting them off from authentic interpersonal relations; it can also divide the family by alienating parents from children and children from parents.

Because the moral and spiritual renewal of the human family as a whole must be rooted in the authentic renewal of individual families, the theme for the 1994 World Communications Day – 'Television and the Family: Guidelines for Good Viewing' – is especially timely, particularly during this International Year of the Family, when the world community is seeking ways to strengthen family life.

In this message, I wish especially to highlight the responsibilities of parents, of the men and women of the television industry, of public authorities and of those with pastoral and educational duties in the Church. In their hands lies the power to make television an ever more effective medium in helping families to fulfil their role as a force for moral and social renewal.

God has entrusted parents with the grave responsibility of helping their children 'to seek the truth from their earliest years and to live in conformity with the truth, to seek the good and promote it (*Message for the 1991 World Day of Peace*, no. 3). It is therefore their duty to lead their children to appreciate 'whatever is true, whatever is honourable, whatever is just, whatever is pure, whatever is lovely, whatever is gracious' (Phil 4:8).

Thus, besides being discriminating television viewers themselves, parents should actively help to form in their children viewing habits conducive to sound development, human, moral and religious. Parents should inform themselves in advance about programme content and make a conscious choice on that basis for the good of the family – to watch or not to watch. Reviews and evaluations provided by religious agencies and other responsible groups – together with sound media education programmes – can be helpful in this regard. Parents should also discuss television with their children, guiding them to regulate the amount and quality of their viewing and to perceive and judge the ethical values underlying particular programmes, because the family is 'the privileged means for transmitting the religious and cultural values which help the person to acquire his or her own identity' (*Message for the 1994 World Day of Peace*, no. 2).

Forming children's viewing habits will sometimes mean simply turning off the television set: because there are better things to do, because consideration for other family members requires it, or because indiscriminate television viewing can be harmful. Parents who make regular, prolonged use of television as a kind of electronic baby-sitter surrender their role as the primary educators of their children. Such dependence on television can deprive family members of opportunities to interact with one another through conversation, shared activities and common prayer. Wise parents are also aware that even good programmes should be supplemented by other sources of news, entertainment, education and culture.

To guarantee that the television industry will safeguard the rights of the family, parents should express their legitimate concerns to media managers and producers. Sometimes they will find it useful to join with others in associations which represent their interests in relation to the media, to sponsors and advertisers and to public authorities.

Television personnel – executives and managers, producers and directors, writers and researchers, journalists, on-camera performers and technical workers – all have serious moral responsibilities to the families that make up such a large part of their audience. In their professional and personal lives, those who work in television should be committed to the family as society's basic community of life, love and solidarity. Recognising the influence of the medium in which they work, they should promote sound moral and spiritual values, and avoid 'anything that could harm the family in its existence, its stability, its balance and its happiness,' including 'eroticism or violence, the defence of divorce or of antisocial attitudes among young people' (Paul VI, *Message for the 1969 World Communications Day*, no. 2).

Television is often required to deal with serious themes: with human weakness and sin and their consequences for individuals and society; with the failings of social institutions, including government and religion; with weighty questions about the meaning of life. It should treat these subjects responsibly – without sensationalism and with a sincere concern for the good of society, as well as with scrupulous regard for the truth. 'The truth shall make you free' (Jn 8:32), Jesus said, and ultimately all truth has its foundation in God, who is also the source of our freedom and creativity.

In fulfilling its public responsibilities, the television industry should develop and observe a code of ethics which includes a commitment to serving the needs of families and to promoting values supportive of family life. Media councils, with members from both the industry and the general public, are also a highly desirable way of making television more responsive to the needs and values of its audiences.

Whether television channels are under public or private management, they represent a public trust for the service of the common good; they are not the mere private preserve of commercial interests or an instrument of power or propaganda for social, economic or political elites; they exist to serve the well-being of society as a whole.

Thus, as the fundamental 'cell' of society, the family deserves to be assisted and defended by appropriate measures of the state and other institutions (cf. *Message for the 1994 World Day of Peace*, no. 5). This points to certain responsibilities on the part of public authorities where television is concerned.

Recognising the importance of a free exchange of ideas and information, the Church supports freedom of speech and of the press (cf. *Gaudium et spes*, 59). At the same time, she insists that 'the rights of individuals, families and society itself to privacy, public decency and the protection of basic values' demand to be respected (*Pontifical Council for Social Communications, Pornography and Violence in the Media: A Pastoral Response*, no. 21). Public authorities are invited to set and enforce reasonable ethical standards for programming which will foster the human and religious values on which family life is built and will discourage whatever is harmful. They should also encourage dialogue between the television industry and the public, providing structures and forums to make this possible.

Church-related agencies, for their part, render an excellent service to families by offering them media education and film and programme evaluation. Where resources permit, Church communications agencies can also help families by producing and disseminating family-oriented programming, or by promoting such programming. Episcopal Conferences and Dioceses should consistently make the 'family dimension' of television part of their pastoral planning for communications (cf. Pontifical Council for Social Communications, *Aetatis novae*, 21-23).

Since television professionals are engaged in presenting a vision of life to a vast audience, which includes children and young people, they can profit from the pastoral ministry of the Church, which can help them to appreciate those ethical and religious principles which give full meaning to human and family life. 'Typically, pastoral programmes of this sort should include ongoing formation which will help these men and women – many of whom sincerely wish to know and to do what is ethically and morally right – to integrate moral norms ever more fully into their professional work as well as their private lives' (Ibid., 19).

The family, founded on marriage, is a unique communion of persons which God has made the 'natural and fundamental group unit of society' (*Universal Declaration of Human Rights*, art. 16, 3). Television and the other communications media have immense power to sustain and strengthen such communion within the family, as well as solidarity with other families and a spirit of service to society. Grateful for the contribution to such communion within the family and among families which television as a communications medium has made and can make, the Church – herself a communion in the truth and love of Jesus Christ, the Word of God – takes the occasion of World Communications Day 1994 to encourage families themselves, media personnel and public authorities to realise to the full their noble calling to strengthen and promote society's first and most vital community, the family.

From the Vatican,
24 January 1994, the Feast of Saint Francis de Sales

IOANNES PAULUS PP. II

MESSAGE OF THE HOLY FATHER JOHN PAUL II FOR THE 29TH WORLD COMMUNICATIONS DAY

Sunday 28 May 1995

Cinema: Communicator of Culture and Values

Dear brothers and sisters

This year, on the occasion of World Communications Day, I would like to invite you to think about the cinema as 'a communicator of culture and of values'. As you certainly will know, during the current year celebrations are being held around the world to commemorate the first centennial of this special and widespread medium of expression, now so easily accessible to all.

The Church has often pointed out the importance of the communications media in transmitting and promoting human and religious values (cf. Pius XII, *Miranda prorsus*, 1957) and the special responsibilities that ensue for those who work in this difficult field. The Church, in fact, considering the progress that has been made and the developments that have taken place in the world of social communication in recent decades, is well aware both of the dangerous conditioning power enjoyed by the mass media as well as of the capacity that they offer, if wisely used, of being useful for evangelization.

As I wrote in the message published on the occasion of the World Communications Day of 1989, 'the question confronting the Church today is not any longer whether the man in the street can grasp a religious message but how to employ the communications media so as to let him have the full impact of the gospel message' (John Paul II, *Message for World Communications Day*, 1989).

Among the media of social communication, the cinema is by now a universal and esteemed medium from which messages are often sent which are capable of influencing and conditioning the choices of the public, and especially young people, in a form of communication that is based not so much on words as on concrete events, expressed in images which impact greatly on the viewers and on their subconscious.

The cinema, since it was invented, while sometimes giving rise to criticism and disapproval on the part of the Church on account of some aspects of its extensive output, has also often dealt with themes of great meaning and value from an ethical and spiritual point of view.

I would like to recall here, for example, the numerous film presentations of the life and passion of Jesus and of the lives of the saints, still available in many film libraries, and which are useful, above all, to animate numerous cultural, recreational and catechetical activities undertaken by many dioceses, parishes and religious institutions. From those beginnings a rich body of religious cinema has been produced, with a large number of films that have had significant influence on many people, albeit with the limitations that the passage of time, inevitably, tends to highlight.

Human and religious values that deserve attention and praise are often present, not only in films that make direct reference to the tradition of Christianity but also in films of different cultures and religions. This confirms the importance of the cinema as a vehicle for cultural exchange and as an invitation to openness and reflection in dealing with realities foreign to our upbringing and mentality. In this sense, the cinema serves to overcome distance and acquires that dignity particular to culture which is 'a specific dimension of the existence and being of man. It creates among the persons within each community a complex of bonds, determining the interpersonal and social character of human existence' (John Paul II, *Message for World Communications Day*, 1984).

To those who work in the field of cinema, I would like to extend a warm invitation not to abandon this important cultural element, because it is not in accordance with the most authentic and deep demands and expectations of the human person to produce films which are devoid of content and which are aimed exclusively at entertainment, or have the sole motive of increasing the size of the audience.

As happens with all the media of social communication, the cinema, as well as having the power and the great merit of contributing to the cultural and human growth of the individual, can oppress freedom – particularly of the most weak – when it distorts the truth (cf. Pius XII, *Miranda prorsus*, 1957) and when it presents itself as the mirror of negative types of behaviour, using scenes of violence and sex offensive to human dignity and 'tending to excite violent emotions to stimulate the attention' of the viewer (John Paul II, *Message for World Communications Day*, 1981). The attitude of those who irresponsibly bring about degrading imitative behaviour whose harmful effects can be read about each day in the pages of the newspapers cannot be defined as free artistic expression. As the gospel reminds us, only in the truth are we made free (cf. Jn 8:32).

The urgency of such a problem in our society, that seems too often to draw negative models from the daily stimuli offered by the cinema, as well as by television and by the newspapers, urges me to extend, once again, a pressing appeal both to those who are responsible for the industry – so that they may commit themselves to working with professionalism and responsibility – as well as to the viewers – so that they may know how to react in a critical way in the face of the ever more demanding proposals offered by the world of the media, including the cinema, and be ready to judge between what may be an opportunity for growth, or an occasion of harm.

When the cinema, in obedience to one of its principal aims, presents us with an image of how we are as human beings, it must provide, from a basis in reality, worthwhile opportunities for reflection on the concrete conditions in which we live. It must therefore offer material for reflection on issues such as social commitment, and the condemnation of violence, of all forms of exclusion, of war and of injustice. These concerns, often dealt with by the cinema in its hundred-year history, cannot leave indifferent all those who are worried about the fate of humanity. This means encouraging those values that the Church has at heart and contributing directly to their spread through a medium which so easily and effectively reaches the public (cf. Pius XII, *The Ideal Film*, 1955).

On this day above all, on the threshold of the third millennium, it is essential to ask ourselves definite questions, not avoiding the problems but looking for answers and solutions. In this context there is no question of not giving the cinema the place and the value that is its due. However, I would appeal to the responsible persons at every level to be fully aware of the great influence that they exercise on people and of the mission that they are called upon to pursue at this present time which has such urgent need of universal assertions of peace and tolerance. This is simply to recall those values which are to be found at the heart of that dignity which has been given to each one of us by God the Creator.

Those that work in the sensitive field of cinema must as communicators remain open to dialogue and to the reality that surrounds them. They must undertake to highlight the most important realities with films that provoke reflection, in the awareness that this approach, which permits the drawing together of different cultures and of the people that live them, will bring about positive results for all.

In order to be sure that the messages that cinema might offer for the human and spiritual growth of those who use it are fully understood, it is also important to take care of the education of viewers in the language of film which often departs from the direct representation of reality in order to use systems of symbols not always easy to comprehend. It is very useful when, even in school, teachers devote attention to this problem, sensitizing the students to images and gradually developing their critical attitude towards an idiom that is by now an integral part of our culture; because 'the application of communications technology has been a mixed blessing, and its use for good purposes requires sound values and wise choices on the part of individuals, the private sector, governments and society as a whole' (*Aetatis novae*, 1992).

While the memory of the statements and of the reflections that accompanied the celebration of the Year of the Family just completed is still with us, I think it important to remind families that to them also is entrusted the duty of educating their children in an accurate reading and understanding of the films that enter their homes each day, thanks to television, and to the videocassette recorder which even the youngest children seem capable of using.

In the context of the necessary education of viewers, the social component of the cinema must not be forgotten. This could offer suitable opportunities for dialogue among those that use the medium, through an exchange of opinions on the issue in question. It is also very useful – especially for young people – to organise film circles where, with the guidance of qualified persons, they may learn to express themselves and to listen to others, in a constructive and serene exchange of opinions.

Before concluding this message, I could not but draw attention to the distinctive duty that this matter of the cinema requires from all those who profess themselves to be Christians, who are aware of their own special mission in the world and who know well that their task is the proclamation of the gospel, the good news of Jesus, 'the saviour of all', to the people of their time.

The cinema, with its vast possibilities, could become a powerful means of evangelization. The Church urges directors, film-makers and all those involved who profess themselves to be Christians and who work in the complex and unique world of the cinema, to act in complete consistency with their own faith and to take courageous initiatives – even in the area of production – in order that through their professionalism the Christian message that is for each man and woman the good news of salvation might be more present in the world.

The Church feels obliged to offer, above all to young people, that spiritual and moral help without which it becomes almost impossible to function in a worthwhile manner. It must take concrete steps, where necessary, with suitable initiatives of support and encouragement.

In the hope that these words could be for all a motive of reflection and an occasion of renewed commitment, I send from my heart a special blessing to all those who, with their different tasks, work in the cinema industry and also to those who endeavor to use the cinema as an authentic vehicle of culture for the integral growth of each person and of society as a whole.

From the Vatican,
January 6, 1995, The Epiphany of the Lord

IOANNES PAULUS PP. II

MESSAGE OF THE HOLY FATHER JOHN PAUL II FOR THE 30TH WORLD COMMUNICATIONS DAY

Sunday 19 May 1996

The Media: Modern Forum for Promoting the Role of Women in Society

Dear brothers and sisters

This year, the theme for World Communications Day, 'The Media: Modern Forum for Promoting the Role of Women in Society', recognises that the communications media play a crucial role not only in promoting justice and equality for women but in fostering appreciation for their specific feminine gifts, which elsewhere I have called the 'genius' of women (cf. *Mulieris Dignitatem*, 30; *Letter to Women*, 10).

Last year, in my letter to women, I sought to advance a dialogue, especially with women themselves, on what it means to be a woman in our time (cf. no. 1). I also pointed out some of 'the obstacles which in so many parts of the world still keep women from being fully integrated into social, political and economic life' (no. 4). This is a dialogue which people in the communications media can, indeed have an obligation to, foster and support. People in the media often become advocates, and commendably so, of the voiceless and the marginalised. They are in a unique position also to stimulate public consciousness with regard to two serious issues concerning women in today's world.

First, as I noted in my letter, motherhood is often penalised rather than rewarded, even though humanity owes its very survival to those women who have chosen to be wives and mothers (cf. no. 4). It is certainly an injustice that such women should be discriminated against, economically or socially, precisely for following that fundamental vocation. Likewise I pointed out that there is an urgent need to achieve real equality in every area: equal pay for equal work, protection for working mothers, fairness in career advancement, equality of spouses with regard to family rights and the recognition of everything that is part of the rights and duties of citizens in a democratic state (cf. no. 4).

Secondly, the advancement of women's genuine emancipation is a matter of justice, which can no longer be overlooked; it is also a question of society's welfare. Fortunately, there is a growing awareness that women must be enabled to play their part in the solution of the serious problems of society and of society's future. In every area, 'a greater presence of women in society will prove most valuable, for it will help to manifest the contradictions present when society is organined solely according to the criteria of efficiency and productivity, and it will force systems to be redesigned in a way which favours the processes of humanination which mark the "civilization of love"' (Ibid., no. 4).

The 'civilization of love' consists, most particularly, in a radical affirmation of the value of life and of the value of love. Women are especially qualified and privileged in both of these areas. Regarding life, although not alone responsible for affirming its intrinsic value, women enjoy a unique capacity for doing so because of their intimate connection with the mystery of life's transmission. Regarding love, women can bring to every aspect of life, including the highest levels of decision-making, that essential quality of femininity which consists in objectivity of judgement, tempered by the capacity to understand in depth the demands of interpersonal relationships.

The communications media, including the press, the cinema, radio and television, the music industry and computer networks, represent the modern forum where information is received and transmitted rapidly to a global audience, where ideas are exchanged, where attitudes are formed – and, indeed, where a new culture is being shaped. The media are therefore destined to exercise a powerful influence in determining whether society fully recognises and appreciates not only the rights but also the special gifts of women.

Sadly though, we often see not the exaltation but the exploitation of women in the media. How often are they treated not as persons with an inviolable dignity but as objects whose purpose is to satisfy others' appetite for pleasure or for power?

How often is the role of woman as wife and mother undervalued or even ridiculed? How often is the role of women in business or professional life depicted as a masculine caricature, a denial of the specific gifts of feminine insight, compassion and understanding, which so greatly contribute to the 'civilization of love'?

Women themselves can do much to foster better treatment of women in the media: by promoting sound media education programmes, by teaching others, especially their families, to be discriminating consumers in the media market, by making known their views to production companies, publishers, broadcasting networks and advertisers with regard to programmes and publications which insult the dignity of women or debase their role in society. Moreover, women can and should prepare themselves for positions of responsibility and creativity in the media, not in conflict with or imitation of masculine roles but by impressing their own 'genius' on their work and professional activity.

The media would do well to focus on the true heroines of society, including the saintly women of the Christian tradition, as role models for the young and for future generations. Nor can we forget, in this respect, the many consecrated women who have sacrificed all to follow Jesus and to dedicate themselves to prayer and to the service of the poor, the sick, the illiterate, the young, the old, the handicapped. Some of these women are themselves involved in the communications media – working so that 'the poor have the Gospel preached to them' (cf. Lk 4:18).

'My soul proclaims the greatness of the Lord' (Lk 1:46). The Blessed Virgin Mary used these words in responding to the salutation of her cousin Elizabeth, thus acknowledging the 'great things' that God had done in her. The image of women communicated by the media should include the recognition that every feminine gift proclaims the greatness of the Lord, the Lord who has communicated life and love, goodness and grace, the Lord who is the source of the dignity and equality of women and of their special 'genius'.

My prayer is that this thirtieth World Communications Day will encourage all those involved in the media of social communication, especially the sons and daughters of the Church, to promote the genuine advancement of women's dignity and rights, by projecting a true and respectful image of their role in society and by bringing out 'the full truth about women' (*Letter to Women*, no. 12).

From the Vatican,
24 January 1996, the Feast of Saint Francis de Sales

IOANNES PAULUS PP. II

MESSAGE OF THE HOLY FATHER JOHN PAUL II FOR THE 31ST WORLD COMMUNICATIONS DAY

Sunday 11 May 1997

Communicating Jesus: The Way, the Truth and the Life

Dear brothers and sisters

As the present century and millennium draw to a close, we see an unprecedented expansion of the means of social communications, with ever new products and services. We see the lives of more and more people being touched by the spread of new technologies of information and communication. Yet, there are still great numbers of people who have no access to the media, old or new.

Those who do benefit from this development experience an ever growing choice of sources. The greater the choice, the harder it may be to choose responsibly. The fact is that it is increasingly difficult to protect one's eyes and ears from images and sounds which arrive through the media unexpectedly and uninvited. It is particularly hard for parents to guard their children from unwholesome messages, and to ensure that their education in human relations and their learning about the world comes about in a way that is appropriate to their age and sensibility and to their developing sense of right and wrong. Public opinion has been shocked at how easily the advanced communication technologies can be exploited by those whose intentions are evil. At the same time, can we not observe a relative slowness on the part of those who wish to do good to use the same opportunities?

We must hope that the gap between the beneficiaries of the new means of information and expression and those who as yet do not have access to them will not become another intractable source of inequity and discrimination. In some parts of the world voices are being raised against what is seen as domination of the media by so-called western culture. Media products are seen as in some way representing values that the west holds dear and, by implication, they supposedly present Christian values. The truth of the matter may well be that the foremost value they genuinely represent is commercial profit.

In addition, the proportion of media programmes which deal with religious and spiritual aspirations, programmes which are morally uplifting and help people to live better lives, is apparently decreasing. It is not easy to remain optimistic about the positive influence of the mass media when they appear either to ignore the vital role of religion in people's lives, or when the treatment that religious belief receives seems consistently negative and unsympathetic. Some elements of the media – especially in the entertainment sectors – often seem to wish to portray religious believers in the worst possible light. Is there still a place for Christ in the traditional mass media? May we claim a place for him in the new media?

In the Church, the year 1997, as the first part of a three-year period of preparation for the Great Jubilee of the Year 2000, is being devoted to reflection on Christ, the Word of God, made man by the power of the Holy Spirit (cf. *Tertio millennio Adveniente*, 30). Appropriately, therefore, the theme of World Communications Day is 'Communicating Jesus Christ: the Way, the Truth and the Life' (cf. Jn 14:6).

This theme provides an opportunity for the Church to meditate and act on the specific contributions which the communications media can offer in making known the good news of salvation in Jesus Christ. It also provides an opportunity for professional communicators to reflect on how religious and specifically Christian themes and values can enrich media productions and the lives of those whom the media serve.

The modern media are addressed not only to society in general, but most of all to families, to young people and also to very young children. What 'way' do the media point out? What 'truth' do they propose? What 'life' do they offer?

This is of concern not only to Christians, but to all people of good will.

The 'way' of Christ is the way of a virtuous, fruitful and peaceful life as children of God and as brothers and sisters in the same human family; the 'truth' of Christ is the eternal truth of God, who has revealed himself to us not only in the created world but also through sacred scripture, and especially in and through his son, Jesus Christ, the word made flesh; and the 'life' of Christ is the life of grace, that free gift of God which is a created share in his own life and which enables us to live for ever in his love. When Christians are truly convinced of this, their lives are transformed. This transformation results not only in a credible and compelling personal witness but also in an urgent and effective communication – likewise through the media – of a living faith which paradoxically increases as it is shared.

It is consoling to know that all who bear the name Christian share this same conviction. With due respect for the communications activities of the individual Churches and ecclesial communities, it would be a significant ecumenical achievement if Christians could cooperate more closely with one another in the media as they prepare to celebrate the forthcoming great jubilee (cf. *Tertio millennio Adveniente*, 41). Everything ought to focus on the primary objective of the jubilee: the strengthening of faith and of Christian witness (Ibid., 42).

Preparing for the 2000th-anniversary of the birth of the saviour has become, as it were, the key to interpreting what the Holy Spirit is saying to the Church and to the Churches at this time (cf. Ibid., 23). The mass media have a significant role to play in proclaiming and explaining this grace to the Christian community itself and to the world at large.

The same Jesus who is 'the way, the truth and the life' is also 'the light of the world' – the light that illumines our path, the light that enables us to perceive the truth, the light of the son who gives us supernatural life here and hereafter. The two thousand years which have passed since the birth of Christ represent an extraordinary commemoration for humanity as a whole, given the prominent role played by Christianity during these two millennia (cf. Ibid., 15). It is surely appropriate that the mass media should pay tribute to that contribution.

Perhaps one of the finest gifts which we could offer to Jesus Christ on the 2000th-anniversary of his birth would be that the good news will at last be made known to every person in the world – first of all through the living witness of Christian example, but also through the media: 'Communicating Jesus Christ: the Way, the Truth and the Life'. May this be the aim and commitment of all who profess the uniqueness of Jesus Christ, the source of life and truth (cf. Jn 5:26; 10:10, 28), and who have the privilege and the responsibility of working in the vast and influential world of social communications.

From the Vatican,
24 January 1997, the Feast of Saint Francis de Sales

IOANNES PAULUS PP. II

MESSAGE OF THE HOLY FATHER JOHN PAUL II FOR THE 32ND WORLD COMMUNICATIONS DAY

Sunday 24 May 1998

Sustained by the Spirit, Communicate Hope

Dear brothers and sisters

1. In this second of the three years leading to the great jubilee of the year 2000, we turn our attention to the Holy Spirit and to his action in the Church, in our lives and in the world. The Spirit is the 'guardian of hope in the human heart' (*Dominum et Vivificantem*, 67). For this reason, then, the theme for the 32nd World Communications Day is 'Sustained by the Holy Spirit, Communicate Hope'.

The hope in which the Spirit sustains believers is above all eschatological. It is hope for salvation – hope of heaven, hope for perfect communion with God. Such hope is, as the letter to the Hebrews puts it, 'a sure and steadfast anchor of the soul, a hope that enters into the inner shrine behind the curtain, where Jesus has gone as a forerunner on our behalf' (Heb 6:19-20).

2. But the eschatological hope dwelling in Christian hearts is deeply related to the search for happiness and fulfilment in this life. Hope of heaven stirs genuine concern for the well being of men and women here and now. 'If any one says, 'I love God,' and hates his brother, he is a liar; for he who does not love his brother whom he has seen, cannot love God whom he has not seen' (1 Jn 4:20). Redemption, which is God's healing of the divine-human relationship, goes hand in hand with the healing of our relationships with one another, and the hope born of the redemption looks to this double healing.

This is why it is so important that Christians prepare for the great jubilee of the dawn of the third millennium by renewing their hope in the final coming of the Kingdom of God, while also reading more perceptively the signs of hope found in the world around them. Among the signs of hope are these: scientific, technological and especially medical progress in the service of human life, a greater awareness of our responsibility for the environment, efforts to restore peace and justice where they have been violated, a desire for reconciliation and solidarity among peoples, particularly in the complex relationship between the north and south of the world. In the church too there are many signs of hope, among them a more attentive listening to the voice of the Holy Spirit prompting the acceptance of charisms and the promotion of the laity, a deeper commitment to Christian unity and a growing recognition of the importance of dialogue with other religions and with contemporary culture (cf. *Tertio millennio Adveniente*, 46).

3. Christian communicators will communicate hope credibly if they first experience hope in their own lives and this will happen only if they are men and women of prayer. Empowered by the Holy Spirit, prayer enables us to be 'ready always with an answer to everyone who asks a reason for the hope' they see in us (1 Pt 3:15). This is how the Christian communicator learns to present the message of hope to the men and women of our times with the force of truth.

4. It can never be forgotten that communication through the media is not a utilitarian exercise intended simply to motivate, persuade or sell. Still less is it a vehicle for ideology. The media can at times reduce human beings to units of consumption or competing interest groups, or manipulate viewers and readers and listeners as mere ciphers from whom some advantage is sought, whether product sales or political support; and these things destroy community. It is the task of communication to bring people together and enrich their lives, not to isolate and exploit them. The means of social communication, properly used, can help to create and sustain a human community based on justice and charity; and, in so far as they do that, they will be signs of hope.

5. The means of social communication are indeed the new 'Areopagus' of today's world – a great forum which, at its best, makes possible the exchange of truthful information, constructive ideas and sound values and so creates community. This in turn challenges the Church in her approach to communications not only to use the media to spread the gospel but actually to integrate the gospel message into the 'new culture' created by modern communications, with their 'new languages, new techniques and a new psychology' (*Redemptoris missio*, 37).

Christian communicators need a formation which enables them to work effectively in a media environment of this kind. Such a formation will have to be comprehensive: training in technical skills; training in ethics and morality, with particular attention to values and norms relevant to their professional work; training in human culture, in philosophy, history, social sciences and aesthetics. But, before all else, it will have to be a formation in the interior life, the life of the spirit.

Christian communicators need to be men and women of spirit-filled prayer, entering ever more deeply into communion with God in order to grow in their ability to foster communion among their fellow human beings. They must be schooled in hope by the Holy Spirit, 'the principal agent of the new evangelization' (*Tertio millennio Adveniente*, 45), so that they can communicate hope to others.

The Virgin Mary is the perfect model of the hope which Christian communicators seek to stir in themselves and share with others. 'Mary gave full expression to the longing of the poor of Yahweh and is a radiant model for those who entrust themselves with all their hearts to the promises of God' (*Tertio millennio Adveniente*, 48). As the Church takes her pilgrim path towards the great jubilee, we turn to Mary whose deep listening to the Holy Spirit opened the world to the great event of the incarnation, the source of all our hope.

From the Vatican,
24 January 1998, the Feast of Saint Francis de Sales

IOANNES PAULUS PP. II

MESSAGE OF THE HOLY FATHER JOHN PAUL II FOR THE 33RD WORLD COMMUNICATIONS DAY

Sunday 16 May 1999

Mass Media: A Friendly Companion for those in Search of the Father

Dear brothers and sisters

1. We are approaching the great jubilee, the 2000th-anniversary of the birth of Jesus Christ, the word of God made flesh, the celebration which will open the door to the third Christian millennium. In this last year of preparation, the Church turns to God our Father, contemplating *the mystery of his infinite mercy*. He is the God from whom all life comes and to whom it will return; and he is the one who journeys with us from birth to death as our friend and companion on the way.

I have chosen as the theme for this year's World Communications Day 'Mass media: a friendly companion for those in search of the Father'. The theme implies two questions: how might the media work with God rather than against him, and how might the media be a friendly companion to those searching for God's loving presence in their lives? It also implies a statement of fact and a reason for thanks: that the media do at times make it possible for those who are searching for God to read in new ways both the book of nature, which is the realm of reason, and the book of revelation, the Bible, which is the realm of faith. Finally, the theme implies an invitation and a hope: that those responsible for the world of social communications will be ever more committed to help rather than hinder the search for meaning which is at the very heart of human life.

2. To be human is to go in search; and, as I stressed in my recent Encyclical Letter *Fides et ratio*, all human searching is in the end a search for God: 'Faith and reason are like two wings upon which

the human spirit rises to the contemplation of truth, and God has placed in the human heart a desire to know the truth – in a word, to know himself – so that, by knowing and loving God, men and women may come to know the truth of themselves' (1). The great jubilee will be a celebration of God who is the goal of all human searching, a celebration of the endless mercy which all men and women desire – even though they often find themselves thwarted by sin which, in the expression of Saint Augustine, is like looking for the right thing in the wrong place (cf. *Confessions*, X, 38). We sin when we look for God where he cannot be found.

Therefore, in speaking of 'those who are searching for the Father', this year's theme for World Communications Day speaks of every man and woman. All are searching, though not all are looking in the right place. The theme recognises the exceptional influence of the media in contemporary culture and therefore the media's special responsibility to witness to the truth about life, about human dignity, about the true meaning of our freedom and mutual interdependence.

3. On the journey of human searching, the Church wishes to befriend the media, knowing that every form of cooperation will be for the good of everyone. Cooperation also means that we come to know each other better. At times, relations between the Church and the media can be marred by mutual misunderstanding which breeds fear and distrust. It is true that Church culture and media culture are different; indeed at certain points there is a stark contrast. But there is no reason why differences should make friendship and dialogue impossible. In many of the deepest friendships it is precisely differences that encourage creativity and bridge-building.

The Church's culture of remembrance can save the media culture of transitory 'news' from becoming a forgetfulness which corrodes hope, and the media can help the Church to proclaim the Gospel in all its enduring freshness in the everyday reality of people's lives. The Church's culture of wisdom can save the media culture of information from becoming a meaningless accumulation of facts, and the media can help the Church's wisdom to remain alert to the array of new knowledge now emerging. The Church's culture of joy can save the media culture of entertainment from becoming a soulless flight from truth and responsibility, and the media can help the Church to understand better how to communicate with people in a way that appeals and even delights. These are just some examples of how closer cooperation in a spirit of friendship and at a deeper level can help both the Church and the media to serve the men and women of our time in their search for meaning and fulfilment.

4. With the recent explosion of information technology, the possibility for communication between individuals and groups in every part of the world has never been greater. Yet, paradoxically, the very forces which can lead to better communication can also lead to increasing self-centredness and alienation. We find ourselves therefore in *a time of both threat and promise*. Nobody of good will wants the threat to prevail in a way that will lead to still more human sorrow – least of all at the end of a century and a millennium which have had more than their share of sorrow.

Let us look instead with great hope to the new millennium, trusting that there will be people in both the Church and the media prepared to cooperate to ensure that the promise prevails over the threat, communication over alienation. This will ensure that the world of the media becomes a more and more friendly companion to all people, presenting them with 'news' wedded to remembrance, information wedded to wisdom and entertainment wedded to joy. It will also ensure a world where the Church and the media can work together for the good of humanity. That is what is required if the power of the media is to be, not a force which destroys, but a love which creates, a love which reflects the love of God 'who is Father of all, who is over all and through all and in all' (Eph 4:6).

May all who work in the world of social communications know the joy of divine companionship, so that in knowing the friendship of God they may be enabled to befriend all men and women on their journey to the house of the Father, to whom be honour and glory, praise and thanksgiving, with the Son and the Holy Spirit, for ever and ever.

From the Vatican,
24 January 1999, the Feast of Saint Francis de Sales

IOANNES PAULUS PP. II

MESSAGE OF THE HOLY FATHER JOHN PAUL II FOR THE 34TH WORLD COMMUNICATIONS DAY

Sunday 4 June 2000

Proclaiming Christ in the Media at the Dawn of the New Millennium

Dear brothers and sisters

The theme of the thirty-fourth World Communications Day, 'Proclaiming Christ in the Media at the Dawn of the New Millennium', is an invitation to look ahead to the challenges we face and also back to the dawn of Christianity itself, for the light and courage we need. The substance of the message which we proclaim is always Jesus himself: 'the whole of human history in fact stands in reference to him: our own time and the future of the world are illumined by his presence' (*Incarnationis mysterium*, 1).

The early chapters of the Acts of the Apostles contain a moving account of the proclamation of Christ by his first followers – a proclamation at once spontaneous, faith-filled and persuasive, and carried out through the power of the Holy Spirit.

First and most important, the disciples proclaim Christ in response to the mandate he had given them. Before ascending into heaven he tells the apostles: 'You shall be my witnesses in Jerusalem and in all Judea and Samaria and to the end of the earth' (Acts 1:8). And even though these are 'uneducated, common men' (Acts 4:13), they respond quickly and generously.

Having spent time in prayer with Mary and other followers of the Lord, and acting at the Spirit's prompting, the apostles begin the work of proclamation at Pentecost (cf. Acts 2). As we read about those marvellous events, we are reminded that the history of communication is a kind of journey, from the pride-driven project of Babel and the collapse into confusion and mutual incomprehension to which it gave rise (cf. Gen 11:1-9), to Pentecost and the gift of tongues: a restoration of communication, centred on Jesus, through the action of the Holy Spirit. Proclaiming Christ therefore leads to a meeting between people in faith and charity at the deepest level of their humanity; the Risen Lord himself becomes a medium of genuine communication among his brothers and sisters in the Spirit.

Pentecost is only the beginning. Even when threatened with reprisals, the apostles are not deterred from proclaiming the Lord: 'We cannot but speak of what we have seen and heard,' Peter and John tell the Sanhedrin (Acts 4:20). Indeed, trials themselves become instrumental to the mission. When a violent persecution breaks out in Jerusalem after Stephen's martyrdom, forcing Christ's followers to flee, 'those who were scattered went about preaching the word' (Acts 8:4).

The living heart of the message which the apostles preach is Jesus' crucifixion and resurrection – life triumphant over sin and death. Peter tells the centurion Cornelius and his household: 'They put him to death by hanging him on a tree; but God raised him on the third day and made him manifest ... And he commanded us to preach to the people, and to testify that he is the one ordained by God to be judge of the living and the dead. To him all the prophets bear witness that every one who believes in him receives forgiveness of sins through his name' (Acts 10:39-43).

It goes without saying that circumstances have changed enormously in two millennia. Yet the same need to proclaim Christ still exists. Our duty to bear witness to the death and resurrection of Jesus and to his saving presence in our lives is as real and pressing as was the duty of the first disciples. We must tell the good news to all who are willing to listen.

Direct, personal proclamation – one person sharing faith in the risen Lord with another – is essential; so are other traditional forms of spreading the word of God. But, alongside these, proclamation today must take place also in and through the media. 'The Church would feel guilty before the Lord if she did not utilise these powerful means' (Pope Paul VI, *Evangelii nuntiandi*, 45).

The impact of the media in today's world can hardly be exaggerated. The advent of the information society is a real cultural revolution, making the media 'the first Areopagus of the modern age' (*Redemptoris missio*, 37), where facts and ideas and values are constantly being exchanged. Through the media, people come into contact with other people and events and form their opinions about the world they live in – indeed, form their understanding of the meaning of life. For many, the experience of living is to a great extent an experience of the media (cf. Pontifical Council for Social Communications, *Aetatis novae*, 2). The proclamation of Christ must be part of this experience.

Naturally, in proclaiming the Lord, the Church must make energetic and skilful use of her own means of communication – books, newspapers and periodicals, radio, television and other means. And Catholic communicators must be bold and creative in developing new media and methods of proclamation. But, as much as possible, the Church also must use the opportunities that are to be found in the secular media.

Already the media contribute to spiritual enrichment in many ways – for example, the many special programmes being carried to worldwide audiences through satellite telecasts during the year of the great jubilee. In other cases, however, they display the indifference, even hostility, to Christ and his message that exists in certain sectors of secular culture. Often though, there is a need for a kind of 'examination of conscience' on the part of the media, leading to a more critical awareness of a bias or a lack of respect for people's religious and moral convictions.

Media presentations which call attention to authentic human needs, especially those of the weak, the vulnerable and the marginalised, can be an implicit proclamation of the Lord. But besides implicit proclamation, Christian communicators should also seek out ways to speak explicitly of Jesus crucified and risen, of his triumph over sin and death, in a manner suited to the medium used and to the capacities of audiences.

To do this well demands professional training and skill. But it also requires something more. In order to witness to Christ, it is necessary to encounter him oneself and foster a personal relationship with him through prayer, the Eucharist and sacramental reconciliation, reading and reflection on God's word, the study of Christian doctrine and service to others. And always, if it is authentic, this will be the Spirit's work much more than our own.

To proclaim Christ is not only a duty but a privilege. 'The journey of believers towards the third millennium is in no way weighed down by the weariness which the burden of two thousand years of history could bring with it. Rather, Christians feel invigorated in the knowledge that they bring to the world the true light, Christ the Lord. Proclaiming Jesus of Nazareth, true God and perfect Man, the Church opens to all people the prospect of being 'divinized' and thus of becoming more human' (*Incarnationis mysterium*, 2).

The great jubilee of the 2000th anniversary of Jesus' birth at Bethlehem must be an opportunity and a challenge for the Lord's disciples to bear witness in and through the media to the extraordinary, consoling good news of our salvation. In this 'year of favour', may the media give voice to Jesus himself, clearly and joyously, with faith and hope and love. To proclaim Christ in the media at the dawn of the new millennium is not only a necessary part of the Church's evangelizing mission; it is also a vital, inspiring and hope-filled enrichment of the media's message. May God abundantly bless all those who honour and proclaim his son, our Lord Jesus Christ, in the vast world of the means of social communication.

From the Vatican,
24 January 2000, the Feast of Saint Francis de Sales

IOANNES PAULUS PP. II

MESSAGE OF THE HOLY FATHER JOHN PAUL II FOR THE 35TH WORLD COMMUNICATIONS DAY

Sunday 27 May 2001

Preach from the Housetops: The Gospel in the Age of Global Communication

Dear brothers and sisters

1. The theme which I have chosen for World Communications Day 2001 echoes the words of Jesus himself. It could not be otherwise, for it is Christ alone whom we preach. We remember his words to his first disciples: 'What I tell you in the dark, utter in the light; and what you hear whispered, proclaim upon the housetops' (Mt 10:27). In the secret of our heart, we have listened to the truth of Jesus; now we must proclaim that truth from the housetops.

In today's world, housetops are almost always marked by a forest of transmitters and antennae sending and receiving messages of every kind to and from the four corners of the earth. It is vitally important to ensure that among these many messages the word of God is heard. To proclaim the faith from the housetops today means to speak Jesus' word in and through the dynamic world of communications.

2. In all cultures and at all times – certainly in the midst of today's global transformations – people ask the same basic questions about the meaning of life: Who am I? Where have I come from and where am I going? Why is there evil? What is there after this life? (cf. *Fides et ratio*, 1). And in every age the Church offers the one ultimately satisfying answer to the deepest questions of the human heart – Jesus Christ himself, 'who fully reveals man to himself and brings to light his high calling' (*Gaudium et spes*, 22). Therefore, the voice of Christians can never fall silent, for the Lord has entrusted to us the word of salvation for which every

human heart longs. The Gospel offers the pearl of great price for which all are searching (cf. Mt 13:45-46).

It follows that the Church cannot fail to be ever more deeply involved in the burgeoning world of communications. The global communications network is extending and growing more complex by the day and the media are having an increasingly visible effect on culture and its transmission. Where once the media reported events, now events are often shaped to meet the requirements of the media. Thus, the relationship between reality and the media has grown more intricate and this is a deeply ambivalent phenomenon. On the one hand, it can blur the distinction between truth and illusion, but on the other, it can open up unprecedented opportunities for making the truth more widely accessible to many more people. The task of the Church is to ensure that it is the latter which actually happens.

3. The world of the media can sometimes seem indifferent and even hostile to Christian faith and morality. This is partly because media culture is so deeply imbued with a typically postmodern sense that the only absolute truth is that there are no absolute truths or that, if there were, they would be inaccessible to human reason and therefore irrelevant. In such a view, what matters is not the truth but 'the story'; if something is newsworthy or entertaining, the temptation to set aside considerations of truth becomes almost irresistible. As a result, the world of the media can sometimes seem no more friendly an environment for evangelization than the pagan world of the apostles' day. But just as the early witnesses to the good news did not retreat when faced with opposition, neither should Christ's followers do so today. The cry of St Paul echoes among us still: 'Woe to me if I do not preach the Gospel' (1 Cor 9:16).

Yet, as much as the world of the media may at times seem at odds with the Christian message, it also offers unique opportunities for proclaiming the saving truth of Christ to the whole human family. Consider, for instance, satellite telecasts of religious ceremonies which often reach a global audience, or the positive capacities of the internet to carry religious information and teaching beyond all barriers and frontiers. Such a wide audience would have been beyond the wildest imaginings of those who preached the Gospel before us. What is therefore needed in our time is an active and imaginative engagement of the media by the Church. Catholics should not be afraid to throw open the doors of social communications to Christ, so that his good news may be heard from the housetops of the world!

4. It is vital too that at the beginning of this new millennium we keep in mind the mission *ad gentes* which Christ has entrusted to the Church. An estimated two thirds of the world's six billion people do not in any real sense know Jesus Christ; and many of them live in countries with ancient Christian roots, where entire groups of the baptised have lost a living sense of the faith, or no longer consider themselves members of the Church and live lives far removed from the Lord and his gospel (cf. *Redemptoris missio*, 33). Certainly, an effective response to this situation involves much more than the media; but in striving to meet the challenge Christians cannot possibly ignore the world of social communications. Indeed, media of every kind can play an essential role in direct evangelization and in bringing to people the truths and values which support and enhance human dignity. The Church's presence in the media is in fact an important aspect of the inculturation of the Gospel demanded by the new evangelization to which the Holy Spirit is summoning the Church throughout the world.

As the whole Church seeks to heed the Spirit's call, Christian communicators have 'a prophetic task, a vocation: to speak out against the false gods and idols of the day – materialism, hedonism, consumerism, narrow nationalism ...' (*Ethics in Communications*, 31). Above all, they have the duty and privilege to declare the truth – the glorious truth about human life and human destiny revealed in the word made flesh. May Catholics involved in the world of social communications preach the truth of Jesus ever more boldly and joyfully from the housetops, so that all men and women may hear about the love which is the heart of God's self-communication in Jesus Christ, the same yesterday, and today, and for ever (cf Heb 13:8).

From the Vatican,
24 January 2001, the Feast of Saint Francis de Sales

IOANNES PAULUS PP. II

MESSAGE OF THE HOLY FATHER JOHN PAUL II FOR THE 36TH WORLD COMMUNICATIONS DAY

Sunday 12 May 2002

Internet: A New Forum for Proclaiming the Gospel

Dear brothers and sisters

1. The Church in every age continues the work begun on the day of Pentecost, when the apostles, in the power of the Holy Spirit, went forth into the streets of Jerusalem to preach the gospel of Jesus Christ in many tongues (cf. Acts 2:5-11). Through the succeeding centuries, this evangelizing mission spread to the far corners of the earth, as Christianity took root in many places and learned to speak the diverse languages of the world, always in obedience to Christ's command to preach the gospel to every nation (cf. Mt 28:19-20).

But the history of evangelization is not just a matter of geographic expansion, for the Church has also had to cross many cultural thresholds, each of which called for fresh energy and imagination in proclaiming the one gospel of Jesus Christ. The age of the great discoveries, the Renaissance and the invention of printing, the Industrial Revolution and the birth of the modern world: these too were threshold moments which demanded new forms of evangelization. Now, with the communications and information revolution in full swing, the Church stands unmistakably at another decisive gateway. It is fitting therefore that on this World Communications Day 2002 we should reflect on the subject: 'Internet: A New Forum for Proclaiming the Gospel'.

2. The internet is certainly a new 'forum', understood in the ancient Roman sense of that public space where politics and

business were transacted, where religious duties were fulfilled, where much of the social life of the city took place and where the best and the worst of human nature was on display. It was a crowded and bustling urban space, which both reflected the surrounding culture and created a culture of its own. This is no less true of cyberspace, which is as it were a new frontier opening up at the beginning of this new millennium. Like the new frontiers of other times, this one too is full of the interplay of danger and promise and not without the sense of adventure which marked other great periods of change. For the Church the new world of cyberspace is a summons to the great adventure of using its potential to proclaim the Gospel message. This challenge is at the heart of what it means at the beginning of the millennium to follow the Lord's command to 'put out into the deep': *Duc in altum!* (Lk 5:4).

3. The Church approaches this new medium with realism and confidence. Like other communications media, it is a means, not an end in itself. The internet can offer magnificent opportunities for evangelization if used with competence and a clear awareness of its strengths and weaknesses. Above all, by providing information and stirring interest it makes possible an initial encounter with the Christian message, especially among the young who increasingly turn to the world of cyberspace as a window on the world. It is important, therefore, that the Christian community think of very practical ways of helping those who first make contact through the internet to move from the virtual world of cyberspace to the real world of Christian community.

At a subsequent stage, the internet can also provide the kind of follow-up which evangelization requires. Especially in an unsupportive culture, Christian living calls for continuing instruction and catechesis, and this is perhaps the area in which the internet can provide excellent help. There already exist on the net countless sources of information, documentation and education about the Church, her history and tradition, her doctrine and her engagement in every field in all parts of the world. It is clear, then, that while the internet can never replace that profound experience of God which only the living, liturgical and sacramental life of the Church can offer, it can certainly provide a unique supplement and support in both preparing for the encounter with Christ in community and sustaining the new believer in the journey of faith which then begins.

4. There are nevertheless certain necessary, even obvious, questions which arise in using the internet in the cause of evangelization. The essence of the internet in fact is that it provides an almost unending flood of information, much of which passes in a moment. In a culture which feeds on the ephemeral there can easily be a risk of believing that it is facts that matter, rather than values. The internet offers extensive knowledge, but it does not teach values; and when values are disregarded, our very humanity is demeaned and man easily loses sight of his transcendent dignity. Despite its enormous potential for good, some of the degrading and damaging ways in which the internet can be used are already obvious to all, and public authorities surely have a responsibility to guarantee that this marvellous instrument serves the common good and does not become a source of harm.

Furthermore, the internet radically redefines a person's psychological relationship to time and space. Attention is rivetted on what is tangible, useful, instantly available; the stimulus for deeper thought and reflection may be lacking. Yet human beings have a vital need for time and inner quiet to ponder and examine life and its mysteries and to grow gradually into a mature dominion of themselves and of the world around them. Understanding and wisdom are the fruit of a contemplative eye upon the world and do not come from a mere accumulation of facts, no matter how interesting. They are the result of an insight which penetrates the deeper meaning of things in relation to one another and to the whole of reality. Moreover, as a forum in which practically everything is acceptable and almost nothing is lasting, the internet favours a relativistic way of thinking and sometimes feeds the flight from personal responsibility and commitment.

In such a context, how are we to cultivate that wisdom which comes not just from information but from insight, the wisdom which understands the difference between right and wrong and sustains the scale of values which flows from that difference?

5. The fact that through the internet people multiply their contacts in ways hitherto unthinkable opens up wonderful possibilities for spreading the Gospel. But it is also true that electronically-mediated relationships can never take the place of the direct human contact required for genuine evangelization. For evangelization always depends upon the personal witness of the one sent to evangelize (cf. Rom 10:14-15). How does the Church lead from the kind of contact made possible by the internet to the deeper communication demanded by Christian proclamation? How do we build upon the first contact and exchange of information which the internet makes possible?

There is no doubt that the electronic revolution holds out the promise of great positive breakthroughs for the developing world; but there is also the possibility that it will in fact aggravate existing inequalities as the information and communications gap widens. How can we ensure that the information and communications revolution which has the internet as its prime engine will work in favour of the globalisation of human development and solidarity, objectives closely linked to the Church's evangelizing mission?

Finally, in these troubled times, let me ask: how can we ensure that this wondrous instrument first conceived in the context of military operations can now serve the cause of peace? Can it favour that culture of dialogue, participation, solidarity and reconciliation without which peace cannot flourish? The Church believes it can; and to ensure that this is what will happen she is determined to enter this new forum, armed with the gospel of Christ, the prince of peace.

6. The internet causes billions of images to appear on millions of computer monitors around the planet. From this galaxy of sight and sound will the face of Christ emerge and the voice of Christ be heard? For it is only when his face is seen and his voice heard that the world will know the glad tidings of our redemption. This is the purpose of evangelization. And this is what will make the internet a genuinely human space, for if there is no room for Christ, there is no room for man. Therefore, on this World Communications Day, I dare to summon the whole Church bravely to cross this new threshold, to put out into the deep of the

net, so that now as in the past the great engagement of the Gospel and culture may show to the world 'the glory of God on the face of Christ' (2 Cor 4:6). May the Lord bless all those who work for this aim.

From the Vatican,
24 January 2002, the Feast of Saint Francis de Sales

IOANNES PAULUS PP. II

MESSAGE OF THE HOLY FATHER JOHN PAUL II FOR THE 37TH WORLD COMMUNICATIONS DAY

Sunday 1 June 2003

The Communications Media at the Service of Authentic Peace in the Light of 'Pacem in terris'

Dear brothers and sisters

1. In the dark days of the Cold War, Blessed Pope John XXIII's Encyclical Letter *Pacem in terris* came as a beacon of hope to men and women of good will. Declaring that authentic peace requires 'diligent observance of the divinely established order' (*Pacem in terris*, 1), the Holy Father pointed to truth, justice, charity and freedom as the pillars of a peaceful society (Ibid., 37).

The emergence of the power of modern social communications formed an important part of the encyclical's background. Pope John XXIII had the media especially in mind when he called for 'fairness and impartiality' in the use of 'instruments for the promotion and spread of mutual understanding between nations' afforded by science and technology; he decried 'ways of disseminating information which violate the principles of truth and justice, and injure the reputation of another nation' (Ibid., 90).

2. Today, as we observe the fortieth anniversary of *Pacem in terris*, the division of peoples into opposing blocs is mostly a painful memory, but peace, justice and social stability are still lacking in many parts of the world. Terrorism, conflict in the Middle East and other regions, threats and counter-threats, injustice, exploitation and assaults upon the dignity and sanctity of human life both before and after birth are dismaying realities of our times.

Meanwhile, the power of the media to shape human relationships and influence political and social life, both for good and for ill, has enormously increased. Hence the timeliness of the theme chosen for the thirty-seventh World Day of Communications: 'The Communications Media at the Service of Authentic Peace in the Light of *Pacem in terris*.' The world and the media still have much to learn from the message of Blessed Pope John XXIII.

3. Media and Truth: The fundamental moral requirement of all communication is respect for and service of the truth. Freedom to seek and speak what is true is essential to human communication, not only in relation to facts and information but also, and especially, regarding the nature and destiny of the human person, regarding society and the common good, regarding our relationship with God. The mass media have an inescapable responsibility in this sense, since they constitute the modern arena in which ideas are shared and people can grow in mutual understanding and solidarity. This is why Pope John XXIII defended the right 'to freedom in investigating the truth and – within the limits of the moral order and the common good – to freedom of speech and publication' as necessary conditions for social peace (*Pacem in terris*, 12).

In fact, the media often do render courageous service to the truth, but sometimes they function as agents of propaganda and disinformation in the service of narrow interests, national, ethnic, racial and religious prejudices, material greed and false ideologies of various kinds. It is imperative that the pressures brought to bear on the media to err in such ways be resisted first of all by the men and women of the media themselves, but also by the Church and other concerned groups.

4. Media and Justice: Blessed Pope John XXIII spoke eloquently in *Pacem in terris* of the universal human good – 'the good, that is, of the whole human family' (no. 132) – in which every individual and all peoples have a right to share.

The global outreach of the media carries with it special responsibilities in this regard. While it is true that the media often belong to particular interest groups, private and public, the very nature of their impact on life requires that they must not serve to set one group against another – for example, in the name of class conflict, exaggerated nationalism, racial supremacy, ethnic cleansing and the like. Setting some against others in the name of religion is a particularly serious failure against truth and justice, as is discriminatory treatment of religious beliefs, since these belong to the deepest realm of the human person's dignity and freedom.

By accurately reporting events, correctly explaining issues and fairly representing diverse points of view, the media have a strict duty to foster justice and solidarity in human relationships at all levels of society. This does not mean glossing over grievances and divisions but getting at their roots so that they can be understood and healed.

5. Media and Freedom: Freedom is a precondition of true peace as well as one of its most precious fruits. The media serve freedom by serving truth: they obstruct freedom to the extent that they depart from what is true by disseminating falsehoods or creating a climate of unsound emotional reaction to events. Only when people have free access to true and sufficient information can they pursue the common good and hold public authority accountable.

If the media are to serve freedom, they themselves must be free and correctly use that freedom. Their privileged status obliges the media to rise above purely commercial concerns and serve society's true needs and interests. Although some public regulation of the media in the interests of the common good is appropriate, government control is not. Reporters and commentators in particular have a grave duty to follow the demands of their moral conscience and to resist pressures to 'adapt' the truth to satisfy the demands of wealth or political power.

As a practical matter, ways must be found not only to give the weaker sectors of society access to the information which they need for their individual and social development, but also to ensure that they are not excluded from having an effective and responsible role in deciding media content and determining the structures and policies of social communications.

6. Media and Love: 'The anger of man does not work the righteousness of God' (Jas 1:20). At the height of the Cold War, Blessed Pope John XXIII expressed this simple but profound thought on what the path to peace entailed: 'The preservation of peace will

have to be dependent on a radically different principle from the one which is operative at the present time. True peace among nations must depend not on the possession of an equal supply of weapons, but solely upon mutual trust' (*Pacem in terris*, 113).

The communications media are key actors in today's world and they have an immense role to play in building that trust. Their power is such that in a few short days they can create the positive or negative public reaction to events which suits their purposes. Reasonable people will realise that such enormous power calls for the highest standards of commitment to truth and goodness. In this sense the men and women of the media are especially bound to contribute to peace in all parts of the world by breaking down the barriers of mistrust, fostering consideration of the point of view of others, and striving always to bring peoples and nations together in mutual understanding and respect – and beyond understanding and respect, to reconciliation and mercy!

'Where hatred and the thirst for revenge dominate, where war brings suffering and death to the innocent, there the grace of mercy is needed in order to settle human minds and hearts and to bring about peace' (*Homily at the Shrine of Divine Mercy at Krakow-Lagiewniki*, 17 August 2002, no. 5).

Challenging as all this is, it is by no means asking too much of the men and women of the media. For by vocation as well as by profession they are called to be agents of truth, justice, freedom and love, contributing by their important work to a social order 'founded on truth, built up on justice, nurtured and animated by charity and brought into effect under the auspices of freedom' (*Pacem in terris*, 167). My prayer therefore on this year's World Communications Day is that the men and women of the media will ever more wholly live up to the challenge of their calling: service of the universal common good. Their personal fulfilment and the peace and happiness of the world depend greatly on this. May God bless them with light and courage.

From the Vatican,
24 January 2003, the Feast of Saint Francis de Sales

IOANNES PAULUS PP. II

MESSAGE OF THE HOLY FATHER JOHN PAUL II FOR THE 38TH WORLD COMMUNICATIONS DAY

Sunday 23 May 2004

The Media and the Family: A Risk and a Richness

Dear brothers and sisters

1. The extraordinary growth of the communications media and their increased availability has brought exceptional opportunities for enriching the lives not only of individuals, but also of families. At the same time, families today face new challenges arising from the varied and often contradictory messages presented by the mass media. The theme chosen for the 2004 World Communications Day – 'The Media and the Family: A Risk and a Richness' – is a timely one, for it invites sober reflection on the use which families make of the media and, in turn, on the way that families and family concerns are treated by the media.

This year's theme is also a reminder to everyone, both communicators and those whom they address, that all communication has a moral dimension. As the Lord himself has said, it is from the abundance of the heart that the mouth speaks (cf. Mt 12:34-35). People grow or diminish in moral stature by the words which they speak and the messages which they choose to hear. Consequently, wisdom and discernment in the use of the media are particularly called for on the part of communications professionals, parents and educators, for their decisions greatly affect children and young people for whom they are responsible and who are ultimately the future of society.

2. Thanks to the unprecedented expansion of the communications market in recent decades, many families throughout the world, even those of quite modest means, now have access in their own

homes to immense and varied media resources. As a result, they enjoy virtually unlimited opportunities for information, education, cultural expansion and even spiritual growth – opportunities that far exceed those available to most families in earlier times.

Yet these same media also have the capacity to do grave harm to families by presenting an inadequate or even deformed outlook on life, on the family, on religion and on morality. This power either to reinforce or override traditional values like religion, culture and family was clearly seen by the Second Vatican Council, which taught that 'if the media are to be correctly employed, it is essential that all who use them know the principles of the moral order and apply them faithfully' (*Inter mirifica*, 4). Communication in any form must always be inspired by the ethical criterion of respect for the truth and for the dignity of the human person.

3. These considerations apply in particular to the treatment of the family in the media. On the one hand, marriage and family life are frequently depicted in a sensitive manner, realistic but also sympathetic, that celebrates virtues like love, fidelity, forgiveness and generous self-giving for others. This is true also of media presentations which recognise the failures and disappointments inevitably experienced by married couples and families – tensions, conflicts, setbacks, evil choices and hurtful deeds – yet at the same time make an effort to separate right from wrong, to distinguish true love from its counterfeits and to show the irreplaceable importance of the family as the fundamental unit of society.

On the other hand, the family and family life are all too often inadequately portrayed in the media. Infidelity, sexual activity outside of marriage and the absence of a moral and spiritual vision of the marriage covenant are depicted uncritically, while positive support is at times given to divorce, contraception, abortion and homosexuality. Such portrayals, by promoting causes inimical to marriage and the family, are detrimental to the common good of society.

4. Conscientious reflection on the ethical dimension of communications should issue in practical initiatives aimed at eliminating the risks to the well-being of the family posed by the media and ensuring that these powerful instruments of communication will remain genuine sources of enrichment. A

special responsibility in this regard lies with communicators themselves, with public authorities and with parents.

Pope Paul VI pointed out that professional communicators should 'know and respect the needs of the family, and this sometimes presupposes in them true courage, and always a high sense of responsibility' (*Message for the 1969 World Communications Day*). It is not so easy to resist commercial pressures or the demands of conformity to secular ideologies, but that is what responsible communicators must do. The stakes are high, since every attack on the fundamental value of the family is an attack on the true good of humanity.

Public authorities themselves have a serious duty to uphold marriage and the family for the sake of society itself. Instead, many now accept and act upon the unsound libertarian arguments of groups which advocate practices which contribute to the grave phenomenon of family crisis and the weakening of the very concept of the family. Without resorting to censorship, it is imperative that public authorities set in place regulatory policies and procedures to ensure that the media do not act against the good of the family. Family representatives should be part of this policy-making.

Policy-makers in the media and in the public sector also must work for an equitable distribution of media resources on the national and international levels, while respecting the integrity of traditional cultures. The media should not appear to have an agenda hostile to the sound family values of traditional cultures or the goal of replacing those values, as part of a process of globalisation, with the secularized values of consumer society.

5. Parents, as the primary and most important educators of their children, are also the first to teach them about the media. They are called to train their offspring in the 'moderate, critical, watchful and prudent use of the media' in the home (*Familiaris consortio*, 76). When parents do that consistently and well, family life is greatly enriched. Even very young children can be taught important lessons about the media: that they are produced by people anxious to communicate messages; that these are often messages to do something – to buy a product, to engage in dubious behaviour – that is not in the child's best interests or in

accord with moral truth; that children should not uncritically accept or imitate what they find in the media.

Parents also need to regulate the use of media in the home. This would include planning and scheduling media use, strictly limiting the time children devote to media, making entertainment a family experience, putting some media entirely off limits and periodically excluding all of them for the sake of other family activities. Above all, parents should give good example to children by their own thoughtful and selective use of media. Often they will find it helpful to join with other families to study and discuss the problems and opportunities presented by the use of the media. Families should be outspoken in telling producers, advertisers and public authorities what they like and dislike.

6. The media of social communications have an enormous positive potential for promoting sound human and family values and thus contributing to the renewal of society. In view of their great power to shape ideas and influence behaviour, professional communicators should recognise that they have a moral responsibility not only to give families all possible encouragement, assistance and support to that end, but also to exercise wisdom, good judgement and fairness in their presentation of issues involving sexuality, marriage and family life.

The media are welcomed daily as a familiar guest in many homes and families. On this World Communications Day I encourage professional communicators and families alike to acknowledge this unique privilege and the accountability which it entails. May all engaged in the field of communications recognise that they are truly 'stewards and administrators of an immense spiritual power that belongs to the patrimony of mankind and is meant to enrich the whole of the human community' (*Address to Communications Specialists*, Los Angeles, 15 September 1987, 8). And may families always be able to find in the media a source of support, encouragement and inspiration as they strive to live as a community of life and love, to train young people in sound moral values and to advance a culture of solidarity, freedom and peace.

From the Vatican,
24 January 2004, the Feast of Saint Francis de Sales

IOANNES PAULUS PP. II

MESSAGE OF THE HOLY FATHER JOHN PAUL II FOR THE 39TH WORLD COMMUNICATIONS DAY

Sunday 8 May 2005

The Communications Media: At the Service of Understanding Among Peoples

Dear brothers and sisters

1. We read in the letter of St James, 'From the same mouth come blessing and cursing. My brothers and sisters, this ought not to be so' (Jas 3:10). The sacred scriptures remind us that words have an extraordinary power to bring people together or to divide them, to forge bonds of friendship or to provoke hostility.

Not only is this true of words spoken by one person to another, it applies equally to communication taking place at any level. *Modern technology places at our disposal unprecedented possibilities for good, for spreading the truth of our salvation in Jesus Christ and for fostering harmony and reconciliation.* Yet its misuse can do untold harm, giving rise to misunderstanding, prejudice and even conflict. The theme chosen for the 2005 World Communications Day – 'The Communications Media: At the Service of Understanding Among Peoples' – addresses an urgent need: to promote the unity of the human family through the use made of these great resources.

2. One important way of achieving this end is through education. The media can teach billions of people about other parts of the world and other cultures. With good reason they have been called 'the first Areopagus of the modern age ... for many the chief means of information and education, of guidance and inspiration in their behaviour as individuals, families and within society at large' (*Redemptoris missio*, 37). Accurate knowledge promotes understanding, dispels prejudice and awakens the desire to learn

more. Images especially have the power to convey lasting impressions and to shape attitudes. They teach people how to regard members of other groups and nations, subtly influencing whether they are considered as friends or enemies, allies or potential adversaries.

When others are portrayed in hostile terms, seeds of conflict are sown which can all too easily escalate into violence, war or even genocide. Instead of building unity and understanding, the media can be used to demonise other social, ethnic and religious groups, fomenting fear and hatred. Those responsible for the style and content of what is communicated have a grave duty to ensure that this does not happen. Indeed, *the media have enormous potential for promoting peace and building bridges between peoples,* breaking the fatal cycle of violence, reprisal and fresh violence that is so widespread today. In the words of St Paul, which formed the basis of this year's message for the World Day of Peace: 'Do not be overcome by evil, but overcome evil with good' (Rom 12:21).

3. If such a contribution to peace-making is one of the significant ways the media can bring people together, its influence in favour of the swift mobilisation of aid in response to natural disasters is another. It was heartening to see how quickly the international community responded to the recent tsunami that claimed countless victims. The speed with which news travels today naturally increases the possibility for timely practical measures designed to offer maximum assistance. In this way the media can achieve an immense amount of good.

4. The Second Vatican Council reminded us: 'If the media are to be correctly employed, it is essential that all who use them know the principles of the moral order and apply them faithfully' (*Inter mirifica*, 4).

The fundamental ethical principle is this: 'The human person and the human community are the end and measure of the use of the media of social communication; communication should be by persons to persons for the integral development of persons' (*Ethics in Communications*, 21). In the first place, then, the communicators themselves need to put into practice in their own lives the values and attitudes they are called to instil in others. Above all, this must include a genuine commitment to the common good – a good that is not confined by the narrow interests of a particular group or nation but embraces the needs and interests of all, the good of the entire human family (cf. *Pacem in terris*, 132). Communicators have the opportunity to promote a true culture of life by distancing themselves from today's conspiracy against life (cf. *Evangelium vitae*, 17) and conveying the truth about the value and dignity of every human person.

5. The model and pattern of all communication is found in the Word of God himself. 'In many and various ways God spoke of old to our fathers by the prophets; but in these last days he has spoken to us by a Son' (Heb 1:1). The Incarnate Word has established a new covenant between God and his people – a covenant which also joins us in community with one another. 'For he is our peace, who has made us both one, and has broken down the dividing wall of hostility' (Eph 2:14).

My prayer on this year's World Communications Day is that the men and women of the media will play their part in breaking down the dividing walls of hostility in our world, walls that separate peoples and nations from one another, feeding misunderstanding and mistrust. May they use the resources at their disposal to strengthen the bonds of friendship and love that clearly signal the onset of the Kingdom of God here on earth.

From the Vatican,
24 January 2005, the Feast of Saint Francis de Sales

IOANNES PAULUS PP. II

MESSAGE OF THE HOLY FATHER BENEDICT XVI FOR WORLD COMMUNICATIONS DAY 2006

MESSAGE OF THE HOLY FATHER BENEDICT XVI FOR THE 40TH WORLD COMMUNICATIONS DAY

Sunday 28 May 2006

The Media: A Network for Communication, Communion and Cooperation

Dear brothers and sisters

1. In the wake of the fortieth anniversary of the closing of the Second Vatican Ecumenical Council, I am happy to recall its Decree on the Means of Social Communication, *Inter mirifica*, which in particular recognised the power of the media to influence the whole of human society. The need to harness that power for the benefit of all mankind has prompted me, in this my first message for World Communications Day, to reflect briefly on the idea of the media as a network facilitating communication, communion and cooperation.

St Paul, in his letter to the Ephesians, vividly depicts our human vocation to be 'sharers in the divine nature' (*Dei verbum*, 2): through Christ we have access in one spirit to the Father; so we are no longer strangers and aliens but citizens with the saints and members of the household of God, growing into a holy temple, a dwelling place for God (cf. Eph 2:18-22). This sublime portrayal of a life of communion engages all aspects of our lives as Christians. The call to be true to the self-communication of God in Christ is in fact a call to recognise his dynamic force within us, which then seeks to spread outwards to others, so that his love can truly become the prevalent measure of the world (cf. *Homily for World Youth Day*, Cologne, 21 August 2005).

2. Technological advances in the media have in certain respects conquered time and space, making communication between people, even when separated by vast distances, both

instantaneous and direct. This development presents an enormous potential for service of the common good and 'constitutes a patrimony to safeguard and promote' (*Rapid Development*, 10). Yet, as we all know, our world is far from perfect. Daily we are reminded that immediacy of communication does not necessarily translate into the building of cooperation and communion in society.

To inform the consciences of individuals and help shape their thinking is never a neutral task. Authentic communication demands principled courage and resolve. It requires a determination of those working in the media not to wilt under the weight of so much information nor even to be content with partial or provisional truths. Instead it necessitates both seeking and transmitting what is the ultimate foundation and meaning of human, personal and social existence (cf. *Fides et ratio*, 5). In this way the media can contribute constructively to the propagation of all that is good and true.

3. The call for today's media to be responsible – to be the protagonist of truth and promoter of the peace that ensues – carries with it a number of challenges. While the various instruments of social communication facilitate the exchange of information, ideas and mutual understanding among groups, they are also tainted by ambiguity. Alongside the provision of a 'great round table' for dialogue, certain tendencies within the media engender a kind of monoculture that dims creative genius, deflates the subtlety of complex thought and undervalues the specificity of cultural practices and the particularity of religious belief. These are distortions that occur when the media industry becomes self-serving or solely profit-driven, losing the sense of accountability to the common good.

Accurate reporting of events, full explanation of matters of public concern and fair representation of diverse points of view must, then, always be fostered. The need to uphold and support marriage and family life is of particular importance, precisely because it pertains to the foundation of every culture and society (cf. *Apostolicam actuositatem*, 11). In cooperation with parents, the social communications and entertainment industries can assist in the difficult but sublimely satisfying vocation of bringing up children, through presenting edifying models of human life and love (cf. *Inter mirifica*, 11). How disheartening and destructive it is to us all when the opposite occurs. Do not our hearts cry out, most especially, when our young people are subjected to debased or false expressions of love which ridicule the God-given dignity of every human person and undermine family interests?

4. To encourage both a constructive presence and a positive perception of the media in society, I wish to reiterate the importance of three steps, identified by my venerable predecessor Pope John Paul II, necessary for their service of the common good: formation, participation and dialogue (cf. *Rapid Development*, 11).

Formation in the responsible and critical use of the media helps people to use them intelligently and appropriately. The profound impact upon the mind of new vocabulary and of images, which the electronic media in particular so easily introduce into society, cannot be overestimated. Precisely because contemporary media shape popular culture, they themselves must overcome any temptation to manipulate, especially the young, and instead pursue the desire to form and serve. In this way they protect rather than erode the fabric of a civil society worthy of the human person.

Participation in the mass media arises from their nature as a good destined for all people. As a public service, social communication requires a spirit of cooperation and co-responsibility with vigorous accountability of the use of public resources and the performance of roles of public trust (cf. *Ethics in Communications*, 20), including recourse to regulatory standards and other measures or structures designed to effect this goal.

Finally, the promotion of dialogue through the exchange of learning, the expression of solidarity and the espousal of peace presents a great opportunity for the mass media which must be recognised and exercised. In this way they become influential and appreciated resources for building the civilization of love for which all peoples yearn.

I am confident that serious efforts to promote these three steps will assist the media to develop soundly as a network of communication, communion and cooperation, helping men, women and children to become more aware of the dignity of the human person, more responsible and more open to others, especially the neediest and the weakest members of society (cf. *Redemptor hominis*, 15; *Ethics in Communications*, 4).

In conclusion, I return to the encouraging words of St Paul: Christ is our peace. In him we are one (cf. Eph 2:14). Let us together break down the dividing walls of hostility and build up the communion of love according to the designs of the Creator made known through his son!

From the Vatican,
24 January 2006, the Feast of Saint Francis de Sales

BENEDICTUS XVI

SOCIAL COMMUNICATIONS AND THE CHURCH – KEY DOCUMENTS 1963–2005

CONCILIAR DECREE ON THE MEDIA OF SOCIAL COMMUNICATIONS
INTER MIRIFICA

SOLEMNLY PROMULGATED BY HIS HOLINESS POPE PAUL VI

4 DECEMBER 1963

Introduction

1. Among the wonderful technological discoveries which men of talent, especially in the present era, have made with God's help, the Church welcomes and promotes with special interest those which have a most direct relation to men's minds and which have uncovered new avenues of communicating most readily news, views and teachings of every sort. The most important of these inventions are those media, such as the press, movies, radio, television and the like, which can, by their very nature, reach and influence, not only individuals, but the very masses and the whole of human society and thus can rightly be called the media of social communication.

2. The Church recognises that these media, if properly utilised, can be of great service to mankind since they greatly contribute to men's entertainment and instruction as well as to the spread and support of the Kingdom of God. The Church recognises, too, that men can employ these media contrary to the plan of the Creator and to their own loss. Indeed, the Church experiences maternal grief at the harm all too often done to society by their evil use. Hence, this sacred Synod, attentive to the watchful concern manifested by the Supreme Pontiffs and Bishops in a matter of such great importance, judges it to be its duty to treat of the principal questions linked with the media of social communication. It trusts, moreover, that the teaching and regulations it thus sets forth will serve to promote, not only the eternal welfare of Christians, but also the progress of all mankind.

CHAPTER I

On the Teaching of the Church

3. The Catholic Church, since it was founded by Christ our Lord to bear salvation to all men and thus is obliged to preach the Gospel, considers it one of its duties to announce the good news of salvation also with the help of the media of social communication and to instruct men in their proper use.

It is, therefore, an inherent right of the Church to have at its disposal and to employ any of these media insofar as they are necessary or useful for the instruction of Christians and all its efforts for the welfare of souls. It is the duty of pastors to instruct and guide the faithful so that they, with the help of these same media, may further the salvation and perfection of themselves and of the entire human family. In addition, the laity especially must strive to instill a human and Christian spirit into these media, so that they may fully measure up to the great expectations of mankind and to God's design.

4. For the proper use of these media it is most necessary that all who employ them be acquainted with the norms of morality and conscientiously put them into practice in this area. They must look, then, to the nature of what is communicated, given the special character of each of these media. At the same time they must take into consideration the entire situation or circumstances, namely, the persons, place, time and other conditions under which communication takes place and which can affect or totally change its propriety. Among these circumstances to be considered is the precise manner in which a given medium achieves its effect. For its influence can be so great that men, especially if they are unprepared, can scarcely become aware of it, govern its impact, or, if necessary, reject it.

5. It is, however, especially necessary that all parties concerned should adopt for themselves a proper moral outlook on the use of these media, especially with respect to certain questions that have been vigorously aired in our day.

The first question has to do with 'information', as it is called, or the search for and reporting of the news. Now clearly this has become most useful and very often necessary for the progress of contemporary society and for achieving closer links among men. The prompt publication of affairs and events provides every individual with a fuller, continuing acquaintance with them and thus all can contribute more effectively to the common good and more readily promote and advance the welfare of the entire civil society. Therefore, in society men have a right to information, in accord with the circumstances in each case, about matters concerning individuals or the community. The proper exercise of this right demands, however, that the news itself that is communicated should always be true and complete, within the bounds of justice and charity. In addition, the manner in which the news is communicated should be proper and decent. This means that in both the search for news and in reporting it, there must be full respect for the laws of morality and for the legitimate rights and dignity of the individual. For not all knowledge is helpful, but 'it is charity that edifies'.[1]

6. The second question deals with the relationship between the rights, as they are called, of art and the norms of morality. Since the mounting controversies in this area frequently take their rise from false teachings about ethics and aesthetics, the Council proclaims that all must hold to the absolute primacy of the objective moral order, that is, this order by itself surpasses and fittingly coordinates all other spheres of human affairs – the arts not excepted – even though they be endowed with notable dignity. For man who is endowed by God with the gift of reason and summoned to pursue a lofty destiny is alone affected by the moral order in his entire being. And likewise, if man resolutely and faithfully upholds this order, he will be brought to the attainment of complete perfection and happiness.

7. Finally, the narration, description or portrayal of moral evil, even through the media of social communication, can indeed serve to bring about a deeper knowledge and study of humanity and, with the aid of appropriately heightened dramatic effects, can reveal and glorify the grand dimensions of truth and goodness. Nevertheless, such presentations ought always to be subject to moral restraint, lest they work to the harm rather than the benefit of souls, particularly when there is question of treating

matters which deserve reverent handling or which, given the baneful effect of original sin in men, could quite readily arouse base desires in them.

8. Since public opinion exercises the greatest power and authority today in every sphere of life, both private and public, every member of society must fulfil the demands of justice and charity in this area. As a result, all must strive, through these media as well, to form and spread sound public opinion.

9. All who, of their own free choice, make use of these media of communications as readers, viewers or listeners have special obligations. For a proper choice demands that they fully favour those presentations that are outstanding for their moral goodness, their knowledge and their artistic or technical merit. They ought, however, to avoid those that may be a cause or occasion of spiritual harm to themselves, or that can lead others into danger through base example, or that hinder desirable presentations and promote those that are evil. To patronise such presentations, in most instances, would merely reward those who use these media only for profit.

In order that those who make use of these media may fulfil the moral code, they ought not to neglect to inform themselves in time about judgments passed by authorities competent in these matters. They ought also to follow such judgments according to the norms of an upright conscience. So that they may more easily resist improper inducements and rather encourage those that are desirable, let them take care to guide and instruct their consciences with suitable aids.

10. Those who make use of the media of communications, especially the young, should take steps to accustom themselves to moderation and self-control in their regard. They should, moreover, endeavour to deepen their understanding of what they see, hear or read. They should discuss these matters with their teachers and experts and learn to pass sound judgements on them. Parents should remember that they have a most serious duty to guard carefully lest shows, publications and other things of this sort, which may be morally harmful, enter their homes or affect their children under other circumstances.

11. The principle moral responsibility for the proper use of the media of social communication falls on newsmen, writers, actors, designers, producers, displayers, distributors, operators and sellers, as well as critics and all others who play any part in the production and transmission of mass presentations. It is quite evident what gravely important responsibilities they have in the present day when they are in a position to lead the human race to good or to evil by informing or arousing mankind.

Thus, they must adjust their economic, political or artistic and technical aspects so as never to oppose the common good. For the purpose of better achieving this goal, they are to be commended when they join professional associations, which – even under a code, if necessary, of sound moral practice – oblige their members to show respect for morality in the duties and tasks of their craft.

They ought always to be mindful, however, that a great many of their readers and audiences are young people who need a press and entertainment that offer them decent amusement and cultural uplift. In addition, they should see to it that communications or presentations concerning religious matters are entrusted to worthy and experienced hands and are carried out with fitting reverence.

12. The public authority, in these matters, is bound by special responsibilities in view of the common good, to which these media are ordered. The same authority has, in virtue of its office, the duty of protecting and safeguarding true and just freedom of information, a freedom that is totally necessary for the welfare of contemporary society, especially when it is a question of freedom of the press. It ought also to encourage spiritual values, culture and the fine arts and guarantee the rights of those who wish to use the media. Moreover, public authority has the duty of helping those projects which, though they are certainly most beneficial for young people, cannot otherwise be undertaken.

Lastly, the same public authority, which legitimately concerns itself with the health of the citizenry, is obliged, through the promulgation and careful enforcement of laws, to exercise a fitting and careful watch lest grave damage befall public morals and the welfare of society through the base use of these media. Such vigilance in no way restricts the freedom of individuals or groups, especially where there is a lack of adequate precaution on the part of those who are professionally engaged in using these media.

Special care should be taken to safeguard young people from printed matter and performances which may be harmful at their age.

CHAPTER II

On the Pastoral Activity of the Church

13. All the children of the Church should join, without delay and with the greatest effort in a common work to make effective use of the media of social communication in various apostolic endeavors, as circumstances and conditions demand. They should anticipate harmful developments, especially in regions where more urgent efforts to advance morality and religion are needed.

Pastors should hasten, therefore, to fulfil their duty in this respect, one which is intimately linked with their ordinary preaching responsibility. The laity, too, who have something to do with the use of these media, should endeavour to bear witness to Christ, first of all by carrying out their individual duties or office expertly and with an apostolic spirit, and, further, by being of direct help in the pastoral activity of the Church – to the best of their ability – through their technical, economic, cultural and artistic talents.

14. First, a good press should be fostered. To instill a fully Christian spirit into readers, a truly Catholic press should be set up and encouraged. Such a press – whether immediately fostered and directed by ecclesiastical authorities or by Catholic laymen – should be edited with the clear purpose of forming, supporting and advancing public opinion in accord with natural law and Catholic teaching and precepts. It should disseminate and properly explain news concerning the life of the Church. Moreover, the faithful ought to be advised of the necessity both to spread and read the Catholic press to formulate Christian judgements for themselves on all events.

The production and showing of films that have value as decent entertainment, humane culture or art, especially when they are designed for young people, ought to be encouraged and assured by every effective means. This can be done particularly by supporting and joining in projects and enterprises for the production and distribution of decent films, by encouraging worthwhile films through critical approval and awards, by patronising or jointly sponsoring theatres operated by Catholic and responsible managers.

Similarly, effective support should be given to good radio and television programmes, above all those that are suitable for families. Catholic programmes should be promoted, in which listeners and viewers can be brought to share in the life of the Church and learn religious truths. An effort should also be made, where it may be necessary, to set up Catholic stations. In such instances, however, care must be taken that their programmes are outstanding for their standards of excellence and achievement.

In addition, there should be an effort to see that the noble and ancient art of the drama, which now is diffused everywhere by the media of social communication, serves the cultural and moral betterment of audiences.

15. To provide for the needs just set forth, priests, religious and laymen who are equipped with the proper skills for adapting these media to the objectives of the apostolate should be appointed promptly.

Importantly, laymen ought to be afforded technical, doctrinal and moral training. For this purpose, the number of school faculties and institutes should be increased, where newsmen, writers for screen, radio and television and all other interested parties can obtain a sound training that is imbued with the Christian spirit, especially with respect to the social teaching of the Church.

Finally, care must be taken to prepare literary, film, radio, television and other critics, who will be equipped with the best skills in their own crafts and trained and encouraged to render judgements which always put moral issues in their proper light.

16. Since the proper use of the media of social communications which are available to audiences of different cultural backgrounds and ages calls for instruction proper to their needs, programmes which are suitable for the purpose – especially where

they are designed for young people – should be encouraged, increased in numbers and organised according to Christian moral principles. This should be done in Catholic schools at every level, in seminaries and in lay apostolate groups. To speed this along catechetical manuals should present and explain Catholic teaching and regulations on this matter.

17. It is quite unbecoming for the Church's children to idly permit the message of salvation to be thwarted or impeded by the technical delays or expenses, however vast, which are encountered by the very nature of these media. Therefore, this sacred Synod advises them of the obligation they have to maintain and assist Catholic newspapers, periodicals and film projects, radio and television programmes and stations, whose principal objective is to spread and defend the truth and foster Christian influence in human society. At the same time, the Synod earnestly invites those organisations and individuals who possess financial and technical ability to support these media freely and generously with their resources and their skills, inasmuch as they contribute to genuine culture and the apostolate.

18. Moreover, that the varied apostolates of the Church with respect to the media of social communication may be strengthened effectively, each year in every diocese of the world, by the determination of the bishops, there should be celebrated a day on which the faithful are instructed in their responsibilities in this regard. They should be invited to pray and contribute funds for this cause. Such funds are to be expended exclusively on the promotion, maintenance and development of institutes and undertakings of the Church in this area, according to the needs of the whole Catholic world.

19. In fulfilling his supreme pastoral charge with respect to the media of social communication, the Sovereign Pontiff has at hand a special office of the Holy See. Moreover, the Fathers of the Council, freely acceding to the wish of the 'Secretariat for the Supervision of Publications and Entertainment', reverently request that the Sovereign Pontiff extend the duties and competence of this office to include all media of social

communication, including the press, and that experts from various countries be named to it, including laymen.

20. It will be the task of the bishops, however, to watch over such works and undertakings in their own dioceses, to promote them and, as far as the public apostolate is concerned, to guide them, not excluding those that are under the direction of exempt religious.

21. Since an effective apostolate on a national scale calls for unity of planning and resources, this sacred Synod decrees and orders that national offices for affairs of the press, films, radio and television be established everywhere and given every aid. It will be the special task of these offices to see to it that the consciences of the faithful are properly instructed with respect to these media. Likewise they should foster and guide whatever is done by Catholics in these areas.

In each country the direction of such offices should be entrusted to a special committee of bishops, or to a single bishop. Moreover, laymen who are experts in Catholic teaching and in these arts or techniques should have a role in these offices.

22. Since the effectiveness of these media reaches beyond national boundaries and has an impact on individual members of the whole human family, national offices should cooperate among themselves on an international plane. The offices spoken of in number 21 should assiduously work together with their own international Catholic associations. These Catholic international associations are legitimately approved by the Holy See alone and depend on it.

APPENDICES

23. So that the general principles and norms of this sacred Synod with respect to the media of social communications may be put into effect, by the express will of the Council, the office of the Holy See mentioned in number 19 should undertake, with the assistance of experts from various countries, to issue a pastoral instruction.

24. As for the rest, this sacred Synod is confident that its issuance of these instructions and norms will be gladly accepted and religiously kept by all the Church's children. By using these helps they will experience no harm and, like salt and light, they will give savour to the earth and brighten the world. Moreover, the Synod invites all men of good will, especially those who have charge of these media, to strive to turn them solely to the good of society, whose fate depends more and more on their proper use. Thus, as was the case with ancient works of art, the name of the Lord may be glorified by these new discoveries in accordance with those words of the Apostle: 'Jesus Christ, yesterday and today, and the same forever.'[2]

Notes

1. Corinthians 8:1.
2. Hebrews 13:8.

PASTORAL INSTRUCTION
COMMUNIO ET PROGRESSIO

ON THE MEANS OF SOCIAL COMMUNICATION WRITTEN BY ORDER OF THE SECOND VATICAN COUNCIL

23 MAY 1971

Foreword

1. The *unity* and *advancement* of men living in society: these are the chief aims of social communication and of all the means it uses. These means include the press, the cinema, radio and television. The constant improvement in the media puts them at the disposal of more and more people who in their daily lives make increasing use of them. More than ever before, the way men live and think is profoundly affected by the means of communication.

2. The Church sees these media as 'gifts of God'[1] which, in accordance with his providential design, unite men in brotherhood and so help them to cooperate with his plan for their salvation. A deeper and more penetrating understanding of social communication and of the contribution which the media it uses can make to modern society can be derived from a number of documents issued by the Second Vatican Council. These are, notably the Constitution on *The Church in the World Today,*[2] the Decree on *Ecumenism,*[3] the Declaration on *Religious Freedom,*[4] the Decree on *The Missionary Activity of the Church*[5] and the Decree on *The Pastoral Duties of Bishops.*[6] And, of course, there is a Decree that is wholly devoted to a discussion of *The Media of Social Communication.*[7]

The deeper understanding based on the teaching and spirit of this Council will now guide Christians in their attitudes to the media and will make them the more eager to commit themselves in this field.

3. This pastoral instruction which is being published at the direction of the Second Vatican Council[8] sets out basic doctrinal principles and general pastoral guidelines. It carefully refrains from going into minute details on a subject which is continually changing and developing and which varies so much according to time and place.

4. It will therefore be the task of bishops and their conferences and, equally, of the Synods of the Eastern Churches, to consult experts and their diocesan, national and international councils. This should be done not only to implement this instruction efficiently and in a spirit of collegiality, but also to discover the best way of explaining it and suiting it, as precisely as possible, to the needs of the people in their care. And while they do this, they will keep in mind the unity of the Church.

In this task episcopal conferences will lean upon the professional assistance which priests, religious and laity can offer. For a proper use of the media of social communication is the responsibility of the entire people of God.

5. This instruction, it is hoped, will be well received by all those who are professionally involved in the field of communications and, indeed, by all who, from good will, seek the progress of mankind. So, as a result of exchanges of views and cooperation with such men, the vast potential that lies in the means of social communication will be made good and this for the advancement of all.

PART ONE

The Christian View of the Means of Social Communication: Basic Points of Doctrine

6. The channels of social communication, even though they are addressed to individuals, reach and affect the whole of society.[9] They inform a vast public about what goes on in the world and about contemporary attitudes and they do it swiftly. That is why they are indispensable to the smooth functioning of modern society with its complex and ever changing needs and the continual and often close consultations all this involves. This

exactly coincides with the Christian conception of how men should live together. These technical advances have the high purpose of bringing men into closer contact with one another. By passing on knowledge of their common fears and hopes they help men to resolve them. A Christian estimate of the contribution that the media make to the well being of mankind is rooted in this fundamental principle.

7. All over the world, men are at work on improving the conditions for human living and the latest scientific wonders and technical achievements play their part in this. The Christian vision of man, of his motives and of his history sees in this development a response – though usually an unconscious one – to the divine command to 'possess and master the world'.[10] It also sees it as an act of cooperation in the divine work of creation and conservation.[11]

It is within this vision that the means of social communication fall into their proper place. They help men share their knowledge and unify their creative work. Indeed, by creating man in his own image, God has given him a share in his creative power. And so man is summoned to cooperate with his fellow man in building the earthly city.[12]

8. Social communications tend to multiply contacts within society and to deepen social consciousness. As a result the individual is bound more closely to his fellow men and can play his part in the unfolding of history as if led by the hand of God.[13] In the Christian faith, the unity and brotherhood of man are the chief aims of all communication and these find their source and model in the central mystery of the eternal communion between the Father, Son and Holy Spirit who live a single divine life.

9. The media of social communication can contribute a great deal to human unity. If, however, men's minds and hearts are ill disposed, if good will is not there, this outpouring of technology may produce an opposite effect so that there is less understanding and more discord and, as a result, evils are multiplied. Too often, we have to watch social communications used to contradict or corrupt the fundamental values of human life. The Christian

considers these evils evidence of man's need to be redeemed and freed from that sin which entered human history with man's first fall.[14]

10. When, by his own fault, man turned away from his Creator, chaos succeeded crime and man became embroiled in discord and deadly fraternal strife.[15] He was no longer able to communicate with his fellow men. But for all that, God's love for man persisted, despite its rejection by man. It was he who made the first move to make contact with mankind[16] at the start of the history of salvation. In the fullness of time, he communicated his very self to man[17] and 'the Word was made flesh'.[18]

When, by his death and resurrection, Christ the Incarnate Son, the Word and Image of the invisible God,[19] set the human race free, he shared with everyone the truth and the life of God. And he did this more richly and lavishly than ever before. As the only mediator between the Father and mankind he made peace between God and man and laid the foundations of unity among men themselves.[20] From that moment, communication among men found its highest ideal and supreme example in God who had become man and brother. He ordered his disciples, always and everywhere,[21] to spread the good tidings 'in the light of day' and 'from the roof tops'.[22]

11. While he was on earth Christ revealed himself as the perfect communicator. Through his 'incarnation', he utterly identified himself with those who were to receive his communication and he gave his message not only in words but in the whole manner of his life. He spoke from within, that is to say, from out of the press of his people. He preached the divine message without fear or compromise. He adjusted to his people's way of talking and to their patterns of thought. And he spoke out of the predicament of their time.

Communication is more than the expression of ideas and the indication of emotion. At its most profound level it is the giving of self in love. Christ's communication was, in fact, spirit and life.[23] In the institution of the Holy Eucharist, Christ gave us the most perfect and most intimate form of communion between God and man possible in this life, and, out of this, the deepest possible unity between men. Further, Christ communicated to us his life-giving spirit, who brings all men together in unity.[24] The Church is Christ's mystical body, the hidden completion of Christ glorified who 'fills the whole creation'.[25] As a result we move, within the Church and with the help of the word and the sacraments, towards the hope of that last unity where 'God will be all in all'.[26]

12. So, 'among the wonderful technical inventions'[27] which foster communication among human beings, Christians find means that have been devised under God's providence for the encouragement of social relations during their pilgrimage on earth. These means, in fact, serve to build new relationships and to fashion a new language which permits men to know themselves better and to understand one another more easily. By this, men are led to a mutual understanding and shared ambition. And this, in turn, inclines them to justice and peace, to good will and active charity, to mutual help, to love and, in the end, to communion. The tools of communication, then, provide some of the most effective means for the cultivation of that charity among men which is at once the cause and the expression of fellowship.

13. All men of good will, then, are impelled to work together to ensure that the media of communication do in fact contribute to the pursuit of truth and the speeding up of progress. The Christian will find in his faith an added incentive to do this. And the message of the Gospel thus spread will promote this idea which is the brotherhood of man under the fatherhood of God.

Contact and cooperation among men depend, in the last resort, on man's free choice which, in its turn, is affected by psychological, sociological and technical factors. And so the importance and ultimate significance of the media of communication depend upon the working of man's free choice in their use.

14. Since it is man himself who decides how the available means of communication shall be used, the moral principles at issue here are those based on a true interpretation of the dignity of man. And man, it should be recalled, must be accounted a member of

the family of the adopted children of God. At the same time, these principles derive from the essential character of social communication and the innate qualities of the medium in question. This also follows from what is said in *Gaudium et spes*: 'By the very fact of their having been created, all things are endowed with their own stability, truth, goodness, proper laws and order which man must respect ...'[28]

15. Whoever wants to see the media take their allotted place in the history of creation, in the incarnation and redemption, and to consider the morality that governs their use, must have a full and proper understanding of man. He must also have a sound knowledge both of the true nature of social communication and of the tools at its service. 'Communicators' are all those who actively employ the media. These have a duty in conscience to make themselves competent in the art of social communication in order to be effective in their work.[29] And as a man's influence on the process of communication grows, so does this duty. All this applies even more to those who have to instruct the tastes and judgements of others. It applies to those who have to teach the young or the uneducated. And it applies to all who can in any way enrich or impoverish man's nature, whether that man be a man alone or a man engulfed in a crowd.

'Recipients' are those who, for their own purpose, read, listen to or view the various media. Everything possible should be done to enable these to know about the media. So they will be able to interpret their message accurately, to reap their benefit in full and play their part in the life of society. Only if this is done will the media function in the best possible way.

16. The total output of the media in any given area should be judged by the contribution it makes to the common good.[30] Its news, culture and entertainment should meet the growing needs of society. The news of something that has happened must be given and so too must the background of the event so that people can understand society's problems and work for their solution. A proper balance must be kept, not only between hard news, educational material and entertainment but also between the light and the more serious forms of that entertainment.

17. Every communication must comply with certain essential requirements and these are sincerity, honesty and truthfulness. Good intentions and a clear conscience do not thereby make a communication sound and reliable. A communication must state the truth. It must accurately reflect the situation with all its implications. The moral worth and validity of any communication does not lie solely in its theme or intellectual content. The way in which it is presented, the way in which it is spoken and treated and even the audience for which it is designed – all these factors must be taken into account.[31]

18. A deeper understanding and a greater sympathy between men, as well as fruitful cooperation in creative work, these are the marvellous benefits that should come from social communication. Those are ideals which are completely in tune with the aims of the people of God. Indeed they are strengthened and reinforced by them. 'For the promotion of unity belongs to the innermost nature of the Church,' since she is 'by her relationship with Christ, both a sacramental sign and an instrument of intimate union with God, and of the unity of all mankind'.[32]

PART TWO

The Contribution of the Communications Media to Human Progress

CHAPTER I

The Work of the Media in Human Society

19. The modern media of social communication offer men of today a great round table. At this they are able to participate in a world-wide exchange in search of brotherhood and cooperation. It is not surprising that this should be so, for the media are at the disposal of all and are channels for that very dialogue which they themselves stimulate. The torrent of information and opinion pouring through these channels makes every man a partner in the business of the human race. This interchange creates the proper conditions for that mutual and sympathetic understanding which leads to universal progress.

20. The swift advances of the means of social communication tear down the barriers that time and space have erected between men. They can make for greater understanding and closer unity. A mass of information is continually on the move to and from all parts of the world and, as a result, men can learn what goes on and how other men live. Teaching at all levels has benefited by the use of these aids. These media play their part in eliminating illiteracy and in providing both basic and further education. They can, very effectively, help people in developing countries to achieve progress and freedom. They can establish a measure of universal equality in which all men, whatever their place in society can enjoy the delights of culture and leisure. They enrich men's minds. They help them to keep in touch with reality by providing the sights and sounds which are the very stuff of life. They bring far away times and places within their grasp. And when illiteracy is rife – and this is not in any way to question the validity of traditional cultures – citizens can quickly be brought in touch with recent developments in modern ways of life.

21. In the light of these advantages, the communications media can be seen as powerful instruments for progress. It is true they present difficulties but these must be faced and overcome. Both the communicators and the recipients ought to be aware of their inherent dangers and difficulties. For instance, how can we ensure that this swift and haphazard and endless stream of news is properly evaluated and understood? The media are bound to seek a mass audience and so they often adopt a neutral stance in order to avoid giving offence to any section of their audience. How, in a society that is committed to the rights of dissent, is the distinction between right and wrong and true and false to be made?

How in the face of competition to capture a large popular audience are the media to be prevented from appealing to and inflaming the less admirable tendencies in human nature? How can one avoid the concentration of the power to communicate in too few hands so that any real dialogue is killed? How can one avoid allowing communications made indirectly and through machinery to weaken direct human contact, especially when these communications take the form of pictures and images? When the media invite men to escape into fantasy, what can be done to bring them back to present reality? How can one stop the media encouraging mental idleness and passivity? And how can one be certain that the incessant appeal to emotion does not sap reason?

22. It is obvious that there has been a decline in moral standards in many areas of life today and this decline is the cause of profound concern to all honest men. It is easy to find evidence of this decline in all the means of social communication. But how far these means must be blamed for the decline is open to question. Many responsible men hold that these means are only a reflection of what already exists in society. Others hold that they increase and spread those tendencies and that, by making them commonplace, lead to their gradual acceptance. And still others would put most of the blame squarely upon the means of social communication. What is certainly true is that the weakness lies in society itself and that the attempt to restore standards must involve the whole of society, its parents, teachers, pastors and all who care about the common good. In this attempt the means of social communication have no small part to play. It is however impossible to put the means of social communication into a quite separate category from that of the everyday life and attitudes of the people.

23. In order that the benefits offered to society by social communications can be better understood and used to the full and the incidental difficulties they present set aside, the chief aspects of the working of the media among men must be investigated.

1. Public Opinion

24. The means of social communication are a public forum where every man may exchange ideas. The public expression and the confrontation of different opinions that occur within this dialogue influence and enrich the development of society and further its progress.

25. Public opinion is an essential expression of human nature organised in a society. This opinion is formed in the following

way. In everyone there is an innate disposition to give vent to opinions, attitudes and emotions in order to reach a general acceptance on convictions and customs. Pius XII describes public opinion as 'the natural echo of actual events and situations as reflected more or less spontaneously in the minds and judgements of men'.[33] So freedom of speech is a normal factor in the growth of public opinion which expresses the ideas and reactions of the more influential circles in a society defined by geography, culture and history.

26. If public opinion is to emerge in the proper manner, it is absolutely essential that there be freedom to express ideas and attitudes. In accordance with the express teaching of the Second Vatican Council it is necessary unequivocally to declare that freedom of speech for individuals and groups must be permitted so long as the common good and public morality be not endangered.[34] In order that men may usefully cooperate and further improve the life of the community, there must be freedom to assess and compare differing views which seem to have weight and validity. Within this free interplay of opinion there exists a process of give and take, of acceptance or rejection, of compromise or compilation. And within this same process, the more valid ideas can gain ground so that a consensus that will lead to common action becomes possible.

27. Communicators have, therefore, a most important part to play in forming public opinion. They have to gather up different views and compare them and transmit them so that people can understand and make a proper decision.

28. Every citizen is expected to play his part in the formation of public opinion. If needs be, he must do this through representatives who reflect his own views.[35] Those who exert influence because of the office they hold or because of their natural talent or for any other reason have an important part to play in forming public opinion: they help to do so whenever they express their views. The greater their quality of leadership, the greater is their responsibility to exert it in this way.

29. The process of promoting – in what is sometimes referred to as a 'propaganda campaign' – with a view to influencing public opinion is justified only when it serves the truth and its objectives and methods accord with the dignity of man and when it promotes causes that are in the public interest. These causes may concern either individuals or groups, one's own country or the world at large.

30. Some types of propaganda are inadmissable. These include those that harm the public interest or allow of no public reply. Any propaganda that deliberately misrepresents the real situation, or that distorts men's minds with half-truths, selective reporting or serious omissions that diminishes man's legitimate freedom of decision, this propaganda should be rejected. It is necessary to stress this because the power of propaganda is increasing. And its power is being augmented by the growth of behavioural sciences like that of psychology and of the technical resources at the disposal of the communications media.

31. Not every opinion that is given publicity should be taken as a true expression of that public opinion which is held by a significant number of people. A number of differing opinions can flourish at the same time in the same area, though, usually, one has a greater following than the others. The opinion of the majority, however, is not necessarily the best or the closest to the truth.

Public opinion, moreover, changes often. The same idea sometimes gains and sometimes loses hold of the public. Because of this, it is prudent to maintain a certain detachment toward the opinions currently in public vogue. There may well be good reasons that require one to oppose them.

32. However, views openly and commonly expressed which reflect the aspirations of the people should always be carefully considered. This is especially binding on those in authority, whether civil or religious.

2. The Right to be Informed and to Inform

33. If public opinion is to be formed in a proper manner, it is necessary that, right from the start, the public be given free access

both to the sources and channels of information and be allowed freely to express its own views. Freedom of opinion and the right to be informed go hand in hand. Pope John XXIII,[36] Pope Paul VI[37] and the Second Vatican Council[38] have all stressed this right to information which today is essential for the individual and for society in general.

a) Access to the Sources and Channels of News

34. Modern man cannot do without information that is full, consistent, accurate and true. Without it, he cannot understand the perpetually changing world in which he lives nor be able to adapt himself to the real situation. This adaptation calls for frequent decisions that should be made with a full knowledge of events. Only in this way can he assume a responsible and active role in his community and be a part of its economic, political, cultural and religious life.

With the right to be informed goes the duty to seek information. Information does not simply occur; it has to be sought. On the other hand, in order to get it, the man who wants information must have access to the varied means of social communication. In this way he can freely choose whatever means best suit his needs both personal and social. It is futile to talk about the right to information if a variety of the sources for it are not made available.

35. Society, at all levels, requires information if it is to choose the right course. The community requires well-informed citizens. The right to information is not merely the prerogative of the individual, it is essential to the public interest.

36. Those whose job it is to give news have a most difficult and responsible role to play. They face formidable obstacles and these obstacles will sometimes include persons interested in concealing the truth. This is especially the case for reporters who give close-up impressions of the news and who, in order to do this, often travel to the four corners of the earth in order to witness events as they actually happen.[39] At times they risk their lives and indeed a number of them have been killed in this line of duty.[40] The safety of such correspondents should be ensured in every possible way

because of the service they render to man's right to know about what is happening. This is particularly true in the case of wars which involve and concern the whole human race. So the Church utterly condemns the use of violence against newsmen or against anyone in any way involved in the passing on of news. For these persons vindicate and practice the right of finding out what is happening and of passing on this information to others.

37. It is hard for anyone to learn the whole truth and to pass this on to others, but newsmen face an additional problem. Of its nature, news is about what is new. So journalists deal with what has just happened and with what is of present interest. More than that, out of a mass of material, they must select what they judge to be the significant facts that will concern their audience. So it can happen that the news reported is only a part of the whole and does not convey what is of real importance.

38. Communicators must give news that is quick, complete and comprehensible. So more and more they have to seek out competent men for comments, background briefing and discussion. Often these comments are required immediately, sometimes even before the expected event has happened. Men of trust, especially when they are in a position of responsibility or authority, are rightly reluctant to make hasty or unprepared comments before they have had a chance to study a situation and its context. And so because the media are impelled to demand quick comment, the initiative often passes to men who are less responsible and less well informed but who are more willing to oblige. Those acquainted with a given situation should try to prevent this happening. As far as they can, they should keep themselves up to date so that they themselves can reply and ensure that the public is properly informed.

39. Then there is another problem. Those who have to keep the public informed must give the news quickly if it is to appear fresh and interesting. Competition also obliges them to do this and speed is often won at the price of accuracy. The communicator has also to know the tastes and cultural level of his public and to take into account its known preferences. And when he comes to

present the news, it is in the face of such hazards that a communicator must remain faithful to the truth.

40. But as well as these problems which are inherent in the nature of the news and communications media, there is another. Communicators must hold the wandering attention of a harried and hurried public by vivid reporting. And yet they must not give way to the temptation of making the news sensational in such a way that they risk distorting it by taking it out of context or by exaggerating it out of all proportion.

41. The recipients who piece together the news that comes to them in fragments may well end up with an unbalanced or distorted idea of the whole picture. To a certain extent, accuracy can be restored by the continuity of the flow from different sources, which must always be carefully assessed. The recipients of information should have a clear conception of the predicament of those that purvey information. They should not look for a superhuman perfection in the communicators. What they do have a right and duty to expect, however, is that a rapid and clear correction should follow any mistake or misrepresentation that has found its way into a report. They are to protest whenever omissions or distortions occur. They are to protest whenever events have been reported out of context or in a biased manner. They are to protest whenever the significance of events has been wildly exaggerated or underplayed. This right should be guaranteed for recipients by agreement among the communicators themselves and, if this cannot be got, then by national law or international convention.

42. But the right to information is not limitless. It has to be reconciled with other existing rights. There is the right of privacy, which protects the private life of families and individuals.[41] There is the right of secrecy, which obtains if necessity or professional duty or the common good itself requires it. Indeed, whenever public good is at stake, discretion and discrimination and careful judgement should be used in the preparation of news.

43. The reporting of violence and brutality demands a special care and tact. There is no denying that human life is debased by

violence and savagery and that such things happen in our own time and perhaps more now than ever before. It is possible to delineate all this violence and savagery so that men will recoil from it. But if these bloody events are too realistically described or too frequently dwelt upon, there is a danger of perverting the image of human life. It is also possible that such descriptions generate an attitude of mind and, according to many experts, a psychosis which escapes the control of the very forces that unleashed it. All this may leave violence and savagery as the accepted way of resolving conflict.

b) Freedom of Communication

44. This right to information is inseparable from freedom of communication. Social life depends on a continual interchange, both individual and collective, between people. This is necessary for mutual understanding and for cooperative creativity. When social intercourse makes use of the mass media, a new dimension is added. Then vast numbers of people get the chance to share in the life and progress of the community.

45. Because man is social by nature, he feels the need to express himself freely and to compare his views with those of other people. This applies today more than ever before now that man's intellect and genius are often enough served more by teamwork than by individual effort. So the result is that when people follow their natural inclination to exchange ideas and declare their opinions, they are not merely making use of a right. They are also performing a social duty.

46. Those societies which tolerate diverse component groups and are called 'pluralist' can well understand the importance of the free flow of information and opinion that enables the citizens to play an active part in the community. Laws have been passed in such countries to guard this freedom. Moreover, the Universal Declaration of Human Rights has proclaimed this freedom to be fundamental and thereby implies that the same freedom is essential in the use of the means of social communication.

47. This freedom of communication also implies that individuals and groups must be free to seek out and spread information. It also means that they should have free access to the media. On the other hand, freedom of communication would be more to the benefit of those who communicate news rather than for the good of those who receive it, if this freedom existed without proper limits and without thought of those real and public needs upon which the right to information is based.

3. Education, Culture and Leisure

48. The means of social communication have an ever growing role to play in the vast field of human education. In many places audiovisual aids, the new video cassettes and the regular use of radio and television have become accepted teaching instruments. They make the work of experts in different fields accessible to more and more people. Elsewhere the means of social communication are used to complement the established ways of teaching. They also give opportunities for further education to adolescents and adults. In places where the educational facilities are inadequate, they can provide religious instruction and basic education and fight illiteracy. They are useful instruments for instructing people in agriculture, medicine, hygiene and many forms of community development. As far as possible, this use of the media for education should have a creative quality and elicit an active response. In this way, the pupil is not only led to knowledge but learns to express himself by using the media.

49. Moreover in a manner that is unique, the media, which are already a conspicuous element in daily life, bring artistic and cultural achievements within the orbit of a great part of the human race. And soon, perhaps, they will do the same for the whole of it. This is as authentic a mark of social progress as is the removal of economic and social inequality.

50. The media can deepen and enrich contemporary culture and communicators should recognise that everyone has a right to this enrichment. They should not hesitate therefore to take the chance offered by the so-called 'mass media' to reach great numbers of people. The media also make it possible to cater for differing

needs and interests since, in a professional and attractive manner, they can produce the fruits of every type of artistic expression.

People, then, will find no difficulty in using the media to deepen and refine their cultural life as long as they supplement this use with the exercise of personal reflection and an exchange of views with others.

51. An example of the cultural potential of the media can be found in their service to the traditional folk arts of countries where stories, plays, song and dance still express an ancient national inheritance. Because of their modern techniques, the media can make these achievements known more widely. They can record them so that they can be seen and heard again and again and make them accessible even in districts where the old traditions have vanished. In this way, the media help to impress on a nation a proper sense of its cultural identity and by expressing this, delight and enrich other cultures and countries as well.

52. It should be recalled that many great works recognised as the products of genius, particularly in music, drama and literature, were first presented to the public as entertainment. So entertainment need not lack cultural validity.[42]

Today, through the media, the noblest forms of artistic expression offer true recreation – in the fullest sense of that word – to more and more people. And there is more and more call for this in our complex society. Simple entertainment, too, has a value of its own. It lightens the burden of daily problems and it occupies men's leisure. The wide variety of productions that the media offer for these hours of leisure is in fact a remarkable service to mankind. But recipients should exercise self-control. They must not allow themselves to be so beguiled by the charms of the media's products or by the curiosity that these arouse that they neglect urgent duties or simply waste time.

53. The media are themselves new factors in contemporary culture, serving as they do large numbers of people at the same time. But as well as enriching culture, they can occasionally degrade it. They often play for the applause of the lowest cultural

levels of their audience. And because they take so much of modern man's time, they can easily divert him from higher and more profitable cultural pursuits.

An unrelieved diet of productions geared to the lowest cultural level within a population would tend to debase the taste of those who have already attained a higher level. These dangers can be avoided if communicators really care about the well-being of culture and buttress their good intentions with a sound knowledge of the science of education. Moreover, it will be recalled that the media are perfectly capable of productions on the highest artistic level, and these are not necessarily the most difficult to follow and to enjoy for the great majority.

4. Forms of Artistic Expression

54. The media of social communication do more than present the traditional forms of artistic expression; they themselves create new ones. And now that the media cover the whole earth and multiply the opportunities for international cultural cooperation, especially in co-productions using the talents of artists from many nations, it is only right that both communicators and recipients should seek to acquire a truly catholic taste, one that includes both the traditional and the latest forms of artistic expression, one that appreciates and understands the production of all nations, of all cultures and of all sub-cultures within the same areas of civilization.

55. Artistic expression both for its own excellence and for what it does for man should be highly appreciated. Of itself, beauty ennobles the mind that contemplates it. The work of the artist can also penetrate and illumine the deepest recesses of the human spirit. It can make spiritual reality immediate by expressing it in a way that the senses can comprehend. And as a result of this expression man comes to know himself better. This is not only a cultural benefit but a moral and religious one as well. 'It is a fact that when you writers and artists are able to reveal in the human condition, however lowly or sad it may be, a spark of goodness, at that very instant a glow of beauty pervades your whole work. We are not asking of you that you should play the part of moralists. We are only asking you to have confidence in your

mysterious power of opening up the glorious regions of light that lie behind the mystery of man's life.'[43]

56. Those who would truly understand the spirit of another age have to study not only its history, but also its literature and artefacts. And this is so because, in a very precise and lucid way, the creative arts are more revealing than conceptual descriptions of the character of people, of their aspirations, emotions and thoughts. Even when the artist takes flight from the tangible and solid world and pursues his creative fantasies, he can give priceless insight into the human condition. Stories fashioned out of imagination in which the artist creates characters that live and evolve in a world of fiction, these too communicate their special truth. Even though they are not real, they are realistic; for they are made of the very stuff of human life. They even affect those deep causes that rouse men to blaze with life.[44] For, in the light they throw on these causes, the sensitive man may know them for what they are. And with this knowledge he can begin to foresee the direction that humanity will take.

57. Pope Pius XII taught that human life 'certainly cannot be understood, at least when considering violent and serious conflicts, if one deliberately turns one eyes from the crimes and evils from which they often have their origin. How, then, can ideal films take this as their subject? The greatest poets and writers of all times have occupied themselves with this difficult and rough matter, and they will continue to do so in the future ... When the conflict with evil, not excluding cases when evil prevails for a while, is treated within the context of a work as a whole, in an effort to understand life better, to see how it should be ordered, or to show how man should conduct himself, how he should think and act with more consistency, then, in such cases, such matter can be chosen as an integral part of the development of the whole film'.[45] Such a work would contribute to moral progress. Even though they are quite distinct, genuine artistic values do not clash with moral standards. Each in fact confirms the validity of the other.

58. Moral problems may at times arise in productions that deal with evil. For instance, these may occur when the audience is

unable to grasp, as it should, the full implications of evil, either because its members are young or undeveloped or because their education is inadequate. The artist is faced with life in its entirety, with its good as well as its bad aspects. Good sense and judgement are therefore called for when a work is destined for a large audience with different backgrounds. This is especially true when the subject is man confronted by evil.

5. Advertising

59. The importance of advertising is steadily on the increase in modern society. It makes its presence felt everywhere; its influence is unavoidable. It offers real social benefits. It tells buyers of the goods and services available. It thus encourages the widest distribution of products and, in doing this, it helps industry to develop and benefit the population. All this is to the good so long as there is respect for the buyer's liberty of choice, even though in trying to sell some particular objects appeal is made to a person's basic need. Advertising too must respect the truth, taking into account accepted advertising conventions.

60. If harmful or utterly useless goods are touted to the public, if false assertions are made about the goods for sale, if less admirable human tendencies are exploited, those responsible for such advertising harm society and forfeit their good name and credibility. More than this, unremitting pressure to buy articles of luxury can arouse false wants that hurt both individuals and families by making them ignore what they really need. And those forms of advertising which, without shame, exploit the sexual instincts simply to make money or which seek to penetrate into the subconscious recesses of the mind in a way that threatens the freedom of the individual, those forms of advertising must be shunned. It is therefore desirable that advertisers make definite rules for themselves lest their sales methods affront human dignity or harm the community.

61. It is true that a judicious use of advertising can stimulate developing countries to improve their standard of living. But serious harm can be done them if advertising and commercial pressure become so irresponsible that communities that seek to

rise from poverty to a reasonable standard of living are persuaded to seek this progress by satisfying wants that have been created artificially. The result of this is that they waste their resources and neglect their real needs and genuine development falls behind.

62. In fact the vast sums of money spent in advertising threaten the very foundations of the mass media. People can get the impression that the instruments of communication exist solely to stimulate men's appetites so that these can be satisfied later by the acquisition of the things that have been advertised. Moreover, because of economic demands and pressures, the essential freedom of the media is at stake. Since advertising revenue is vital for these media, only those can ultimately survive which receive the greatest share of advertising outlays. Consequently, the door is open for monopolies to develop in the media which may impede the right to receive and give information and inhibit the exchange of views within the community. A variety of independent means of social communication must therefore be carefully safeguarded even if this requires legislative action. This will ensure that there is an equitable distribution of advertising revenue among the most deserving media of communication and prevent the lion's share from going to those that are already the most powerful.

CHAPTER II

The Best Conditions for their Proper Working

63. If the media of social communication are to give their best service to mankind, the importance of the human element must be recognised. This element plays a more decisive role than the most marvellous electronic and mechanical instruments by themselves. For the proper functioning of the media in society does not occur of its own accord. Both communicators and recipients, each according to his own requirements, need a suitable grounding if full advantage is to be taken of the opportunities offered by these instruments. All should know what their particular role requires of them and then proceed to play it, both as individuals and members of society. Civil authorities, as well as religious leaders

and educators, should play their part too in order that the rich promise of the media be effectively realised for the good of society.

1. Training

64. A training that grounds a man in the basic principles governing the working of the media in human society, as explained above, is nowadays clearly necessary for all. The means of communication genuinely enrich men's minds if their character and function is understood. On the other hand, men who do not sufficiently appreciate their importance may find their liberty diminished. Training should include a practical consideration of the special nature of each medium and of its status in the local community and how it can best be utilised. And this should be done with special reference to man and society.

a) The Recipients

65. Recipients need some basic training if they are to benefit to the full from what the instruments of social communication have to offer. This training is not merely for their personal advantage, but it should help them to make their contribution to the give and take of society as well as to the constructive work of the community. Such a training will also help them to discover the best way of achieving these ends. It will help them to play their part in the process of striving for justice among nations and for the elimination of glaring inequalities between the richer and poorer countries.

66. For this they require a knowledge of the media that will keep pace with their maturing. And the processs of education, which should be available to all, does not come to an end. It is to be supplemented continually by lectures and discussions, by special courses and study sessions that make use of the help of professionals in this field.

67. It is never too early to start encouraging in children artistic taste, a keen critical faculty and a sense of personal responsibility that is based on sound morality. They need all these so that they can use discrimination in choosing from the publications, films

and broadcasts that are set before them. This is necessary because the young are naturally vulnerable, but this self-discipline acquired in childhood will richly serve the adult too. Generosity and idealism are admirable qualities in young people; so are their frankness and sincerity. But these qualities, along with self-discipline, will only survive if they are guarded and fostered from an early age. This is why parents and teachers should urge children to make their own choice even if the educators should reserve at times the final decision to themselves. And if they find themselves forced to disapprove of the way their children are using some aspect of the media, they must clearly explain the reasons for their objections. Persuasion works better than prohibition and this is especially true in education. Adults should realise that the psychology of children differs from that of adults. Because of this, programmes that seem meaningless to them may be useful to children and even to teenagers.

Young people can, without doubt, influence one another for the better when it comes to culture. Their very years serve as a passport to the new forms it takes and gives them an entrance to their own circle. There is ample evidence to prove how effective they can be.

68. It is useful for educators to take note of some of the broadcasts, films and publications that most interest the young in their care. They can then discuss them together and this helps to develop the child's critical powers. As for the more difficult or even controversial artistic productions, here the parent should, at the right moment, help his young to discover the human values in the production and to interpret its details within the context of the work as a whole.

69. This sort of training must be given a regular place in school curricula. It must be given, and systematically, at every stage of education. In this way, young people can be helped gradually to develop a new perception in their interpretation of what is offered them by the press, the other media and the literary publishing houses. All this should be taught in study courses planned to include special sessions where the teacher can call on the help of professional communicators for lectures and for practical exercises.

70. It is obvious that parents and other educators cannot meet these obligations unless they themselves are reasonably well grounded in an understanding of the media. Here it must be remembered that parents who have not grown up to be at home with the media often find it harder to comprehend the language used than do the young people of today. Often parents are disturbed by the frankness with which the media treat every question and these include the problems that face both the civil government and the Church. Naturally they wish their children to use the media in a proper manner. Nevertheless, let them trust the young because these have been born and have grown up in a different kind of society. Because of this, they are better forewarned and better forearmed to meet the pressures that come from every side.

b) The Communicators

71. Many are the communicators who handle well the tools of their profession, but lack a deep understanding of the art of communicating with all it implies. It is obvious that the communicators in the media who wish to excel, need a serious and specialised training in every aspect of their work. The growing trend to found faculties of social communication in institutions of higher learning, and these with authority to confer degrees, is a welcome development. For if communicators are to meet their professional obligations, they must have sound knowledge as well as experience.

72. In the training of a communicator, human qualities as well as professional competence should be developed. Since the media of social comunication are for mankind, communicators should be consumed by the desire to serve men. They can only achieve this if they really do know and love their fellow man. The more communicators remember that beyond the lifeless instruments which pass on their words and images are countless men and women alive, the more satisfaction they will get from their work and the better they will help others. The more they get to know their audience, the more they understand it and appreciate it, the more they will suit what they communicate to those who receive it. If they do this, they help to make the process of communication a communion of the spirit.

2. Opportunities and Obligations

a) Of Communicators

73. Communicators breathe life into the dialogue that happens within the family of man. It is they who preside while the exchange proceeds around the vast 'round table' that the media have made. Their vocation is nobly to promote the purpose of social communication. This purpose is to accelerate every sort of human progress and to increase cooperation among men until there exists a genuine communion among them.

74. When they come to choose the subjects for their productions, communicators will attempt to match all the needs of their public. They will be scrupulous in seeing that every relevant group is fairly represented. To do this, they have to try to foresee the kind of audience they serve. There should, accordingly, be close cooperation between communicators and recipients. Only in this way can these social communications set up a working and workable dialogue between free and adequately prepared people. And this dialogue must not ignore the age, culture and social background of the participants. The media of social communication are the right instruments for the propagation of this sort of interchange between men.

75. Pope Paul said of communicators that they are obliged to pay continual attention to and to carry on an uninterrupted observation of the external world: 'You must continually stand at the window, open to the world; you are obliged to study the facts, the events, the opinions, the current interests, the thought of the surrounding environment.'[46] Because factual information provides a public service, not only must news reporting keep to the facts and bear down upon the most important of these but the meaning of what it reports should be brought out by explanation. The real bearing of one item of news upon another should be pointed out especially when different items reach the recipient without evidence of any discernible pattern. In this way the recipient will be able to use this information as a basis for his judgement and decision in matters affecting the community.

76. Communicators should not allow themselves to forget that the nature of the mass media makes their audience a vast one. While they must keep faith with their artistic integrity, they will remember at the same time both their power and the grave responsibilities that it brings with it. For they have been given a rare chance to promote the happiness and progress of men. In their productions justice and integrity of judgement will impel artists to be concerned both with the needs of minorities as well as of larger and more numerous groups. And if some of the means of social communication, whether by law or local practice, in fact enjoy a monopoly, then a scrupulous impartiality must be sought since, in such a situation, the danger is that monologue may replace dialogue.

77. Communicators who debase their skills and their work for money or for easy popularity and passing acclaim are not only failing their public. In the end, they are demeaning their profession.

78. Critics have a commanding role in getting communicators to maintain the highest standards of integrity and service and continually to make progress. As they themselves are also communicators, they provide the self-criticism within the profession and in this way they are able to protect creative artists from external pressures. They must be convinced that integrity and incorruptibility are the essence of their profession. They will be inspired by fidelity to truth and a passion for justice. In a cool and objective way, they should try to display both the strength and the weakness of the work under review so that the public can make its own fair judgement. The importance of their own creative art should not be underrated, especially when through their wide knowledge and their penetrating judgement they are able to discover in works of art meaning and riches that may have escaped even the artists themselves. Yet they should not attract all attention to themselves at the expense of the work under study.

79. The founding of professional associations for communicators is most valuable. They are very useful as places where opinions and experiences can be exchanged. They form a basis for

organised cooperation. They help in coping with the sort of difficulties that are inherent in the communicator's task. These associations can draw up codes of ethics on a basis of principle and experience. Through the guidance they offer, these codes can help in producing work that meets the needs of social communication. Fundamentally, the codes of these associations ought to be positive. They should not be wholly preoccupied with forbidding; rather they should concentrate on how to improve what can be done for the communicators' fellow men.

80. In order to survive and to expand, the means of social communication require reliable financial backing. It therefore happens that communicators must at times, either directly or indirectly, seek funds from public or private sources. The men who provide these funds can powerfully influence the quality of the product. But they must be discerning in choosing which enterprises to support and desire the good of mankind rather than financial advantage. As long as they bear in mind that the means of social communication are more than commercial enterprises, are, in fact, at one and the same time, cultural and social services, these investors will not exercise any undue pressure that might distort the proper liberty of the communicators, the artists or what we have called the recipients.

b) Recipients

81. The recipients can do more to improve the quality of the media than is generally realised; so their responsibility to do this is all the greater. Whether or not the media can set up an authentic dialogue with society depends very largely upon these recipients. If they do not insist on expressing their views, if they are content with a merely passive role, all the efforts of the communicators to establish an uninhibited dialogue will be useless.

82. Recipients can be described as active when they know how to interpret communications accurately and can judge them in the light of their origin, background and total content. They will be active when they make their selection judiciously and critically, when they fill out incomplete information that comes their way

with more news which they themselves have obtained from other sources and, finally, when they are ready to make their views heard in public, whether they agree or partly agree or totally disagree.

83. There is the obvious objection that there is little a man can do alone at the receiving end. This is necessarily pessimistic. Recipients can find strength in unity. There exists no reason why they should not work closely together. They can band themselves into associations, just as communicators have been advised to do. Their organisations need not be set up with the single end of giving expression to what the man in the street feels about the products of the media. They could just as well avail themselves of organisations that already exist and which have a wider scope but compatible aims.

3. Cooperation between:

a) Citizens and the Civil Authorities

84. The media are there for the good of everyone and to serve everyone. So, at once, they concern both citizens and public authorities These authorities have the essential duty of maintaining freedom of speech and of seeing that the right conditions exist for it. Every individual must have the chance of following his informed judgement. Human dignity must be fully respected. The good of the country and the interests of international cooperation must both be given due consideration.

85. The well-being of society requires absolutely that individuals and groups be free to exercise initiative. It also requires that citizens exercise responsibility and self-control both as communicators and as recipients. With this end in view, voluntary associations may not only be desirable, they may even be essential.

86. The role of the civil authorities in this matter is essentially a positive one. Their chief task is not to create difficulties or to suppress, though, at times, corrective measures may become necessary. The Second Vatican Council explained that man's freedom is to be respected as far as possible and curtailed only

when and in so far as necessary.[47] Censorship therefore should only be used in the very last extremity. Moreover the civil authorities should respect the principle of subsidiarity which has often been affirmed in the official teaching of the Church, the gist of which is: 'Let them not undertake to do themselves what can be done just as well, or even better, by individuals or private groups.'

87. Therefore, it is right that, in the light of these principles, freedom of communication and the right to be informed be established in law and guarded from excessive economic, political and ideological pressures that might weaken them. There should be legislation to guarantee to citizens the right to criticise the actual working of the communications media. This is particularly desirable where the media are conducted as a monopoly. This is all the more necessary if the monopoly is exercised by the civil authorities themselves. It is undoubtedly the task of the lawmakers to legislate about the media. In fact the media must have the support of law so that they can survive, and survive in a sufficient variety and independence in the face of the encroachment of economic interests that make for harmful concentration. Again, the good name of the private citizen and of minority groups needs the protection of the law. Cultural and human values require protection. Religious liberty in the use of the media should be guaranteed.

88. It is highly recommended that professionals in the media or their institutions set up councils on their own account. These will have their own statutes and will be concerned with all aspects of social communication. Representatives of the different sections of the populations should be invited to sit on these councils. This, it is hoped, will eliminate the wrong sort of interference from state or economic interests. It will strengthen cooperation and fellow feeling between communicators and that will be to the benefit of the whole community. In some cases, however, the state may have to intervene in order to set up these advisory boards to supervise the media. In these cases, the boards should be, by law, representative of all shades of opinion within the community.

89. As far as possible, the law should protect the young from what can do them permanent psychological or moral harm. It is the task of legislation in this field to give the necessary support to the family and the school in the task of educating the young.

90. Legislation should be encouraged to provide financial support to initiatives in the use of communications that clearly serve the general good. These would include organisations that provide information, specialist educational publications, films and broadcasts, particularly when these are made for children. This support is more desirable when the initiatives have little hope of financial success. This encouragement also applies to feature films of high artistic quality and to publications and performances which are destined for a restricted public and which are therefore unlikely to pay their way.

91. The responsibility of civil authorities over the means of social communication now covers the world, for they have to guarantee the development of social communication for the good of all mankind, and this without selection or discrimination. This development can be secured by the use of international agreements including those that touch on the use of space satellites. In this way, all nations will be guaranteed a fair place within the dialogue and interplay of mankind.

b) Nations

92. Those forms of aid which emerging nations need to develop their own means of social communication are of great importance among the many forms of international effort which the media demand. The lack of proper means of social communication is, in fact, a sign of slow development in a community, as well as being one of the causes of it. Without the use of modern techniques of social communication no country can provide its citizens with necessary information or proper education. This inability endangers political, social and economic progress.

93. 'Progress,' said Pope Paul VI, 'is the new term for peace.'[48] Countries that are well equipped should provide technical assistance to those which are not. This is as true in the field of

social communication as in any other. The developed countries are to help in the training of professionals and provide the necessary equipment. Their responsibilities for the common good do not end at their national frontiers. They extend to the whole of mankind. This requirement is all the more pressing now that developments in the field are progressing so swiftly. Developing countries should be helped with training centres for social communication set up within their own boundaries. Otherwise the trainees may be forced wastefully to leave their own country. Such centres will prevent a 'brain drain' from the developing countries.

94. It goes without saying that the aid given to developing countries can never be at the expense of their own cherished traditions, of their culture and art forms, for these are rich in human significance. Cultural cooperation is not the giving of alms. It is an exchange that is mutually advantageous.

95. In developing countries, particularly in those where illiteracy hinders progress, audiovisual means are very effective in spreading knowledge. These means can help to improve agriculture, industry, commerce, hygiene and public health. They can serve to develop the individual's personality, to strengthen family life, social relations and civic responsibility. It is virtually impossible to do such works at a profit. It is therefore necessary to appeal to the generosity of private citizens and of private organisations in the richer countries as well as to the support of international bodies.

c) All Christians, all Believers and all Men of Good Will

96. The means of social communication are not likely to achieve their purpose – which is actively to further human progress – unless they face the formidable problems that beset modern man and strengthen his hopes and lead to a concerted effort on the part of all who believe in the living God. This is especially true in the case of those who are united in the sacrament of Baptism. So teaches the Second Council in the documents on ecumenism and non-Christian religions.[49]

97. As a result of the work of the communications media, Christians are better able to understand the state of contemporary world society, a society which is frequently alienated from God. Dramatists and journalists describe this alienation in significant terms asserting human liberty with all the force of their genius and with all the depth of their thought. Their creative power and descriptive skill have our admiration and gratitude.[50]

98. When their faith gives them real inspiration, people of different religions can render notable service to social communications. This will do more than further human progress both social and cultural. It can, under divine providence, institute a universal dialogue on the highest level that can lead man to cherish and foster in his daily life his common brotherhood under the one eternal God, the father of all.

99. There is almost no end to the opportunities for such collaboration. Some are obvious: joint programmes on radio and television; educational projects and services especially for parents and young people; meetings and discussions between professionals that may be on an international level; recognition of achievement in these fields by annual awards; cooperation in research in the media, especially in professional training and education. All these can help towards the fair and equal advancement of all peoples.

100. To make practical the possibilities that are inherent in the media there should be a joint programme of action. Resources will have to be made available for this. As a practical step the Vatican Council suggested the establishment of World Communications Day. Every man who believes in God is invited to spend one particular day every year to pray and think about the future and the problems of the media. They are also invited to friendly meetings with the different sorts of professionals. In this way it should be possible to explore what projects can be started and what initiatives encouraged whereby the media can be used to further the progress of mankind. The people of God (both pastors and laymen) commits itself, in the fulfilment of these duties, to give support to the initiatives of men of good will

everywhere so that the means of social communication may be used for justice, peace, freedom and human progress.

PART THREE

The Commitment of Catholics in the Media

101. Catholics have been asked by the Second Vatican Council to consider still more carefully and in the light of the faith what new work and responsibility the modern means of social communication place upon them. In the first part of this instruction, we have suggested how the history of salvation implied a vital role for social communications in God's creative and redeeming work among men. In interpreting her responsibilities in this, the Church tries to give a coherent vision that will embrace both the faith and the practical working of social communication. It is in this light that she will fulfil her divine mission, which is the object of all her pastoral activity and which has the dual aspects of helping men and of announcing the good news. The aspect of human progress by the media has been generally discussed in the second part of this document. The specifically Christian and Catholic contribution to human advancement will be dealt with briefly in the following chapter of this third part which is concerned with the role of the media in the life of Catholics.

CHAPTER I

The Contribution of Catholics to Social Communication

102. If Catholics are to be of service to the means of social communication and to act so that these may serve humanity's ends, it goes without saying that it is in the spiritual sphere that the Church can best help. The Church hopes that, as a result of her spiritual contribution, the basic nature of social communication will be more clearly appreciated. The Church hopes, too, that the dignity of the human person, both communicator and recipient, will be better understood and respected. In this way this social interplay that makes neighbours of men can lead to true communion.

103. Therefore, the active cooperation of Christians who are professionally competent in this field is a major service to social communication. The excellence which they bring to their professional duty is itself a powerful testimony to Christianity. Moreover, as members of companies or organisations without religious affiliations, they will bring to the fore a Christian point of view on all questions that exercise men in society. They can help news editors and newscasters not to overlook news items about religious life which will interest their audience. They can give the religious dimension to human life. It goes without saying that they are not at this work in order to dominate the media with their viewpoint. Rather they aim to give a service which will earn the sympathy of their colleagues simply by its quality.

104. It is a source of strength for Catholic commumicators that they receive from the Church spiritual help to meet the needs of their important and difficult role.

105. Fully aware of the importance of their profession and of the special difficulties it involves, the Church is very willing to undertake a dialogue with all communicators of every religious persuasion. She would do this so that she may contribute to a common effort to solve the problems inherent in their task and do what is best for the benefit of man.

106. As representatives of the Church, bishops, priests, religious and laity are increasingly asked to write in the press or appear on radio and television or to collaborate in filming. They are warmly urged to undertake this work, which has consequences that are far more important than is usually imagined. But the complexity of the media requires a sound knowledge of their work, of their impact and of the best way to use them. It is therefore the task of the national centres and of the specialised organisations to make certain that those who have to use the media receive sufficient and timely training.

107. The Church considers it to be one of her most urgent tasks to provide the means for training recipients in Christian principles. This also is a service to social communication. The

well-trained recipient will be able to take part in the dialogue promoted by the media and will demand high quality in communications. Catholic schools and organisations cannot ignore the urgent duty they have in this field. These schools and institutions will take care to teach young people not only to be good Christians when they are recipients but also to be active in using all the aids to communication that lie within the media, now called the 'total language'. So, young people will be true citizens of that age of social communication which has already begun.

108. The whole question of social communications deserves attention from theologians, particularly in the areas of moral and pastoral theology. Religious education too ought to include instruction on the modern media and their principal implications. This will be more readily achieved when theologians have studied the suggestions in the first part of this instruction and enriched them with their research and insight.

109. Parents, educators, priests and Christian organisations should encourage young people with the right qualities to take up a career in social communication. To do this and to provide properly trained candidates, funds are necessary. In developing areas, the national hierarchies should get financial help for the training of local candidates both in theory and practice.

110. Bishops, priests, religious and laity, all in their own ways, have a clear duty to contribute to Christian education in this field. They must make this contribution with the social teaching of the Church in mind. They will of their own accord keep in touch with the latest developments in communications so as to be well informed themselves. Otherwise they will lack that familiarity with the media which their actual use requires. Working with professional communicators, they will be wise to go more deeply into the problems presented by communicating through the media and to exchange their experiences and ideas.

111. If students for the priesthood and religious in training wish to be part of modern life and also to be at all effective in their

apostolate, they should know how the media work upon the fabric of society and the technique of their use. This knowledge should be an integral part of their ordinary education. Indeed, without this knowledge an effective apostolate is impossible in a society which is increasingly conditioned by the media.[51] It is also desirable that priests and religious understand how public opinion and popular attitudes come into being so that they can suit both the situation and the people of their time. They can find the media of great help in their effort to announce the Word of God to modern men. Students who show a special gift in the handling of the media should be given higher training.

112. Reviews of radio and television broadcasts, of films and illustrated magazines can be of help in cultural and religious education. They will also help those who wish to make a wise choice of what the media have to offer, particularly for the family. In this connection, particular attention should be paid to reviews that have real competence. These include assessment of the worth, the morality and the Christian value of films, broadcasts and writings issued under the pastoral care of bishops in different regions by specially appointed boards.

113. Catholic universities and educational institutions should be more assiduous in the promotion of scientific studies and research on social communications. They will try to collate all the findings of research, themselves play a part in this research, and make all of it available to the service of Christian education. While they will need financial help from others for these projects, they too will readily cooperate with other institutions.

CHAPTER II

The Contribution of the Communications Media to Catholics

1. Public Opinion and a Closer Communication in the Life of the Church

114. The Church looks for ways of multiplying and strengthening the bonds of union between her members. For this reason, communication and dialogue among Catholics are indispensable. The Church lives her life in the midst of the whole community of

man. She must therefore maintain contacts and lines of communication in order to keep a relationship with the whole human race. This is done both by giving information and by listening carefully to public opinion inside and outside the Church. Finally, by holding a continuous discussion with the contemporary world, she tries to help in solving the problems that men face at the present time.

a) Dialogue within the Church

115. Since the Church is a living body, she needs public opinion in order to sustain a giving and taking between her members. Without this, she cannot advance in thought and action. 'Something would be lacking in her life if she had no public opinion. Both pastors of souls and lay people would be to blame for this.'[52]

116. Catholics should be fully aware of the real freedom to speak their minds, which stems from a 'feeling for the faith' and from love. It stems from that feeling for the faith which is aroused and nourished by the spirit of truth in order that, under the guidance of the teaching Church which they accept with reverence, the people of God may cling unswervingly to the faith given to the early Church, with true judgement penetrate its meaning more deeply, and apply it more fully in their lives.[53] This freedom also stems from love. For it is with love that the liberty of the people of God are raised to an intimate sharing in the freedom of Christ himself, who cleansed us from our sins, in order that we might be able freely to make judgements in accordance with the will of God. Those who exercise authority in the Church will take care to ensure that there is responsible exchange of freely held and expressed opinion among the people of God. More that this, they will set up norms and conditions for this to take place.[54]

117. There is an enormous area where members of the Church can express their views on domestic issues. It must be taken that the truths of the faith express the essence of the Church and therefore do not leave room for arbitrary interpretations. Nonetheless, the Church moves with the movement of man. She

therefore has to adapt herself to the special circumstances that arise out of time and place. She has to consider how the truths of the faith may be explained in different times and cultures. She has to reach a multitude of decisions while adjusting her actions to the changes around her. While the individual Catholic follows the magisterium, he can and should engage in free research so that he may better understand revealed truths or explain them to a society subject to incessant change.

This free dialogue within the Church does no injury to her unity and solidarity. It nurtures concord and the meeting of minds by permitting the free play of the variations of public opinion. But in order that this dialogue may go in the right direction it is essential that charity is in command even when there are differing views. Everyone in this dialogue should be animated by the desire to serve and to consolidate unity and cooperation. There should be a desire to build not to destroy. There should be a deep love for the Church and a compelling desire for its unity. Christ made love the sign by which men can recognise his true Church and therefore his true followers.[55]

118. For this reason, distinction must be born in mind between, on the one hand, the area that is devoted to scientific investigation and and on the other the area that concerns the teaching of the faithful. In the first, experts enjoy the freedom required by their work and are free to comunicate to others in books and commentaries the fruits of their research. In the second, only those doctrines may be attributed to the Church which are declared to be such by her authentic magisterium. These last, obviously, can be aired in public without fear of giving scandal. It sometimes happens, however, because of the very nature of social communication that new opinions circulating among theologians, at times, circulate too soon and in the wrong places. Such opinions, which must not be confused with the authentic doctrine of the Church, should be examined critically. It must also be remembered that the real significance of such theories is often badly distorted by popularisation and by the style of presentation used in the media.

119. Since the development of public opinion within the Church is essential, individual Catholics have the right to all the

information they need to play their active role in the life of the Church. In practice this means that communications media must be available for the task. These should not only exist in sufficient number but also reach all the people of God. Where necessary, they may even be owned by the Church as long as they truly fulfil their purpose.

120. The normal flow of life and the smooth functioning of government within the Church require a steady two-way flow of information between the ecclesiastical authorities at all levels and the faithful as individuals and as organised groups. This applies to the whole world. To make this possible various institutions are required. These might include news agencies, official spokesmen, meeting facilities, pastoral councils, all properly financed.

121. On those occasions when the affairs of the Church require secrecy, the rules normal in civil affairs equally apply. On the other hand, the spiritual riches which are an essential attribute of the Church demand that the news she gives out of her intentions as well as of her works be distinguished by integrity, truth and openness. When ecclesiastical authorities are unwilling to give information or are unable to do so, then rumour is unloosed and rumour is not a bearer of the truth but carries dangerous half-truths. Secrecy should therefore be restricted to matters that involve the good name of individuals or that touch upon the rights of people whether singly or collectively.

b) Dialogue between the Church and the World

122. The Church does not speak and listen to her own members alone; her dialogue is with the whole world. By virtue of a divine command[56] and by the right to knowledge possessed by the people whose lot she shares on earth, the Church is in duty bound publicly to communicate her belief and her way of life. Moreover, as the Second Vatican Council teaches, she is 'to read the signs of the times', for these too reveal the message of God and indicate the unfolding of the history of salvation under divine providence. This is another reason why the Church needs to know contemporary reactions to ideas and events, whether they be Catholic or not. The greater the extent to which the means of

social communication reflect these reactions, the more do they contribute towards this knowledge required by the Church.

123. It is the mission of those with responsible positions in the Church to announce without fail or pause the full truth by the means of social communication, so as to give a true picture of the Church and her life. Since the media are often the only channels of information that exist between the Church and the world, a failure to use them amounts to 'burying the talent given by God'. The Church naturally expects of the news agencies that they give religious news, with all the care and attention that the subject demands. On her part, the Church is consequently bound in duty to give complete and ertirely accurate information to the news agencies so that they, in their turn, can carry out their task.

124. What was contained above[57] where commentaries on the news were discussed retains its full force here where Church news is under consideration. Responsible leaders in the Church then should try in advance to be ready to deal with a difficult situation and should not abandon the initiative. Further, it is wise to see that important decisions and statements be made available in advance, using time embargo on publication. In this way, arrangements could be made in the interests of the Church for proper explanation and discussion.

125. The means of social communication help Catholics in three ways. They help the Church reveal herself to the modern world. They foster dialogue within the Church. They make clear to the Church contemporary opinions and attitudes. For the Church has been ordered by God to give men the message of salvation in a language they can understand and to concern herself with the concerns of man.

2. The Use of the Media for Giving the Good News

126. Christ commanded the apostles and their successors to 'teach all nations',[58] to be 'the light of the world'[59] and to announce the good news in all places at all times. During his life on earth, Christ showed himself to be the perfect communicator, while the apostles used what means of social communication

were available in their time. It is now necessary that the same message be carried by the means of social communication that are available today. Indeed it would be difficult to suggest that Christ's command was being obeyed unless all the opportunities offered by the modern media to extend to vast numbers of people the announcement of his good news were being used. Therefore, the Second Vatican Council invited the people of God 'to use effectively and at once the means of social communication, zealously availing themselves of them for apostolic purposes'.[60]

127. The necessity for doing this is quite obvious once it is realised that modern men are immersed in the tide of social communication when they are forming their profound convictions and adopting their attitudes. This is as true of religious convictions and attitudes as it is of any other sort.

128. The modern media offer new ways of confronting people with the message of the gospel, of allowing Christians even when they are far away to share in sacred rites, worship and ecclesiastical functions. In this way they can bind the Christian community closer together and invite everyone to participate in the intimate life of the Church. Of course the mode of presentation has to suit the special nature of the medium being used. The media are not the same as a church pulpit. It cannot be overstressed that the standard of such presentations must at least equal in quality the other productions of the media.

129. The media are invaluable helps for Christian education. They can call on the services of the greatest specialists in religious teaching as well as of experts on all the questions that arise. The media have at their command all the technical facilities required for attractive and contemporary presentation. They can back up most effectively the personal work of the daily teacher. Their resources make possible the radical changes that are required in the whole style of religious instruction today.

Since the instruments of social communication are the usual channels for giving the news and voicing contemporary man's attitudes and views, they offer marvellous opportunities to all for considering the deeper implications of their religious convictions through the discussion of events and problems of the day. The Christian can then apply these deepened convictions to his daily life.

130. People today have grown so used to the entertaining style and skilful presentation of communications by the media that they are intolerant of what is obviously inferior in any public presentation. It makes no difference if this be a religious occasion, such as, for example, a liturgical ceremony, a sermon or religious instruction.

131. In order to make the teaching of Christianity more interesting and effective the media should be used as much as possible. Every effort should be made to use the most appropriate technique and style in fitting a communication to its medium.

132. The Church can use means of communication that are not under her control but which, under agreed conditions, are offered for her use. Where it is necessary, she may also herself own and administer means of communication. No hard and fast rules can here be laid down; the situation varies from place to place. Religious authorities will advise those who are involved in this apostolate what to do within the differing conditions of different countries. They should give this advice when they have consulted the local experts and, if it should be necessary, after seeking international advice.

133. Considerable financial resources are required if Catholics are to meet their different commitments to further human progress in the light of the Gospel both by making their proper contribution to social communication and by using these God-given methods themselves. Catholics are called upon to ponder their responsibilities in this field and to meet them with generosity '... as it would ill become the faithful to suffer the word of salvation to be confined and circumscribed'.[61]

134. In view of the mounting importance of the means of social communication – to the life of mankind in general and of the Church in particular – the media should receive a great deal more

emphasis than they presently get in the overall plans for pastoral action made by episcopal conferences. These plans should make the necessary funds available for use in the areas under their jurisdiction. Funds should also be made available for international cooperation.

CHAPTER III

The Active Commitment of Catholics in the Different Media

135. We have considered what should be the right approach of dedicated Catholic communicators towards their work,[62] an approach shared by colleagues, whatever the nature of their beliefs. For the Catholic, his faith provides an extra incentive.

Then we dealt with the special duties of communicators who work as Catholics. In this we confined ourselves to general discussion, without dealing with the media one by one.[63] Here we deal with the duties of Catholic communicators in each separate medium of social communication. These are duties that affect anyone who appears in the name of the Church, whether he appears in media that are officially Catholic or as a spokesman in some uncommitted institution that opens its facilities to the expression of a Catholic point of view.

1. The Printed Word

136. The press, of its power and nature, is of towering importance. Because of its adaptability, because of its variety and of the number of its publications, it can go into detail when reporting the news. It can also comment on the news and, without boring the reader, interpret it in a way that makes him think for himself. It is a most useful complement to the audio-visual means of communication. It is a most effective means of stimulating men's critical faculties and of helping them form their own opinions. Since it is able to deal with such a variety of material and since it can so admirably encourage men to think, it has prime place in the promotion of social dialogue.

Moreover, today all the classics of religious literature are available to everybody in the form of paperbacks, booklets and every sort of leaflet. So also are the accepted masterpieces of every nation, scientific works and every sort of light reading that can provide pleasant relaxation. 'Comics' and illustrated stories are not to be despised. They can for instance be used to illustrate the sacred scriptures and the lives of the saints. All these productions of the printing press deserve our interest and support.

137. The Catholic press – and this includes reviews, magazines and periodicals – can be marvellously effective in bringing a knowledge of the Church to the world and a knowledge of the world to the Church. It does this by imparting information and by stimulating those processes by which public opinion is formed. There is, however, no advantage in founding new publications if quantity is achieved at the cost of quality and if the new injure the old.

138. That part of the Catholic press which is of general interest publishes news and opinions and background articles about all the facets and problems and worries of modern life. This it does in the light of Christian principles. It is the task of the Catholic press to balance, to complete and, if necessary, to correct the news and comments about religion and the Christian life. At one and the same time it will be a glass that reflects the world and a light to show it the way. It will be a forum, a meeting place for the exchange of views. This press needs talented men and funds if its professional competence is to be above dispute.

139. The Catholic press must be able to acquire suitable offices and the proper facilities for obtaining news reports and features. Otherwise, a Catholic-run press cannot effectively promote dialogue inside the Church and between the Church and the outside world. It must also achieve professional standards in printing up-to-date, accurate and comprehensive news about the life of the Church. In the collecting, collating and passing on of the news throughout the world there is need for cooperation at the international level.

140. Catholics are encouraged to read Catholic publications regularly. Naturally these must deserve the name of being Catholic. It is hard to see how people can keep in touch with

what is happening in the Church without the Catholic press. Neither can people keep a Catholic attitude towards what happens in the world without the help of commentaries on the news written in the light of Christian principles. This is certainly not intended as an interference in the individual's right to read what he chooses. Still less is it intended as an interference with the freedom of expression of writers with different convictions nor is it intended to discourage diversity, ordinarily taken for granted in a particular area. It is self-evident that Catholic writers must earn their popularity and following by the high standard of their work.

141. When the events of the day raise questions that touch fundamental Christian principles the Catholic press will try to interpret these in accordance with the magisterium of the Church. Apart from this, clergy and laity will encourage a free expression of opinion and a wide variety of publications and points of view. They should do this because it will satisfy the different interests and concerns of readers and because it contributes to the formation of public opinion in the Church and the world.[64] Those Catholic newspapers which are recognised as the official organs of the various authorities and institutions of the Church will always, in accordance with usual press practice, try to explain fully the thinking of the organisation for which they are accepted as public spokesmen. In these newspapers, an unrestricted liberty of expression will be maintained in those pages where it is made quite clear that the editors are not committing themselves in a particular question that is still under discussion.

2. Cinema

142. The cinema is part of contemparary life. It exerts a strong influence on education, knowledge, culture and leisure. The artist finds in film a very effective means for expressing his interpretation of life and one that well suits his times. The improvement of techniques that increase audience participation and the general availability at low cost of filming and projecting equipment, presage an even wider use of films in the future. Because of all this, it is possible to derive a deeper appreciation and a richer cultural dividend from the film and filming.

143. These developments should be carefully studied in pastoral planning, for there are many openings for a greater use of this medium in pastoral action. There has been a growth of international cooperation in this field. And it is easier now to produce films that are completely adapted to various needs and circumstances and to project these, not only in large cinemas, but also in small halls and even in homes.

144. Many films have compellingly treated subjects that concern human progress or spiritual values. Such works deserve everyone's praise and support. The Catholic organisations specialising in films should be among the first to support them. They should also promote these films in an organised manner. In this connection, it will be recalled that among films which have been widely accepted as classics, many have dealt with specifically religious themes. This not only proves that the cinema is a proper vehicle for such noble themes, but it is a strong encouragement to produce films of this kind.

145. Catholic organisations for the cinema will collaborate with their counterparts in the other media in endeavours to plan, produce, distribute and exhibit films imbued with religious principles. With discrimination they should also use for religious teaching all the new developments in this field which make inexpensive productions possible. These include gramophone records, audio and video tape recorders, videocassettes and all the machines that record and playback either sound or static or moving images.

146. In regions where there is illiteracy films can make a very effective contribution to the provision of basic education. The illiterate are profoundly affected by images and can readily grasp the facts and ideas presented through them. The media should be used effectively in the effort to promote human and religious progress. But, of course, the films chosen for use must be suited to the cultural traditions of the local population.

147. Since professional film-makers have to face many difficulties in the course of their creative work, all Catholics, but especially

Catholic film organisations, should be ready and anxious to engage in dialogue with them. Based, as they will be, on a shared belief in the good that the cinema can do for man, these contacts will bear witness to the nobility of the vocation of those involved in film production.

3. Radio and Television

148. Radio and television have given society new patterns of communication. They have changed ways of life. Broadcasting stretches out, further and further, towards every corner of the earth. Instantaneous transmissions break through political and cultural barriers. What they have to say reaches men in their own homes. Broadcasters have access to the minds and hearts of everyone. Rapid technological advances, especially those that involve satellite transmissions and the recording and storage of programmes, have done still more to free the media from the restrictions of time and space and these promise still more effectiveness and influence. For the listener and viewer, radio and television open up the whole world of events, of culture and of entertainment. Television, especially, brings individuals and events before the general public, as though the viewers were actually present. And besides the established forms of artistic expression, broadcasters have created art forms of their own which can affect man in new ways.

149. The religious aspects of human life will find a place in daily broadcasting, both on radio and television.

150. Religious programmes that utilise all the resources of radio and television enrich people's religious life and create new bonds between the faithful. They help in religious education and in the Church's active commitment in the world. They are bonds of union for those who cannot share physically in the life of the Church because of their sickness or old age. In addition they create new relationships between the faithful and those people – and today they are legion – who have no affiliation with any Church and yet subconsciouly seek spiritual nourishment. They carry the message of the Gospel to countries where the Church is not. The Church cannot afford to ignore such opportunities. On

the contrary, she will make the fullest use of any fresh opportunities that the improvement of those instruments may disclose.

151. The transmission of the Mass and of other sacred rites is to be included in religious broadcasting. Both in their technical and in their religious aspects, such transmissions must be carefully prepared in advance. The vastness of the audience must be considered and, if transmissions cross national frontiers, so too must the religious sensitivities and conditions of other nations. How often such programmes are transmitted and how long they should last must be decided upon in the light of the popular demand.

152. Sermons and homilies must be adapted to the nature of the medium that is used. Those who are given the task of preaching in this way, should, therefore, be carefully chosen from among those who have a sound practical knowledge of the technique of broadcasting.

153. Religious broadcasts, such as newscasts, commentaries, reports and discussions, can contribute a great deal towards education and dialogue. What has already been said about the Catholic commitment in the press, applies here too. And here, also, the general rules for giving a fair hearing to different points of view are equally valid, especially when the medium in question enjoys, in practice, a monopoly in a given region.

154. Well known Catholics who go on the air, whether they are clerical or lay, are automatically regarded as spokesmen of the Church. They must keep this in mind and try to avoid any confusion arising therefrom. Even so they will be conscious of their responsibility when they express their views, when they decide on the style of their broadcast and, indeed, on their whole manner of behaviour. If they can do so in time, they will consult with competent ecclesiastical authorities for whatever counsel and advice they feel they need.

155. Listeners and viewers will contribute to the betterment of religious programmes by making their reactions known.

156. If the active presence of the Church in general in religious programmes is to be ensured, then a close collaboration based on mutual trust must be established between the responsible Catholic authorities and the broadcasting companies.

157. In those countries where the Church is forbidden the use of the media of social communication, listening to foreign religious broadcasts may be the only way the faithful can learn about the life of the Universal Church and hear the Word of God. In the name of Christian solidarity, such a situation puts a grave obligation upon the Catholics of other countries. It is necessary to organise religious broadcasts that are specially suited to the needs of fellow Christians who suffer this sort of deprivation.

4. The Theatre

158. The theatre is one of the most ancient and lively forms of human expression and communication. Still, today, it commands a large audience, not only of those who go to plays, but also of those who follow drama on radio and television. Moreover, many plays have been adapted for films.

159. The partnership of the theatre with the mass media of communication has brought about forms of dramatic expression that, aptly, have been called 'multi-media', adding something of their own to the traditional theatre. These, using their different resources, have created a kind of synthesis of the potentials of each of the media of communication.

160. Finally and most significantly, the contemporary theatre is, without doubt, an experimental workshop for the expression of new, daring and challenging ideas about modern man and his predicament. The impact of all this goes far beyond the audience attending a particular play, which may be quite small. Ultimately it extends to all the media of communication.

161. The Church has always shown considerable interest in the theatre which, in its origins, was closely connected with manifestations of religion. This ancient interest in the theatre should be maintained by Christians today and full use be made of

its possibilities. Playwrights should be encouraged and helped to set man's religious preoccupation on the platform of the public stage. This is often the first step in a much wider diffusion made possible by the communications media.

CHAPTER IV

Equipment, Personnel and Organisation

162. The place of the instruments of social communication in human destiny, the opportunities and the problems that they set before the Christian conscience: all this makes it essential that a way be found for a pastoral approach to this field. Trained and experienced men must be found for this work. The proper pastoral structures, with all the necessary funding, rights and resources should also be set up. Finally, special organisations should be devoted to the apostolate of each of the media.

163. This modern mission of the Church will mean a great deal to the faithful. They will offer their prayers and support so that she will be adequately equipped to fulfil it. The latest media of social communication are indispensable means for evangelization and enlightening the minds and heart of men. They also contribute towards cooperation in furthering human progress by a Christian leavening of the social order.

164. The official Catholic organisations and enterprises that work in social communications with a pastoral end in view should be able to call upon trained personnel. The training of laymen, priests and religious is to be given a high priority by those responsible for this work in the Church.

165. A careful appraisal of the entire range of the communications media, a prudent and well-informed planning for pastoral work and in every apostolic enterprise, all this is the rightful province of the ecclesiastical authorities. They, in their turn, should depend upon the advice of experienced experts in the different branches of communication. According to the ground rules laid down in *Inter mirifica* this duty devolves upon every bishop in every diocese,[65] upon a special commission of bishops

or a bishop-delegate in each country[66] and, for the universal Church, upon the Pontifical Commission for Social Communications.[67]

166. The different sorts of projects and organisations for the specialised apostolate in social communications should everywhere be promoted and coordinated one with another.[68] The ecclesiastical authorities should encourage the free flowering of Catholic initiative in this, but they should retain guidance over those works which properly belong to the priestly ministry and over those which – according to the circumstances of time and place – demand a commitment on the part of the hierarchy on behalf of the faithful.

167. The competent ecclesiastical authorities at all levels (mentioned in para. 165) will lend their full support to the preparation and celebration of World Communications Day. This day has been designed specially to honour the professionals in the media and to encourage their cooperation.[69] The ecclesiastical authorities will present regularly to the episcopal conferences projects for financing pastoral activity in the field of social communications.

168. The local hierarchies will take a keen interest in the apostolate of social communications. They will seek the advice of their priests and laity. Wherever possible, diocesan, or at least, interdiocesan offices will be set up. One of the chief tasks of these is to organise this pastoral apostolate within the diocese, penetrating right down to parish level. Another task is to prepare for the celebration of World Communications Day mentioned above within the diocese.

169. A national office for the communications media should be set up in every country. It can be divided into specialised and reasonably autonomous departments for each of the separate media. Or it can have separate offices for the press, motion pictures and broadcasting that work closely together.[70] In any case, the whole of this apostolate should be placed under a single, overall direction.

170. It is the mission of the national and diocesan offices to stimulate, promote and harmonise Catholic activities in the field of social communications. They will take particular pains about the training of the faithful, clerical and lay, by means of organised courses, conferences, study sessions and critical assessments prepared by their experts. So, the public will be enabled to make wise decisions. The offices will also be ready to give advice to producers engaged on films, performance or broadcasts that concern religious subjects.

171. The national and diocesan offices will maintain these contacts with the professional world of social communications. They will furnish the documentary material, the advice and the pastoral assistance that professional communicators may require. They also are to organise World Communications Day on the national level and organise the collection of funds that the Decree of the Council suggests should be made on that day.[71]

172. The national espiscopal commission for social communications or the delegated bishop are in charge of the direction of all the activities of the national offices. They are to lay down general guidelines for the development of the apostolate of social communications on the national level. They will keep in touch with the other national episcopal commissions and collaborate with the Pontifical Commission for Social Communications. The status of this commission is described in the Conciliar Decree, *Inter mirifica*[72] and in the apostolic letter, *In Fructibus multis.*[73]

173. On continents or in regions where an episcopal conference exists that embraces several countries, this episcopal conference will have an office for social communications under the overall direction of a bishop or a number of bishops.

174. Every bishop, all episcopal conferences or bishops' assemblies and the Holy See itself should each have their own official and permanent spokesman or press officer to issue the news and give clear explanations of the documents of the Church so that people can grasp precisely what is intended. These

spokesmen will give, in full and without delay, information on the life and work of the Church in that area for which they are responsible. It is highly recommended that individual dioceses and the more weighty Catholic organisations also have their own permanent spokesmen with the sort of duties explained above. All these officials and, indeed, all those who are identified with the Church in the mind of the public, should take into account the principles of public relations. They should consider the sort of audience they are, at various times, addressing and establish a relationship that is based on mutual trust and understanding. This can only be maintained as long as people have a genuine regard and consideration for one another and a scrupulous respect for the truth.

175. It is not enough to have a public spokesman. There must be a continual two-way flow of news and information. On the one hand, this aims to present a true image of the Church in a way that makes it visible to all. On the other, this exchange reveals to the ecclesiastical authorities the surges, currents and ideas that stir the world of men. Clearly this calls for the cultivation of friendly relations based on mutual reverence between the Church, people and groups. In this way continual exchanges can be fostered, with each side both giving and receiving.[74]

176. To make sure of an effective dialogue, both within the Church and with the outside world, on the subject of recent events and their religious significance, official news bulletins are indispensable. These will publicise relevant news items as quickly as possible. The public, in this way, will get their information in good time. Needless to say, all the necessary means are to be used to make these bulletins absolutely accurate and so avoid the necessity for subsequent corrections. News flashes, telex, all the latest techniques will be used to convey precise meanings in the most dependable way.

177. Religious orders and congregations will give thought to the many pressing tasks of the Church in the field of social communications and consider what they themselves can do to fulfil them under their constitutions. Their own specialised

institutions for social communications will collaborate with one another and they will keep abreast of the overall pastoral planning of the diocesan offices and of the national, continental or regional offices since these are, usually, the competent bodies for the aspostolate of social communications.

178. The national offices[75] and the corresponding central offices of the religious congregations will cooperate with the international organisations for the press (UCIP), for motion pictures (OCIC) and for radio and television (UNDA). This will be done in accord with the statutes of these international organisations as approved by the Holy See.[76]

179. These international Catholic organisations for social communications – each in its own sphere and in a way that fits its statutes – will help professionals and the national professional bodies of Catholics who have given themselves to these tasks. The way to do this is to keep abreast of research and development in the media. They will foster mutual aid and international cooperation. They will keep themselves informed on Catholic activity in the field. They will prepare the coordination of international programmes and projects. They will continually seek advice on the best ways to help developing countries. They will encourage fresh initiatives. They will produce and distribute films and recorded broadcasts and every sort of audiovisual material, including the printed word. They will do all this for the advancement of social progress and for the betterment of Catholic life. These international Catholic organisations are exhorted to undertake and to coordinate research for the solution of their common problems.

180. The episcopal conferences, through their specialised offices, and the Catholic professional associations will assure for the international Catholic organisation the funds necessary for doing this work.

Conclusion

181. The question is posed whether we are on the threshold of an utterly new sort of era in social communications or whether we

face merely a change in degree and not in kind. There is no easy answer to this question and it continually increases in complexity. What is certain is that soon, due to the latest technical developments, especially those that concern communication satellites, sounds, images and the messages that they bear will soon be reaching men, simultaneously, all over the world. It will be possible to record these and play them back at will – either for entertainment or instruction. So it will be possible for all peoples to learn more of each other as a result of this real dialogue. They can then work together for the unity of mankind and the establishment of peace.

182. Suddenly and in proportion with these changes, the responsibilities of the people of God will enormously increase. Never before will they have been offered such opportunities. It will be possible to ensure that the media promote the advance of the whole human race and the development of those countries in what is called the ' third world'. It will be possible to strengthen the brotherhood of man. And then the Good News can be given everywhere, bearing witness to Christ, the Saviour.

183. This pastoral instruction lays down some guidelines chosen after considering the general situation that prevails in social communications. As things stand at present, it would not be reasonable to try to be more precise and detailed. The Christian outlook is based on certain immutable principles that are founded on that message of love which is the Gospel's good news and upon the dignity of man who has been called to be an adopted son of God. It is obvious that directions and practical applications, as well as pastoral guidelines, will have to be adapted to the different conditions that obtain in different places – depending on their degree of technical progress and their social situation. They will change too with the changing conditions of the media and of their inherent laws, and the future is certain to bring changes in this area of social communications. In so fluid a situation, it is clear that those who are responsible for pastoral planning must stay flexible and be always willing to try to keep pace with new discoveries in this field.

184. Even today there is a great deal that must still be learnt about the present media and how the fullest use can be made of them, in education particularly and indeed at every level. There is room for study, in much greater depth, of the effects of social communications on different cultural environments and on different types of people. In order to be able to understand the functioning of the media of social communication within the family of man, and to comprehend both their potential and present performance, to reach a better assessment of their varying psychological and cultural effects, it is necessary to concentrate on a rigorous programme of scientific research. Indeed, a much greater effort than that now being made is required of all the concerned parties in furthering this research.

Universities, whether of new or ancient foundation, have an open field before them. The problems they face are not only urgent, they are also fully consonant with the dignity of the traditional disciplines. For her part, the Church wishes to let researchers know how eager she is to learn from their work in all these areas and to follow out its practical conclusions. Thus she herself may the better serve the process of social communication and use its means to the best advantage of all men.

185. In this connection, it appears necessary to discover through scientific research the true effectiveness of the Church in the field of social communications. It will then be possible to deploy her resources so that they suit the importance of the tasks she faces throughout the world. Catholics will then find it easier to start new projects that match the ever growing importance of the media.

186. In the meantime, faced by the most urgent need for making closer contact with the professional world of social communication, for engaging these men in dialogue, for making her contribution in this field and for urging all men to use the media to serve both the progress of man and the glory of God, the Church could no longer delay this pastoral instruction. The Pontifical Commission for Social Communications issues this instruction in accordance with the mandate from the Second Vatican Council but only after intensive consultations on a

worldwide basis. It is hoped that this publication marks not so much the end of a phase as the start of a new one.

187. The people of God walk in history. As they, who are, essentially, both communicators and recipients, advance with their times, they look forward with confidence and even with enthusiasm to whatever the development of communications in a space age may have to offer.

His Holiness, Pope Paul VI has graciously approved in its entirety this pastoral instruction on the means of social communication, and confirmed it with his authority. He ordered it to be published so that it can be put into effect by all concerned, anything to the contrary notwithstanding.

Given in Rome on the twenty-third day of May, in the year of the Lord nineteen seventy-one, being the fifth World Communications Day.

Martin J. O'Connor
Tit. Archbishop of Laodicea in Syria, President

Augustine Ferrari-Toniolo
Tit. Bishop of Tarasa in Byzacena, Pro-President

Andrew M. Deskur
Secretary

Notes

1. *Miranda prorsus* A.A.S., XXIV (1957), p. 765.
2. *Gaudium et spes*, A.A.S., LVIII (1966), pp. 1025–1120.
3. *Unitatis redintegratio*, A.A.S., LVII (1965), pp. 90–112.
4. *Dignitatis humanae*, A.A.S., LVIII (1966), pp. 929–946.
5. *Ad gentes*, A.A.S., LVIII (1966), pp. 947–990.
6. *Christus Dominus*, A.A.S., LVIII (1966), pp. 673–696.
7. *Inter mirifica*, A.A.S., LVI (1964), pp. 145–157.
8. Cf. Ibid., 23.
9. *Inter mirifica*, 1.
10. Gen 1:26-28; cf. Gen 9:2-3; Wis 9:2-3; *Gaudium et spes*, 34.
11. Cf. *Gaudium et spes*, 34.
12. Cf. Ibid., 57.
13. Cf. *Gaudium et spes*, 36; The Encyclical by Pope John XXIII, *Pacem in terris*, A.A.S., LV (1963), p. 257 and passim.
14. Cf. Rom 5:12-14.

15. Cf. Gen 4:1-16; 11:1-9.
16. Cf. Gen 3:15; 9:1-17; 12:1-3.
17. Cf. Heb 1:1-2.
18. Jn 1:14.
19. Col 1:15; II Cor 4:4.
20. Cf. *Ad gentes*, 3.
21. Mt 28:19.
22. Mt 10:27; Lk 12:3.
23. Jn 6:53.
24. Cf . *Lumen gentium*, A.A.S., LVII (1965), no. 9, p. 14.
25. Eph 1:23; 4:10.
26. I Cor 15:28.
27. *Inter mirifica*, 1.
28. *Gaudium et spes*, 36.
29. Cf. Ibid., 43.
30. The 'Common Good' is defined in the Encylical by Pope John XXIII, *Mater et Magistra,* as the 'sum of those conditions of social life by which men can attain their perfection more fully and with greater ease'. A.A.S., LIII (1961), p. 417. See also *Pacem in terris*, A.A.S., LV (1963), pp. 272-274; *Dignitatis humanae*, 6; *Gaudium et spes*, 26 and 74.
31. Cf Cf. *Inter mirifica*, 4.
32. *Gaudium et spes*, 42; *Lumen gentium*, 1.
33. In his Allocution to Catholic Journalists on February 17, 195O. A.A.S., XLII (l950), p. 251. See also *Gaudium et spes*, 59; *Pacem in terris*, A.A.S., LV (1963), p. 283.
34. *Gaudium et spes*, 59.
35. Cf. *Inter mirifica*, 8.
36. Cf. *Pacem in terris*, A.A.S., LV (1963), p. 260
37. Cf. Allocution given on April 17, 1964 to 'Seminaire des Nations Unies sur la liberté de l'information', A.A.S., LVI (1964), pp. 387ff.
38. Cf. *Inter mirifica*, 5.
39. Pius XII in an address given to American journalists on July 21, 1945. *L'Osservatore Romano*, July 22, 1945.
40. An address to a similar group on April 27, 1946. *L'Osservatore Romano*, April 28, 1946.
41. 'The manner of the [communication] should be honorable and appropriate, namely, one which keeps sacred the laws of morality and the legitimate rights and dignity of man in reporting the news'. *Inter mirifica*, 5.
42. Cf. *Miranda prorsus*, A.A.S., XLIX (1957), p. 765.
43. Paul VI: Allocution given on May 6, 1967 to a large number of those who devote themselves to the theatre, the cinema, radio and

television and other media of social communication. A.A.S., LIX (1967), p. 509.

44. Pius XII: Allocution given on June 21, 1955 to the patrons of the art of the cinema in Italy meeting in Rome. A.A.S., XLVI (1955), p. 509. Roma, 21 Giugno 1955, in AAS, XLVII (1955), p. 509.
45. Pius XII: Allocution given on October 28, 1955 to the patrons of the art of the cinema gathered in Rome for their International Convention. A.A.S. XLVII (1955), pp. 822–823.
46. Paul VI: Allocution given on January 24, 1969 to the Officers of the Catholic Association of Italian Journalists (U.C.S.I.). *L'Osservatore Romano*, January 24, 1969.
47. Cf. *Dignitatis humanae*, 7.
48. Paul VI: Letter to the Honorable U Thant, Secretary General of the United Nations. A.A.S., LVIII (1966), p. 480. See also the Holy Father's Allocution to the delegates present at Milan for the second meeting of the Administrative Council of the United Nations' Programme for Development. A.A.S., LVIII (1966), p. 589.
49. Cf. *Unitatis redintegratio*, A.A.S., LVII (1965), pp. 90–112. See also *Nostra aetate*, A.A.S., LVIII (1966), pp. 740–744.
50. This was expressed by the World Council of Churches in their ' Instruction' issued at Upsala in 1968, p. 381.
51. Cf. The Sacred Congregation for Catholic Education, 'The Fundamental Characteristic of Priestly Education'. A.A.S. XLII (1970), pp. 321–384. See especially para. 4 and no. 68.
52. Pius XII: Allocution given on February 17, 1950 to those who were in Rome to participate in the International Congress for Editors of Catholic Periodicals. A.A.S., XVIII (1950), p. 256.
53. Cf. *Lumen gentium*, 12.
54. Cf. 'Réflexions et suggestions concernant le dialogue oecuménique', L'Osservatore Romano, September 21–22, 1970.
55. Cf. Jn 17:21.
56. Cf. Mt 28:19.
57. Cf. paragraph 38 above.
58. Mt 28:19.
59. Mt 5:14.
60. *Inter mirifica*, 13.
61. Ibid., 17.
62. Cf. paragraphs 102–113 above.
63. Cf. paragraphs 126–134 above.
64. Cf. paragraphs 114–121 above, where dialogue in the Church is discussed. Cf. Paul VI: *Ecclesiam suam*. See also the outline of the principles for ecumenical dialogue in document 'Réflexions et suggestions concernant le dialogue oecuménique', especially nos.

IV, 4, b and IV, 5. *L'Osservatore Romano*, September 21–22, 1970.
65. Cf. *Inter mirifica*, 20.
66. Cf. Ibid., 21.
67. Cf. Ibid., 19.
68. Cf. *Apostolicam actuositatem*, 19 and 21.
69. Cf. *Inter mirifica*, 18.
70. Cf. Ibid., 21.
71. Cf. Ibid., 18.
72. Cf. Ibid., 19.
73. Cf. In *Fructibus multis,* A.A.S., LVI (1964), pp. 289–292.
74. Cf. paragraphs 138–141 above.
75. Cf. paragraph 169 above.
76. Cf. *Inter mirifica*, 22.

PASTORAL INSTRUCTION *AETATIS NOVAE*

ON SOCIAL COMMUNICATIONS ON THE TWENTIETH ANNIVERSARY OF *COMMUNIO ET PROGRESSIO*

23 FEBRUARY 1992

Introduction

A Revolution in Human Communications

1. At the dawn of a new era, a vast expansion of human communications is profoundly influencing culture everywhere. Revolutionary technological changes are only part of what is happening. Nowhere today are people untouched by the impact of media upon religious and moral attitudes, political and social systems and education.

It is impossible to ignore, for instance, that geographical and political boundaries were both of very little avail in view of the role played by communications during the 'radical transformations' of 1989 and 1990, on whose historical significance the Pope reflects in *Centesimus annus*.[1]

It becomes equally evident that 'the first Areopagus of the modern age is the world of communications which is unifying humanity and turning it into what is known as a 'global village'. The means of social communications have become so important as to be for many the chief means of information and education, of guidance and inspiration in their behaviour as individuals, families and within society at large'.[2]

More than a quarter century after the promulgation of the Second Vatican Council's decree on social communications, *Inter mirifica*, and two decades after the pastoral instruction *Communio et progressio*, the Pontifical Council for Social Communications wishes to reflect on the pastoral implications of this situation.

We do so in the spirit expressed by the closing words of *Communio et progressio*: 'The people of God walk in history. As they ... advance with their times, they look forward with confidence and even with enthusiasm to whatever the development of communications in a space age may have to offer.'[3]

Taking for granted the continued validity of the principles and insights of these conciliar and postconciliar documents, we wish to apply them to new and emerging realities. We do not pretend to say the final word on a complex, fluid, rapidly changing situation, but simply wish to provide a working tool and a measure of encouragement to those confronting the pastoral implications of the new realities.

2. In the years since *Inter mirifica* and *Communio et progressio* appeared, people have grown accustomed to expressions like 'information society', 'mass media culture' and 'media generation'. Terms like these underline a remarkable fact: today, much that men and women know and think about life is conditioned by the media; to a considerable extent, human experience itself is an experience of media.

Recent decades also have witnessed remarkable developments in the technology of communicating. These include both the rapid evolution of previously existing technologies and the emergence of new telecommunications and media technologies: satellites, cable television, fibre optics, video cassettes, compact discs, computerised image making and other computer and digital technology and much else. The use of new media gives rise to what some speak of as 'new languages' and has given birth to new possibilities for the mission of the Church as well as to new pastoral problems.

3. Against this background we encourage the pastors and people of the Church to deepen their understanding of issues relating to communications and media and to translate their understanding into practical policies and workable programs.

'As the Council Fathers looked to the future and tried to discern the context in which the Church would be called upon to carry out her mission, they could clearly see that the progress of technology was already "transforming the face of the earth" and even reaching out to conquer space. They recognised that developments in communications technology, in particular, were likely to set off chain reactions with unforeseen consequences.'[4]

'Far from suggesting that the Church should stand aloof or try to isolate herself from the mainstream of these events, the Council Fathers saw the Church as being in the very midst of human progress, sharing the experiences of the rest of humanity, seeking to understand them and to interpret them in the light of faith. It was for God's faithful people to make creative use of the new discoveries and technologies for the benefit of humanity and the fulfilment of God's plan for the world ... employing the full potential of the 'computer age' to serve the human and transcendent vocation of every person and thus to give glory to the Father from whom all good things come.'[5]

We express our gratitude to those responsible for the creative communications work underway in the Church everywhere. Despite difficulties – arising from limited resources, from the obstacles sometimes placed in the way of the Church's access to media and from a constant reshaping of culture, values and attitudes brought about by the pervasive presence of media – much has been, and continues to be, accomplished. The dedicated bishops, clergy, religious and lay people engaged in this critically important apostolate deserve the thanks of all.

Also welcome are those positive ventures in media-related ecumenical cooperation involving Catholics and their brothers and sisters of other Churches and ecclesial communities, as well as interreligious cooperation with those of other world religions. It is not only appropriate but 'necessary for Christians to work together more effectively in their communications efforts and to act in more direct cooperation with other religions to ensure a united religious presence in the very heart of mass communications'.[6]

The Context of Social Communications

A. Cultural and Social context

4. As more than just a technological revolution, today's revolution in social communications involves a fundamental reshaping of the elements by which people comprehend the world about them and verify and express what they comprehend. The constant availability of images and ideas and their rapid transmission even from continent to continent have profound

consequences, both positive and negative, for the psychological, moral and social development of persons, the structure and functioning of societies, intercultural communications and the perception and transmission of values, world views, ideologies and religious beliefs. The communications revolution affects perceptions even of the Church and has a significant impact on the Church's own structures and modes of functioning.

All this has striking pastoral implications. The media can be used to proclaim the Gospel or to reduce it to silence in human hearts. As media become ever more intertwined with people's daily lives, they influence how people understand the meaning of life itself.

Indeed, the power of media extends to defining not only what people will think but even what they will think about. Reality, for many, is what the media recognise as real; what media do not acknowledge seems of little importance. Thus de facto silence can be imposed upon individuals and groups whom the media ignore; even the voice of the Gospel can be muted, though not entirely stilled, in this way.

It is important therefore that Christians find ways to furnish the missing information to those deprived of it and also to give a voice to the voiceless.

The power of media either to reinforce or override the traditional reference points of religion, culture and family underlines the continued relevance of the Council's words: 'If the media are to be correctly employed, it is essential that all who use them know the principles of the moral order and apply them faithfully in this domain'.[7]

B. Political and Economic Context

5. The economic structures of nations are inextricably linked to contemporary communications systems. National investment in an efficient communications infrastructure is widely regarded as necessary to economic and political development, and the growing cost of such investment has been a major factor leading governments in a number of countries to adopt policies aimed at increasing market competition. For this and other reasons, public telecommunications and broadcasting systems in many instances have been subject to policies of deregulation and privatisation.

While public systems can clearly be misused for purposes of ideological and political manipulation, unregulated commercialisation and privatisation in broadcasting can also have far-reaching consequences. In practice, and often as a matter of public policy, public accountability for the use of the airwaves is devalued. Profit, not service, tends to become the most important measure of success. Profit motives and advertisers' interests exert undue influence on media content: popularity is preferred over quality and the lowest common denominator prevails. Advertisers move beyond their legitimate role of identifying genuine needs and responding to them and, driven by profit motives, strive to create artificial needs and patterns of consumption.

Commercial pressures also operate across national boundaries at the expense of particular peoples and their cultures. Faced with increasing competition and the need to develop new markets, communications firms become ever more 'multinational' in character; at the same time, lack of local production capabilities makes some countries increasingly dependent on foreign material. Thus, the products of the popular media of one culture spread into another, often to the detriment of established art forms and media and the values which they embody.

Even so, the solution to problems arising from unregulated commercialisation and privatisation does not lie in state control of media but in more regulation according to criteria of public service and in greater public accountability. It should be noted in this connection that, although the legal and political frameworks within which media operate in some countries are currently changing strikingly for the better, elsewhere government intervention remains an instrument of oppression and exclusion.

The Work of the Means of Social Communications

6. *Communio et progressio* is rooted in a vision of communication as a way toward communion. For 'more than the expression of ideas and the indication of emotion', it declares, communication is 'the giving of self in love'.[8] In this respect, communication mirrors the Church's own communion and is capable of contributing to it.

Indeed, the communication of truth can have a redemptive power, which comes from the person of Christ. He is God's word made flesh and the image of the invisible God. In and through him God's own life is communicated to humanity by the Spirit's action. 'Since the creation of the world, invisible realities, God's eternal power and divinity have become visible, recognised through the things he has made';[9] and now: 'The Word has become flesh and made his dwelling among us, and we have seen his glory: the glory of an only Son coming from the Father, filled with enduring love.'[10]

Here, in the word made flesh, God's self-communication is definitive. In Jesus' words and deeds the word is liberating, redemptive, for all humankind. This loving self-revelation of God, combined with humanity's response of faith, constitutes a profound dialogue.

Human history and all human relationships exist within the framework established by this self-communication of God in Christ. History itself is ordered toward becoming a kind of word of God, and it is part of the human vocation to contribute to bringing this about by living out the ongoing, unlimited communication of God's reconciling love in creative new ways. We are to do this through words of hope and deeds of love, that is, through our very way of life. Thus communication must lie at the heart of the Church community.

Christ is both the content and the dynamic source of the Church's communications in proclaiming the Gospel. For the Church itself is 'Christ's Mystical Body – the hidden completion of Christ glorified – who 'fills the whole creation'.[11] As a result we move, within the Church and with the help of the word and the sacraments, toward the hope of that last unity where 'God will be all in all'.[12]

A. Media at the Service of Persons and Cultures

7. For all the good which they do and are capable of doing, mass media 'which can be such effective instruments of unity and understanding, can also sometimes be the vehicles of a deformed outlook on life, on the family, on religion and on morality – an outlook that does not respect the true dignity and destiny of the human person'.[13] It is imperative that media respect and

contribute to that integral development of the person which embraces 'the cultural, transcendent and religious dimensions of man and society'.[14]

One also finds the source of certain individual and social problems in the replacement of human interaction by increased media use and intense attachment to fictitious media characters. Media, after all, cannot take the place of immediate personal contact and interaction among family members and friends. But the solution to this difficulty also may lie largely in the media: through their use in ways – dialogue groups, discussions of films and broadcasts – which stimulate interpersonal communication rather than substituting for it.

B. Media at the Service of Dialogue with the World

8. The Second Vatican Council underlined the awareness of the people of God that they are 'truly and intimately linked with mankind and its history'.[15] Those who proclaim God's word are obliged to heed and seek to understand the 'words' of diverse peoples and cultures, in order not only to learn from them but to help them recognise and accept the word of God.[16] The Church therefore must maintain an active, listening presence in relation to the world – a kind of presence which both nurtures community and supports people in seeking acceptable solutions to personal and social problems.

Moreover, as the Church always must communicate its message in a manner suited to each age and to the cultures of particular nations and peoples, so today it must communicate in and to the emerging media culture.[17] This is a basic condition for responding to a crucial point made by the Second Vatican Council: the emergence of 'social, technical and cultural bonds' linking people ever more closely lends 'special urgency' to the Church's task of bringing all to 'full union with Christ'.[18] Considering how important a contribution the media of social communications can make to its efforts to foster this unity, the Church views them as means 'devised under God's Providence' for the promotion of communication and communion among human beings during their earthly pilgrimage.[19]

Thus, in seeking to enter into dialogue with the modern world, the Church necessarily desires honest and respectful dialogue with those responsible for the communications media. On the Church's side this dialogue involves efforts to understand the media – their purposes, procedures, forms and genres, internal structures and modalities – and to offer support and encouragement to those involved in media work. On the basis of this sympathetic understanding and support, it becomes possible to offer meaningful proposals for removing obstacles to human progress and the proclamation of the gospel.

Such dialogue therefore requires that the Church be actively concerned with the secular media and especially with the shaping of media policy. Christians have in effect a responsibility to make their voice heard in all the media and their task is not confined merely to the giving out of Church news. The dialogue also involves support for media artists; it requires the development of an anthropology and a theology of communication – not least, so that theology itself may be more communicative, more successful in disclosing Gospel values and applying them to the contemporary realities of the human condition; it requires that Church leaders and pastoral workers respond willingly and prudently to media when requested, while seeking to establish relationships of mutual confidence and respect, based on fundamental common values, with those who are not of our faith.

C. Media at the Service of Human Community and Progress

9. Communications in and by the Church is essentially communication of the good news of Jesus Christ. It is the proclamation of the Gospel as a prophetic, liberating word to the men and women of our times; it is testimony, in the face of radical secularisation, to divine truth and to the transcendent destiny of the human person; it is the witness given in solidarity with all believers against conflict and division, to justice and communion among peoples, nations and cultures.

This understanding of communication on the part of the Church sheds a unique light on social communications and on the role which, in the providential plan of God, the media are intended to play in promoting the integral development of human persons and societies.

D. Media at the Service of Ecclesial Communion

10. Along with all this, it is necessary constantly to recall the importance of the fundamental right of dialogue and information within the Church, as described in *Communio et progressio*,[20] and to continue to seek effective means, including a responsible use of media of social communications, for realising and protecting this right. In this connection we also have in mind the affirmations of the *Code of Canon Law*, that, besides showing obedience to the pastors of the Church, the faithful 'are at liberty to make known their needs, especially their spiritual needs, and their wishes' to these pastors,[21] and that the faithful, in keeping with their knowledge, competence and position, have 'the right, indeed at times the duty, to express to the pastors their views on matters concerning the good of the Church'.[22]

Partly this is a matter of maintaining and enhancing the Church's credibility and effectiveness. But, more fundamentally, it is one of the ways of realising in a concrete manner the Church's character as communion, rooted in and mirroring the intimate communion of the trinity. Among the members of the community of persons who make up the Church there is a radical equality in dignity and mission which arises from baptism and underlies hierarchical structure and diversity of office and function; and this equality necessarily will express itself in an honest and respectful sharing of information and opinions.

It will be well to bear in mind, however, in cases of dissent, that 'it is not by seeking to exert the pressure of public opinion that one contributes to the clarification of doctrinal issues and renders service to the truth'.[23] In fact, 'not all ideas which circulate among the people of God' are to be 'simply and purely identified with the sense of the Faith'.[24]

Why does the Church insist that people have the right to receive correct information? Why does the Church emphasise its right to proclaim authentic Gospel truth? Why does the Church stress the responsibility of its pastors to communicate the truth and to form the faithful to do the same? It is because the whole understanding of what communication in the Church means is based upon the realisation that the Word of God communicates himself.

E. Media at the Service of a New Evangelization
11. Along with traditional means such as witness of life, catechetics, personal contact, popular piety, the liturgy and similar celebrations, the use of media is now essential in evangelization and catechesis. Indeed, 'the Church would feel guilty before the Lord if she did not utilise these powerful means that human skill is daily rendering more perfect'.[25] The media of social communications can and should be instruments in the Church's programme of re-evangelisation and new evangelisation in the contemporary world. In view of the proven efficacy of the old principle 'see, judge, act', the audiovisual aspect of media in evangelization should be given due attention.

But it will also be of great importance in the Church's approach to media and the culture they do so much to shape always to bear in mind that: 'It is not enough to use the media simply to spread the Christian message and the Church's authentic teaching. It is also necessary to integrate that message into the 'new culture' created by modern communications ... with new languages, new techniques and a new psychology'.[26] Today's evangelization ought to well up from the Church's active, sympathetic presence within the world of communications.

Current Challenges

A. The Need for a Critical Evaluation
12. But even as the Church takes a positive, sympathetic approach to media, seeking to enter into the culture created by modern communications in order to evangelize effectively, it is necessary at the very same time that the Church offer a critical evaluation of mass media and their impact upon culture.

As we have said repeatedly, communications technology is a marvellous expression of human genius, and the media confer innumerable benefits upon society. But, as we have also pointed out, the application of communications technology has been a mixed blessing, and its use for good purposes requires sound values and wise choices on the part of individuals, the private sector, governments and society as a whole. The Church does not presume to dictate these decisions and choices, but it does seek to be of help by indicating ethical and moral criteria which are relevant to the process – criteria which are to be found in both human and Christian values.

B. Solidarity and Integral Development

13. As matters stand, mass-media at times exacerbate individual and social problems which stand in the way of human solidarity and the integral development of the human person. These obstacles include secularism, consumerism, materialism, dehumanisation and lack of concern for the plight of the poor and neglected.[27]

It is against this background that the Church, recognising the media of social communications as 'the privileged way' today for the creation and transmission of culture,[28] acknowledges its own duty to offer formation to communications professionals and to the public, so that they will approach media with 'a critical sense which is animated by a passion for the truth'; it likewise acknowledges its duty to engage in 'a work of defence of liberty, respect for the dignity of individuals and the elevation of the authentic culture of peoples which occurs through a firm and courageous rejection of every form of monopoly and manipulation'.[29]

C. Policies and Structures

14. Certain problems in this regard arise specifically from media policies and structures: for example, the unjust exclusion of some groups and classes from access to the means of communication, the systematic abridgement of the fundamental right to information which is practiced in some places, the widespread domination of media by economic, social and political elites.

These things are contrary to the principal purposes, and indeed to the very nature, of the media, whose proper and essential social role consists in contributing to the realisation of the human right to information, promoting justice in the pursuit of the common good and assisting individuals, groups and peoples in their search for truth. The media carry out these crucial tasks when they foster the exchange of ideas and information among all classes and sectors of society and offer to all responsible voices opportunities to be heard.

D. Defence of the Right to Information and Communications

15. It is not acceptable that the exercise of the freedom of communication should depend upon wealth, education or political power. The right to communicate is the right of all.

This calls for special national and international efforts, not only to give those who are poor and less powerful access to the information which they need for their individual and social development, but to ensure that they are able to play an effective, responsible role in deciding media content and determining the structures and policies of their national institutions of social communications.

Where legal and political structures foster the domination of the media by elites, the Church for its part must urge respect for the right to communicate, including its own right of access to media, while at the same time seeking alternative models of communications for its own members and for people at large. The right to communicate is part also of the right to religious freedom, which should not be confined to freedom of worship.

Pastoral Priorities and Responses

A. Defence of Human Cultures

16. Considering the situation in many places, sensitivity to the rights and interests of individuals may often call for the Church to promote alternative community media. Often, too, for the sake of evangelization and catechesis the Church must take steps to preserve and promote folk media and other traditional forms of expression, recognizing that in particular societies these can be more effective than newer media in spreading the Gospel because they make possible greater personal participation and reach deeper levels of human feeling and motivation.

The overwhelming presence of mass media in the contemporary world by no means detracts from the importance of alternative media which are open to people's involvement and allow them to be active in production and even in designing the process of communications itself. Then, too, grassroots and traditional media not only provide an important forum for local cultural expression but develop competence for active participation in shaping and using mass media.

Similarly, we view with sympathy the desire of many peoples and groups for more just, equitable systems of communications and information which safeguard them against domination and manipulation, whether from abroad or at the hands of their fellow countrymen. This is a concern of developing nations in relation to developed ones; and often, too, it is a concern of minorities within particular nations, both developed and developing. In all cases people ought to be able to participate actively, autonomously and responsibly in the processes of communications which in so many ways help to shape the conditions of their lives.

B. Development and Promotion of the Church's own Media of Social Communications

17. Along with its other commitments in the area of communications and media, the Church must continue, in spite of the many difficulties involved, to develop, maintain and foster its own specifically Catholic instruments and programmes for social communications. These include the Catholic press and Catholic publishing houses, Catholic radio and television, offices for public information and media relations, institutes and programmes for training in and about media, media research and Church-related organisations of communications professionals – including especially the international Catholic communications organisations – whose members are knowledgeable and competent collaborators with the episcopal conferences as well as with the bishops individually.

Catholic media work is not simply one more programme alongside all the rest of the Church's activities: social communications have a role to play in every aspect of the Church's mission. Thus, not only should there be a pastoral plan for communications, but communications should be an integral part of every pastoral plan, for it has something to contribute to virtually every other apostolate, ministry and programme.

C. The Formation of Christian Communicators

18. Education and training in communications should be an integral part of the formation of pastoral workers and priests.[30]

There are several distinct elements and aspects to the education and training which are required. For example, in today's world, so strongly influenced by media, Church personnel require at least a working grasp of the impact which new information technologies and mass media are having upon individuals and society. They must likewise be prepared to minister both to the 'information-rich' and to the 'information-poor'. They need to know how to invite others into dialogue, avoiding a style of communicating which suggests domination, manipulation or personal gain. As for those who will be actively engaged in media work for the Church, they need to acquire professional skills in media along with doctrinal and spiritual formation.

D. Pastoral Care of Communications Personnel

19. Media work involves special psychological pressures and ethical dilemmas. Considering how important a role the media play in forming contemporary culture and shaping the lives of countless individuals and whole societies, it is essential that those professionally involved in secular media and the communications industries approach their responsibilities imbued with high ideals and a commitment to the service of humanity.

The Church has a corresponding responsibility: to develop and offer programmes of pastoral care which are specifically responsive to the peculiar working conditions and moral challenges facing communications professionals. Typically, pastoral programmes of this sort should include ongoing formation which will help these men and women – many of whom sincerely wish to know and do what is ethically and morally right – to integrate moral norms ever more fully into their professional work as well as their private lives.

The Need for Pastoral Planning

A. Responsibilities of the Bishops

20. Recognising the validity, and indeed the urgency, of the claims advanced by communications work, bishops and others responsible for decisions about allocating the Church's limited human and material resources should assign it an appropriate, high priority, taking into account the circumstances of their particular nations, regions and dioceses.

This need may be even greater now than previously, precisely because, to some degree at least, the great contemporary

'Areopagus' of mass media has more or less been neglected by the Church up to this time.[31] As the Holy Father remarks: 'Generally, preference has been given to other means of preaching the Gospel and of Christian education, while the mass media are left to the initiative of individuals or small groups and enter into pastoral planning only in a secondary way.'[32] This situation needs correcting.

B. Urgency of a Pastoral Plan for Social Communications

21. We therefore strongly recommend that dioceses and episcopal conferences or assemblies include a communications component in every pastoral plan. We further recommend that they develop specific pastoral plans for social communications itself, or else review and bring up to date those plans which already exist, in this way fostering the desirable process of periodic re-examination and adaptation. In doing so, bishops should seek the collaboration of professionals in secular media and of the Church's own media-related organisations, including especially the international and national organisations for film, radio-television and the press.

Episcopal conferences in some regions already have been well served by pastoral plans which concretely identify needs and goals and encourage the coordination of efforts. The results of the study, assessment and consultation involved in preparing these documents can and should be shared at all levels in the Church, as useful data for pastoral workers. Practical, realistic plans of this sort also can be adapted to the needs of local Churches. They should of course be constantly open to revision and adaptation in light of changing needs.

This document itself concludes with elements of a pastoral plan which also indicate issues for possible treatment in pastoral letters and episcopal statements at the national and local levels. These elements reflect suggestions received from episcopal conferences and media professionals.

Conclusion

22. We affirm once again that the Church 'sees these media as gifts of God' which, in accordance with his providential design, unite men in brotherhood and so help them to cooperate with his

plan for their salvation'.[33] As the Spirit helped the prophets of old to see the divine plan in the signs of their times, so today the Spirit helps the Church interpret the signs of our times and carry out its prophetic tasks, among which the study, evaluation and right use of communications technology and the media of social communications are now fundamental.

APPENDIX

Elements of a Pastoral Plan for Social Communications

23. Media conditions and the opportunities presented to the Church in the field of social communications differ from nation to nation and even from diocese to diocese within the same country. It naturally follows that the Church's approach to media and the cultural environment they help to form will differ from place to place and that its plans and participation will be tailored to local situations.

Every episcopal conference and diocese should therefore develop an integrated pastoral plan for communications, preferably in consultation with representatives of international and national Catholic communications organisations and with local media professionals. Furthermore, communications ought to be taken into account in formulating and carrying out all other pastoral plans, including those concerning social service, education and evangelization. A number of episcopal conferences and dioceses already have developed such plans in which communications needs are identified, goals are articulated, realistic provision is made for financing and a variety of communications efforts is coordinated.

The following guidelines are offered as assistance to those formulating such pastoral plans or engaged in reassessing plans which exist.

Guidelines for designing Pastoral Plans for Social Communications in a Diocese, Episcopal Conference or Patriarchal Assembly

24. A pastoral plan for social communications should include the following elements:

a) the statement of a vision, based on extensive consultation, which identifies communications strategies for all Church ministries and responds to contemporary issues and conditions;
b) an inventory or assessment which describes the media environment in the territory under consideration, including audiences, public and commercial media producers and directors, financial and technical resources, delivery systems, ecumenical and educational resources and Catholic media organisations and communications personnel, including those of religious communities;
c) a proposed structure for Church-related social communications in support of evangelization, catechesis and education, social service and ecumenical cooperation, and including, as far as possible, public relations, press, radio, television, cinema, cassettes, computer networks, facsimile services and related forms of telecommunications;
d) media education, with special emphasis on the relationship of media and values;
e) pastoral outreach to, and dialogue with, media professionals, with particular attention to their faith development and spiritual growth;
f) means of obtaining and maintaining financial support adequate to the carrying-out of the pastoral plan.

Process for Designing a Pastoral Plan for Social Communications
25. The plan should offer guidelines and suggestions helpful to Church communicators in establishing realistic goals and priorities for their work. It is recommended that a planning team including Church personnel and media professionals be involved in this process, whose two phases are: 1. research and 2. design.

Research Phase
26. The elements of the research phase are needs assessment, information gathering and an exploration of alternative models of a pastoral plan. It includes an analysis of the internal communications environment, including the strengths and weaknesses of the Church's current structures and programmes for communications as well as the opportunities and challenges these face.

Three types of research will assist in gathering the required information: a needs assessment, a communications audit and a resource inventory. The first identifies areas of ministry requiring particular attention on the part of the episcopal conference or diocese. The second considers what is now being done – including its effectiveness – so as to identify strengths and weaknesses of existing communications structures and procedures. The third identifies communications resources, technology and personnel available to the Church – including not only the Church's 'own' resources but those to which it may have access in the business community, the media industries and ecumenical settings.

Design Phase

27. After gathering and studying these data, the planning team should identify conference or diocesan communications goals and priorities. This is the beginning of the design phase. The planning team should then proceed to address each of the following issues as it relates to local circumstances.

28. *Education.* Communications issues and mass communications are relevant to every level of pastoral ministry, including education. A pastoral social communications plan should attempt:

a) to offer educational opportunities in communications as essential components of the formation of all persons who are engaged in the work of the Church: seminarians, priests, religious brothers and sisters and lay leaders;
b) to encourage Catholic schools and universities to offer programmes and courses related to the communications needs of the Church and society;
c) to offer courses, workshops and seminars in technology, management and communications ethics and policy issues for Church communicators, seminarians, religious and clergy;
d) to plan and carry out programmes in media education and media literacy for teachers, parents and students;
e) to encourage creative artists and writers accurately to reflect Gospel values as they share their gifts through the written word, legitimate theatre, radio, television and film for entertainment and education;

f) to identify new strategies for evangelization and catechesis through the application of communications technology and mass communications.

29. *Spiritual Formation and Pastoral Care.* Lay Catholic professionals and others working in either the Church apostolate of social communications or the secular media often look to the Church for spiritual guidance and pastoral care. A pastoral plan for social communications therefore should seek:

a) to offer opportunities for professional enrichment to lay Catholic and other professional communicators through days of recollection, retreats, seminars and professional support groups;
b) to offer pastoral care which will provide the necessary support, nourish the communicators' faith and keep alive their sense of dedication in the difficult task of communicating Gospel values and authentic human values to the world.

30. *Cooperation.* Cooperation involves sharing resources among conferences and/or dioceses and between dioceses and other institutions, such as religious communities, universities and health care facilities. A pastoral plan for social communications should be designed:

a) to enhance relations and encourage mutual consultation between Church representatives and media professionals, who have much to teach the Church about the use of media;
b) to explore cooperative productions through regional and national centres and to encourage the development of joint promotion, marketing and distribution networks;
c) to promote cooperation with religious congregations working in social communications;
d) to collaborate with ecumenical organisations and with other Churches and religious groups regarding ways of securing and guaranteeing access to the media by religion, and to collaborate in 'the more recently-developed media: especially in regard to the common use of satellites, data banks and cable networks and in informatics generally, beginning with system compatibility';[34]

e) to cooperate with secular media, especially in regard to common concerns on religious, moral, ethical, cultural, educational and social issues.

31. *Public Relations.* Public relations by the Church means active communication with the community through both secular and religious media. Involving readiness to communicate Gospel values and to publicise the ministries and programmes of the Church, it requires that the Church do all in its power to ensure that its own true image reflects Christ. A pastoral plan for social communications should seek:

a) to maintain public relations offices with adequate human and material resources to make possible effective communication between the Church and the community as a whole;
b) to produce publications and radio, television and video programmes of excellent quality which give high visibility to the message of the Gospel and the mission of the Church;
c) to promote media awards and other means of recognition in order to encourage and support media professionals;
d) to celebrate World Communications Day as a means of fostering awareness of the importance of social communications and supporting the communications initiatives of the Church.

32. *Research.* The Church's strategies in the field of social communications must be based on the results of sound media research which have been subjected to informed analysis and evaluation. It is important that communications research include topics and issues of particular relevance to the mission of the Church in the particular nation and region involved. A pastoral plan for social communications should be designed:

a) to encourage institutes of higher studies, research centres, and universities to engage in both applied and fundamental research related to communications needs and concerns of the Church and society;
b) to identify practical ways of interpreting current communications research and applying it to the mission of the Church;

c) to support ongoing theological reflection upon the processes and instruments of social communications and their role in the Church and society.

33. *Communications and Development of Peoples.* Accessible point-to-point communications and mass media offer many people a more adequate opportunity to participate in the modern world economy, to experience freedom of expression and to contribute to the emergence of peace and justice in the world. A pastoral plan for social communications should be designed:

a) to bring Gospel values to bear upon the broad range of contemporary media activities – from book publishing to satellite communications – so as to contribute to the growth of international solidarity;
b) to defend the public interest and to safeguard religious access to the media by taking informed, responsible positions on matters of communications law and policy and on the development of communications systems;
c) to analyse the social impact of advanced communications technology and to help prevent undue social disruption and cultural destabilisation;
d) to assist professional communicators in articulating and observing ethical standards, especially in regard to the issues of fairness, accuracy, justice, decency and respect for life;
e) to develop strategies for encouraging more widespread, representative, responsible access to the media;
f) to exercise a prophetic role by speaking out in timely fashion from a gospel perspective concerning the moral dimensions of significant public issues.

Vatican City, 22 February 1992
Feast of the Chair of St Peter the Apostle

✠ **John P. Foley**
President

✠ **Pierfranco Pastore**
Secretary

Notes

1. Cf. JOHN PAUL II, *Centesimus annus*, nn. 12-23, in AAS, LXXXIII (1991), pp. 807–821.
2. JOHN PAUL II, *Redemptoris missio*, n. 37, in AAS, LXXXIII (1991), p. 285.
3. *Communio et progressio*, n. 187, in AAS, LXIII (1971), pp. 655–656.
4. JOHN PAUL II, Message for the World Communications Day 1990, in *L'Osservatore Romano*, 25 January 1990, p. 6; cf. *Gaudium et spes*, n. 5, in AAS, LVIII (1966), p. 1028.
5. Ibid.
6. Pontifical Council for Social Communications, Criteria for Ecumenical and Inter-religious Cooperation in Communications, n. 1, Vatican City, 1989.
7. *Inter mirifica*, n. 4, in AAS, LVI (1964), p. 146.
8. *Communio et progressio*, n. 11, in AAS, LXIII (1971), p. 598.
9. Rm 1:20.
10. John 1:14.
11. Eph 1:23; 4:10.
12. 1 Cor 15:28; *Communio et progressio*, n. 11, in AAS, LXIII (1971), p. 598.
13. Pontifical Council for Social Communications, *Pornography and Violence in the Media: A Pastoral Response*, n. 7, Vatican City, 1989.
14. JOHN PAUL II, *Sollicitudo Rei Socialis*, n. 46, in AAS, LXXX (1988), p. 579.
15. *Gaudium et spes*, n. 11, in AAS, LVIII (1966), p. 1034.
16. Cf. PAUL VI, *Evangelii nuntiandi*, n. 20, in AAS, LXVIII (1976), pp. 18–19.
17. Cf. *Inter mirifica*, n. 3, in AAS, LVI (1964), p. 146.
18. *Lumen gentium*, n. 1, in AAS, LVII (1965), p. 5.
19. Cf. *Communio et progressio*, n. 12, in AAS, LXIII (1971), p. 598.
20. Ibid., nn. 114–121, pp. 634–636.
21. Cf. Canon 212.2, in AAS, LXXV, 2 (1983), p. 34.
22. Cf. Canon 212.3, p. 34.
23. Congregation for the Doctrine of the Faith, Instruction on the Ecclesial Vocation of the Theologian, n. 30, in AAS, LXXXII (1990), p. 1562.
24. Cf. Ibid., n. 35, p. 1565.
25. PAUL Vl, *Evangelii nuntiandi*, n. 45, in AAS, LXVIII (1976), p. 35.
26. JOHN PAUL II, *Redemptoris missio*, n. 37, in AAS, LXXXIII (1991), p. 285.

27. Cf. JOHN PAUL II, *Centesimus annus*, n. 41, in AAS, LXXXIII (1991), p. 841.
28. JOHN PAUL II, *Christifideles laici*, n. 44, in AAS, LXXXI (1989), p. 480.
29. Ibid., p. 481.
30. Cf. Congregation for Catholic Education, *Guide to the Training of Future Priests Concerning the Instruments of Social Communications*, Vatican City, 1986.
31. Cf. JOHN PAUL II, *Redemptoris missio*, n. 37, in AAS, LXXXIII (1991), p. 285.
32. Ibid.
33. *Communio et progressio*, n. 2, in AAS, LXIII (1971), pp. 593–594.
34. Pontifical Council for Social Communications, *Criteria for Ecumenical and Inter-religious Cooperation in Communications*, n. 14.

PONTIFICAL COUNCIL FOR SOCIAL COMMUNICATIONS

ETHICS IN ADVERTISING

22 FEBRUARY 1997

Introduction

1. The importance of advertising is 'steadily on the increase in modern society'. That observation, made by this Pontifical Council a quarter century ago as part of an overview of the state of communications, is even more true now.

Just as the media of social communication themselves have enormous influence everywhere, so advertising, using media as its vehicle, is a pervasive, powerful force shaping attitudes and behaviour in today's world.

Especially since the Second Vatican Council, the Church has frequently addressed the question of the media and their role and responsibilities. She has sought to do so in a fundamentally positive manner, viewing the media as 'gifts of God' which, in accordance with his providential design, bring people together and 'help them to cooperate with his plan for their salvation'.

In doing so, the Church stresses the responsibility of media to contribute to the authentic, integral development of persons and to foster the well being of society. 'The information provided by the media is at the service of the common good. Society has a right to information based on truth, freedom, justice and solidarity.'

It is in this spirit that the Church enters into dialogue with communicators. At the same time, she also calls attention to moral principles and norms relevant to social communications, as to other forms of human endeavour, while criticising policies and practices that offend against these standards.

Here and there in the growing body of literature arising from the Church's consideration of media, the subject of advertising is discussed. Now, prompted by the increasing importance of advertising and by requests for a more extensive treatment, we turn again to this topic.

We wish to call attention to positive contributions that advertising can and does make; to note ethical and moral problems that advertising can and does raise; to point to moral principles that apply to this field; and, finally, to suggest certain steps for the consideration of those professionally involved in advertising, as well as for others in the private sector, including the churches, and for public officials.

Our reason for addressing these matters is simple. In today's society, advertising has a profound impact on how people understand life, the world and themselves, especially in regard to their values and their ways of choosing and behaving. These are matters about which the Church is and must be deeply and sincerely concerned.

2. The field of advertising is extremely broad and diverse. In general terms, of course, an advertisement is simply a public notice meant to convey information and invite patronage or some other response. As that suggests, advertising has two basic purposes: to inform and to persuade, and – while these purposes are distinguishable – both very often are simultaneously present.

Advertising is not the same as marketing (the complex of commercial functions involved in transferring goods from producers and consumers) or public relations (the systematic effort to create a favourable public impression or 'image' of some person, group, or entity). In many cases, though, it is a technique or instrument employed by one or both of these.

Advertising can be very simple – a local, even 'neighbourhood', phenomenon – or it can be very complex, involving sophisticated research and multimedia campaigns that span the globe. It differs according to its intended audience, so that, for example, advertising aimed at children raises some technical and moral issues significantly different from those raised by advertising aimed at competent adults.

Not only are many different media and techniques employed in advertising; advertising itself is of several different kinds: commercial advertising for products and services; public service advertising on behalf of various institutions, programmes and causes; and – a phenomenon of growing importance today – political advertising in the interests of parties and candidates. Making allowance for the differences among the different kinds and methods of advertising, we intend what follows to be applicable to them all.

3. We disagree with the assertion that advertising simply mirrors the attitudes and values of the surrounding culture. No doubt advertising, like the media of social communications in general, does act as a mirror. But, also like media in general, it is a mirror that helps shape the reality it reflects, and sometimes it presents a distorted image of reality.

Advertisers are selective about the values and attitudes to be fostered and encouraged, promoting some while ignoring others. This selectivity gives the lie to the notion that advertising does no more than reflect the surrounding culture. For example, the absence from advertising of certain racial and ethnic groups in some multi-racial or multi-ethnic societies can help to create problems of image and identity, especially among those neglected, and the almost inevitable impression in commercial advertising that an abundance of possessions leads to happiness and fulfilment can be both misleading and frustrating.

Advertising also has an indirect but powerful impact on society through its influence on media. Many publications and broadcasting operations depend on advertising revenue for survival. This is often true of religious media as well as commercial media. For their part, advertisers naturally seek to reach audiences; and the media, striving to deliver audiences to advertisers, must shape their content so to attract audiences of the size and demographic composition sought. This economic dependency of media and the power it confers upon advertisers carries with it serious responsibilities for both.

The Benefits of Advertising

4. Enormous human and material resources are devoted to advertising. Advertising is everywhere in today's world, so that, as Pope Paul VI remarked, 'No one now can escape the influence of advertising'. Even people who are not themselves exposed to

particular forms of advertising confront a society, a culture – other people – affected for good or ill by advertising messages and techniques of every sort.

Some critics view this state of affairs in unrelievedly negative terms. They condemn advertising as a waste of time, talent and money – an essentially parasitic activity. In this view, not only does advertising have no value of its own, but its influence is entirely harmful and corrupting for individuals and society.

We do not agree. There is truth to the criticisms, and we shall make criticisms of our own. But advertising also has significant potential for good, and sometimes it is realised. Here are some of the ways that happens.

a) Economic Benefits of Advertising

5. Advertising can play an important role in the process by which an economic system guided by moral norms and responsive to the common good contributes to human development. It is a necessary part of the functioning of modern market economies, which today either exist or are emerging in many parts of the world and which – provided they conform to moral standards based upon integral human development and the common good – currently seem to be 'the most efficient instrument for utilising resources and effectively responding to needs' of a socio-economic kind.

In such a system, advertising can be a useful tool for sustaining honest and ethically responsible competition that contributes to economic growth in the service of authentic human development. 'The Church looks with favour on the growth of man's productive capacity, and also on the ever widening network of relationships and exchanges between persons and social groups ... [F]rom this point of view she encourages advertising, which can become a wholesome and efficacious instrument for reciprocal help among men.'

Advertising does this, among other ways, by informing people about the availability of rationally desirable new products and services and improvements in existing ones, helping them to make informed, prudent consumer decisions, contributing to efficiency and the lowering of prices, and stimulating economic progress through the expansion of business and trade. All of this can contribute to the creation of new jobs, higher incomes and a more decent and humane way of life for all. It also helps pay for publications, programming and productions – including those of the Church – that bring information, entertainment and inspiration to people around the world.

b) Benefits of Political Advertising

6. 'The Church values the democratic system inasmuch as it ensures the participation of citizens in making political choices, guarantees to the governed the possibility both of electing and holding accountable those who govern them, and of replacing them through peaceful means when appropriate.'

Political advertising can make a contribution to democracy analogous to its contribution to economic well being in a market system guided by moral norms. As free and responsible media in a democratic system help to counteract tendencies toward the monopolisation of power on the part of oligarchies and special interests, so political advertising can make its contribution by informing people about the ideas and policy proposals of parties and candidates, including new candidates not previously known to the public.

c) Cultural Benefits of Advertising

7. Because of the impact advertising has on media that depend on it for revenue, advertisers have an opportunity to exert a positive influence on decisions about media content. This they do by supporting material of excellent intellectual, aesthetic and moral quality presented with the public interest in view, and particularly by encouraging and making possible media presentations which are oriented to minorities whose needs might otherwise go unserved.

Moreover, advertising can itself contribute to the betterment of society by uplifting and inspiring people and motivating them to act in ways that benefit themselves and others. Advertising can brighten lives simply by being witty, tasteful and entertaining. Some advertisements are instances of popular art, with a vivacity and elan all their own.

d) Moral and Religious Benefits of Advertising

8. In many cases, too, benevolent social institutions, including those of a religious nature, use advertising to communicate their messages – messages of faith, of patriotism, of tolerance, compassion and neighbourly service, of charity toward the needy, messages concerning health and education, constructive and helpful messages that educate and motivate people in a variety of beneficial ways.

For the Church, involvement in media-related activities, including advertising, is today a necessary part of a comprehensive pastoral strategy. This includes both the Church's own media – Catholic press and publishing, television and radio broadcasting, film and audiovisual production, and the rest – and also her participation in secular media. The media 'can and should be instruments in the Church's programme of re-evangelisation and new evangelisation in the contemporary world'. While much remains to be done, many positive efforts of this kind are already underway. With reference to advertising itself, Pope Paul VI once said that it is desirable that Catholic institutions 'follow with constant attention the development of the modern techniques of advertising and ... know how to make opportune use of them in order to spread the Gospel message in a manner which answers the expectations and needs of contemporary man'.

The Harm Done by Advertising

9. There is nothing intrinsically good or intrinsically evil about advertising. It is a tool, an instrument: it can be used well, and it can be used badly. If it can have, and sometimes does have, beneficial results such as those just described, it also can, and often does, have a negative, harmful impact on individuals and society.

Communio et progressio contains this summary statement of the problem: 'If harmful or utterly useless goods are touted to the public, if false assertions are made about goods for sale, if less than admirable human tendencies are exploited, those responsible for such advertising harm society and forfeit their good name and credibility. More than this, unremitting pressure to buy articles of luxury can arouse false wants that hurt both individuals and families by making them ignore what they really need. And those forms of advertising which, without shame, exploit the sexual instincts simply to make money or which seek to penetrate into the subconscious recesses of the mind in a way that threatens the freedom of the individual ... must be shunned.'

a) Economic Harms of Advertising

10. Advertising can betray its role as a source of information by misrepresentation and by withholding relevant facts. Sometimes, too, the information function of media can be subverted by advertisers' pressure upon publications or programmes not to treat of questions that might prove embarrassing or inconvenient.

More often, though, advertising is used not simply to inform but to persuade and motivate – to convince people to act in certain ways: buy certain products or services, patronise certain institutions, and the like. This is where particular abuses can occur.

The practice of 'brand'-related advertising can raise serious problems. Often there are only negligible differences among similar products of different brands, and advertising may attempt to move people to act on the basis of irrational motives ('brand loyalty', status, fashion, 'sex appeal', etc.) instead of presenting differences in product quality and price as bases for rational choice.

Advertising also can be, and often is, a tool of the 'phenomenon of consumerism', as Pope John Paul II delineated it when he said: 'It is not wrong to want to live better; what is wrong is a style of life which is presumed to be better when it is directed toward "having" rather than "being", and which wants to have more, not in order to be more but in order to spend life in enjoyment as an end in itself.' Sometimes advertisers speak of it as part of their task to 'create' needs for products and services – that is, to cause people to feel and act upon cravings for items and services they do not need. 'If ... a direct appeal is made to his instincts – while ignoring in various ways the reality of the person as intelligent and free – then consumer attitudes and lifestyles can be created which are objectively improper and often damaging to his physical and spiritual health.'

This is a serious abuse, an affront to human dignity and the common good when it occurs in affluent societies. But the abuse is still more grave when consumerist attitudes and values are transmitted by communications media and advertising to developing countries, where they exacerbate socio-economic problems and harm the poor. 'It is true that a judicious use of advertising can stimulate developing countries to improve their standard of living. But serious harm can be done them if advertising and commercial pressure become so irresponsible that communities seeking to rise from poverty to a reasonable standard of living are persuaded to seek this progress by satisfying wants that have been artificially created. The result of this is that they waste their resources and neglect their real needs, and genuine development falls behind.'

Similarly, the task of countries attempting to develop types of market economies that serve human needs and interests after decades under centralised, state-controlled systems is made more difficult by advertising that promotes consumerist attitudes and values offensive to human dignity and the common good. The problem is particularly acute when, as often happens, the dignity and welfare of society's poorer and weaker members are at stake. It is necessary always to bear in mind that there are 'goods which by their very nature cannot and must not be bought or sold' and to avoid 'an "idolatry" of the market' that, aided and abetted by advertising, ignores this crucial fact.

b) Harms of Political Advertising

11. Political advertising can support and assist the working of the democratic process, but it also can obstruct it. This happens when, for example, the costs of advertising limit political competition to wealthy candidates or groups, or require that office-seekers compromise their integrity and independence by over-dependence on special interests for funds.

Such obstruction of the democratic process also happens when, instead of being a vehicle for honest expositions of candidates' views and records, political advertising seeks to distort the views and records of opponents and unjustly attacks their reputations. It happens when advertising appeals more to people's emotions and base instincts – to selfishness, bias and hostility toward others, to racial and ethnic prejudice and the like – rather than to a reasoned sense of justice and the good of all.

c) Cultural Harms of Advertising

12. Advertising also can have a corrupting influence upon culture and cultural values. We have spoken of the economic harm that can be done to developing nations by advertising that fosters consumerism and destructive patterns of consumption. Consider also the cultural injury done to these nations and their peoples by advertising whose content and methods, reflecting those prevalent in the first world, are at war with sound traditional values in indigenous cultures. Today this kind of 'domination and manipulation' via media rightly is 'a concern of developing nations in relation to developed ones', as well as a 'concern of minorities within particular nations'.

The indirect but powerful influence exerted by advertising upon the media of social communications that depend on revenues from this source points to another sort of cultural concern. In the competition to attract ever larger audiences and deliver them to advertisers, communicators can find themselves tempted – in fact pressured, subtly or not so subtly – to set aside high artistic and moral standards and lapse into superficiality, tawdriness and moral squalour.

Communicators also can find themselves tempted to ignore the educational and social needs of certain segments of the audience – the very young, the very old, the poor – who do not match the demographic patterns (age, education, income, habits of buying and consuming, etc.) of the kinds of audiences advertisers want to reach. In this way the tone and indeed the level of moral responsibility of the communications media in general are lowered.

All too often, advertising contributes to the invidious stereotyping of particular groups that places them at a disadvantage in relation to others. This often is true of the way advertising treats women; and the exploitation of women, both in and by advertising, is a frequent, deplorable abuse. 'How often are they treated not as persons with an inviolable dignity but as objects whose purpose is to satisfy others' appetite for pleasure or for power? How often is the role of woman as wife and mother undervalued or even ridiculed? How often is the role of women in business or professional life depicted as a masculine caricature, a denial of the specific gifts of feminine insight, compassion, and understanding, which so greatly contribute to the "civilisation of love"?'

d) Moral and Religious Harms of Advertising

13. Advertising can be tasteful and in conformity with high moral standards, and occasionally even morally uplifting, but it can also be vulgar and morally degrading. Frequently it deliberately appeals to such motives as envy, status seeking and lust. Today, too, some advertisers consciously seek to shock and titillate by exploiting content of a morbid, perverse, pornographic nature.

What this Pontifical Council said several years ago about pornography and violence in the media is no less true of certain forms of advertising:

'As reflections of the dark side of human nature marred by sin, pornography and the exaltation of violence are age-old realities of the human condition. In the past quarter century, however, they have taken on new dimensions and have become serious social problems. At a time of widespread and unfortunate confusion about moral norms, the communications media have made pornography and violence accessible to a vastly expanded audience, including young people and even children, and a problem which at one time was confined mainly to wealthy countries has now begun, via the communications media, to corrupt moral values in developing nations.'

We note, too, certain special problems relating to advertising that treats of religion or pertains to specific issues with a moral dimension.

In cases of the first sort, commercial advertisers sometimes include religious themes or use religious images or personages to sell products. It is possible to do this in tasteful, acceptable ways, but the practice is obnoxious and offensive when it involves exploiting religion or treating it flippantly.

In cases of the second sort, advertising sometimes is used to promote products and inculcate attitudes and forms of behaviour contrary to moral norms. That is the case, for instance, with the advertising of contraceptives, abortifacients and products harmful to health, and with government-sponsored advertising campaigns for artificial birth control, so-called 'safe sex', and similar practices.

Some Ethical and Moral Principles

14. The Second Vatican Council declared: 'If the media are to be correctly employed, it is essential that all who use them know the principles of the moral order and apply them faithfully in this domain.' The moral order to which this refers is the order of the law of human nature, binding upon all because it is 'written on their hearts' (Rom 2:15) and embodies the imperatives of authentic human fulfilment.

For Christians, moreover, the law of human nature has a deeper dimension, a richer meaning. 'Christ is the "Beginning" who, having taken on human nature, definitively illumines it in its constitutive elements and in its dynamism of charity towards God and neighbour.' Here we comprehend the deepest significance of human freedom: that it makes possible an authentic moral response, in light of Jesus Christ, to the call 'to form our conscience, to make it the object of a continuous conversion to what is true and to what is good'.

In this context, the media of social communications have two options, and only two. Either they help human persons to grow in their understanding and practice of what is true and good, or they are destructive forces in conflict with human well being. That is entirely true of advertising.

Against this background, then, we point to this fundamental principle for people engaged in advertising: advertisers – that is, those who commission, prepare or disseminate advertising – are morally responsible for what they seek to move people to do; and this is a responsibility also shared by publishers, broadcasting executives, and others in the communications world, as well as by those who give commercial or political endorsements, to the extent that they are involved in the advertising process.

If an instance of advertising seeks to move people to choose and act rationally in morally good ways that are of true benefit to themselves and others, persons involved in it do what is morally good; if it seeks to move people to do evil deeds that are self-destructive and destructive of authentic community, they do evil.

This applies also to the means and the techniques of advertising: it is morally wrong to use manipulative, exploitative, corrupt and corrupting methods of persuasion and motivation. In this regard, we note special problems associated with so-called indirect advertising that attempts to move people to act in certain ways – for example, purchase particular products – without their being fully aware that they are being swayed. The techniques involved here include showing certain products or forms of behaviour in superficially glamorous settings associated with superficially glamorous people; in extreme cases, it may even involve the use of subliminal messages.

Within this very general framework, we can identify several moral principles that are particularly relevant to advertising. We shall speak briefly of three: truthfulness, the dignity of the human person and social responsibility.

a) Truthfulness in Advertising

15. Even today, some advertising is simply and deliberately untrue. Generally speaking, though, the problem of truth in advertising is somewhat more subtle: it is not that advertising says what is overtly false, but that it can distort the truth by implying things that are not so or withholding relevant facts. As Pope John Paul II points out, on both the individual and social levels, truth and freedom are inseparable; without truth as the basis, starting point and criterion of discernment, judgement, choice and action, there can be no authentic exercise of freedom. The Catechism of the Catholic Church, quoting the Second Vatican Council, insists that the content of communication be 'true and – within the limits set by justice and charity – complete'; the content should, moreover, be communicated 'honestly and properly'.

To be sure, advertising, like other forms of expression, has its own conventions and forms of stylisation, and these must be taken into account when discussing truthfulness. People take for granted some rhetorical and symbolic exaggeration in advertising; within the limits of recognised and accepted practice, this can be allowable.

But it is a fundamental principle that advertising may not deliberately seek to deceive, whether it does that by what it says, by what it implies, or by what it fails to say. 'The proper exercise of the right to information demands that the content of what is communicated be true and, within the limits set by justice and charity, complete. ... Included here is the obligation to avoid any manipulation of truth for any reason.'

b) The Dignity of the Human Person

16. There is an 'imperative requirement' that advertising 'respect the human person, his right/duty to make a responsible choice, his interior freedom; all these goods would be violated if man's lower inclinations were to be exploited, or his capacity to reflect and decide compromised'.

These abuses are not merely hypothetical possibilities but realities in much advertising today. Advertising can violate the dignity of the human person both through its content – what is advertised, the manner in which it is advertised – and through the impact it seeks to make upon its audience. We have spoken already of such things as appeals to lust, vanity, envy and greed, and of techniques that manipulate and exploit human weakness. In such circumstances, advertisements readily become 'vehicles of a deformed outlook on life, on the family, on religion and on morality – an outlook that does not respect the true dignity and destiny of the human person'.

This problem is especially acute where particularly vulnerable groups or classes of persons are concerned: children and young people, the elderly, the poor, the culturally disadvantaged.

Much advertising directed at children apparently tries to exploit their credulity and suggestibility, in the hope that they will put pressure on their parents to buy products of no real benefit to them. Advertising like this offends against the dignity and rights of both children and parents; it intrudes upon the parent-child relationship and seeks to manipulate it to its own base ends. Also, some of the comparatively little advertising directed specifically to the elderly or culturally disadvantaged seems designed to play upon their fears so as to persuade them to allocate some of their limited resources to goods or services of dubious value.

c) Advertising and Social Responsibility

17. Social responsibility is such a broad concept that we can note here only a few of the many issues and concerns relevant under this heading to the question of advertising.

The ecological issue is one. Advertising that fosters a lavish lifestyle which wastes resources and despoils the environment offends against important ecological concerns. 'In his desire to have and to enjoy rather than to be and grow, man consumes the resources of the earth and his own life in an excessive and disordered way. ... Man thinks that he can make arbitrary use of the earth, subjecting it without restraint to his will, as though it did not have its own requisites and a prior God-given purpose, which man can indeed develop but must not betray.'

As this suggests, something more fundamental is at issue here: authentic and integral human development. Advertising that reduces human progress to acquiring material goods and cultivating a lavish lifestyle expresses a false, destructive vision of the human person harmful to individuals and society alike.

When people fail to practice 'a rigorous respect for the moral, cultural and spiritual requirements, based on the dignity of the person and on the proper identity of each community, beginning with the family and religious societies', then even material abundance and the conveniences that technology makes available 'will prove unsatisfying and in the end contemptible'. Advertisers, like people engaged in other forms of social communication, have a serious duty to express and foster an authentic vision of human development in its material, cultural and spiritual dimensions. Communication that meets this standard is, among other things, a true expression of solidarity. Indeed, the two things – communication and solidarity – are inseparable, because, as the *Catechism of the Catholic Church* points out, solidarity is 'a consequence of genuine and right communication and the free circulation of ideas that further knowledge and respect for others'.

Conclusion: Some Steps to Take

18. The indispensable guarantors of ethically correct behaviour by the advertising industry are the well formed and responsible consciences of advertising professionals themselves: consciences sensitive to their duty not merely to serve the interests of those who commission and finance their work but also to respect and uphold the rights and interests of their audiences and to serve the common good.

Many women and men professionally engaged in advertising do have sensitive consciences, high ethical standards and a strong sense of responsibility. But even for them, external pressures – from the clients who commission their work as well as from the competitive internal dynamics of their profession – can create powerful inducements to unethical behaviour. That underlines the need for external structures and systems to support and encourage responsible practice in advertising and to discourage the irresponsible.

19. Voluntary ethical codes are one such source of support. These already exist in a number of places. Welcome as they are, though, they are only as effective as the willingness of advertisers to comply strictly with them. 'It is up to the directors and managers of the media which carry advertising to make known to the public, to subscribe to and to apply the codes of professional ethics which already have been opportunely established so as to have the cooperation of the public in making these codes still better and in enforcing their observance.'

We emphasise the importance of public involvement. Representatives of the public should participate in the formulation, application and periodic updating of ethical codes. The public representatives should include ethicists and church people, as well as representatives of consumer groups. Individuals do well to organise themselves into such groups in order to protect their interests in relation to commercial interests.

20. Public authorities also have a role to play. On the one hand, government should not seek to control and dictate policy to the advertising industry, any more than to other sectors of the communications media. On the other hand, the regulation of advertising content and practice, already existing in many places, can and should extend beyond banning false advertising, narrowly defined. 'By promulgating laws and overseeing their application, public authorities should ensure that "public morality and social progress are not gravely endangered" through misuse of the media.'

For example, government regulations should address such questions as the quantity of advertising, especially in broadcast media, as well as the content of advertising directed at groups particularly vulnerable to exploitation, such as children and old people. Political advertising also seems an appropriate area for regulation: how much may be spent, how and from whom may money for advertising be raised, etc.

21. The media of news and information should make it a point to keep the public informed about the world of advertising. Considering advertising's social impact, it is appropriate that media regularly review and critique the performance of advertisers, just as they do other groups whose activities have a significant influence on society.

22. Besides using media to evangelize, the Church for her part needs to grasp the full implications of the observation by Pope John Paul: that media comprise a central part of that great modern 'Areopagus' where ideas are shared and attitudes and values are formed. This points to a 'deeper reality' than simply using media to spread the Gospel message, important as that is. 'It is also necessary to integrate that message into the "new culture" created by modern communications' with its 'new ways of communicating ... new languages, new techniques and a new psychology.'

In light of this insight, it is important that media education be part of pastoral planning and a variety of pastoral and educational programmes carried on by the Church, including Catholic schools. This includes education regarding the role of advertising in today's world and its relevance to the work of the Church. Such education should seek to prepare people to be informed and alert in their approach to advertising as to other forms of communication. As the *Catechism of the Catholic Church* points out, 'the means of social communication ... can give rise to a certain passivity among users, making them less than vigilant consumers of what is said or shown. Users should practice moderation and discipline in their approach to the mass media'.

23. In the final analysis, however, where freedom of speech and communication exists, it is largely up to advertisers themselves to ensure ethically responsible practices in their profession. Besides avoiding abuses, advertisers should also undertake to repair the harm sometimes done by advertising, insofar as that is possible: for example, by publishing corrective notices, compensating injured parties, increasing the quantity of public service advertising, and the like. This question of 'reparations' is a matter

of legitimate involvement not only by industry self-regulatory bodies and public interest groups, but also by public authorities.

Where unethical practices have become widespread and entrenched, conscientious advertisers may be called upon to make significant personal sacrifices to correct them. But people who want to do what is morally right must always be ready to suffer loss and personal injury rather than to do what is wrong. This is a duty for Christians, followers of Christ, certainly, but not only for them. 'In this witness to the absoluteness of the moral good Christians are not alone: they are supported by the moral sense present in peoples and by the great religious and sapiential traditions of east and west.'

We do not wish, and certainly we do not expect, to see advertising eliminated from the contemporary world. Advertising is an important element in today's society, especially in the functioning of a market economy, which is becoming more and more widespread.

Moreover, for the reasons and in the ways sketched here, we believe advertising can, and often does, play a constructive role in economic growth, in the exchange of information and ideas, and in the fostering of solidarity among individuals and groups. Yet it also can do, and often does, grave harm to individuals and to the common good.

In light of these reflections, therefore, we call upon advertising professionals and upon all those involved in the process of commissioning and disseminating advertising to eliminate its socially harmful aspects and observe high ethical standards in regard to truthfulness, human dignity and social responsibility. In this way, they will make a special and significant contribution to human progress and to the common good.

Vatican City, 22 February 1997
Feast of the Chair of St Peter the Apostle

✠ **John P. Foley**
President

✠ **Pierfranco Pastore**
Secretary

PONTIFICAL COUNCIL FOR SOCIAL COMMUNICATIONS

ETHICS IN COMMUNICATIONS

2 JUNE 2000

Introduction

1. Great good and great evil come from the use people make of the media of social communication. Although it typically is said – and we often shall say here – that 'media' do this or that, these are not blind forces of nature beyond human control. For even though acts of communicating often do have unintended consequences, nevertheless people choose whether to use the media for good or evil ends, in a good or evil way.

These choices, central to the ethical question, are made not only by those who receive communication – viewers, listeners, readers – but especially by those who control the instruments of social communication and determine their structures, policies and content. They include public officials and corporate executives, members of governing boards, owners, publishers and station managers, editors, news directors, producers, writers, correspondents, and others. For them, the ethical question is particularly acute: Are the media being used for good or evil?

2. The impact of social communication can hardly be exaggerated. Here people come into contact with other people and with events, form their opinions and values. Not only do they transmit and receive information and ideas through these instruments but often they experience living itself as an experience of media (cf. Pontifical Council for Social Communications, *Aetatis novae,* 2).

Rapid technological change is making the media of communication even more pervasive and powerful. 'The advent of the information society is a real cultural revolution' (Pontifical Council for Culture, *Toward a Pastoral Approach To Culture*, 9); and the twentieth century's dazzling innovations may have been only a prologue to what this new century will bring.

The range and diversity of media accessible to people in well-to-do countries already are astonishing: books and periodicals, television and radio, films and videos, audio recordings, electronic communication transmitted over the airwaves, over cable and satellite, via the Internet. The contents of this vast outpouring range from hard news to pure entertainment, prayer to pornography, contemplation to violence. Depending on how they use media, people can grow in sympathy and compassion or become isolated in a narcissistic, self-referential world of stimuli with near-narcotic effects. Not even those who shun the media can avoid contact with others who are deeply influenced by them.

3. Along with these reasons, the Church has reasons of her own for being interested in the means of social communication. Viewed in the light of faith, the history of human communication can be seen as a long journey from Babel, site and symbol of communication's collapse (cf. Gn 11:4-8), to Pentecost and the gift of tongues (cf. Acts 2:5-11) – communication restored by the power of the Spirit sent by the Son. Sent forth into the world to announce the Good News (cf. Mt 28:19-20; Mk 16:15), the Church has the mission of proclaiming the Gospel until the end of time. Today, she knows, that requires using media (cf. Vatican Council II, *Inter mirifica*, 3; Pope Paul VI, *Evangelii nuntiandi*, 45; Pope John Paul II, *Redemptoris missio*, 37; Pontifical Council for Social Communications, *Communio et progressio*, 126-134, *Aetatis novae*, 11).

The Church also knows herself to be a *communio*, a communion of persons and eucharistic communities, 'rooted in and mirroring the intimate communion of the Trinity' (*Aetatis novae*, 10; cf. Congregation for the Doctrine of the Faith, *Some Aspects of the Church Understood as Communion*). Indeed, all human communication is grounded in the communication among Father, Son and Spirit. But more than that, Trinitarian communion reaches out to humankind: the Son is the Word, eternally 'spoken' by the Father; and in and through Jesus Christit,

Son and Word made flesh, God communicates himself and his salvation to women and men. 'In many and various ways God spoke of old to our fathers by the prophets; but in these last days he has spoken to us by a Son' (Heb 1:1-2). Communication in and by the Church finds its starting point in the communion of love among the divine Persons and their communication with us.

4. The Church's approach to the means of social communication is fundamentally positive, encouraging. She does not simply stand in judgement and condemn; rather, she considers these instruments to be not only products of human genius but also great gifts of God and true signs of the times (cf. *Inter mirifica*, 1; *Evangelii nuntiandi*, 45; *Redemptoris missio*, 37). She desires to support those who are professionally involved in communication by setting out positive principles to assist them in their work, while fostering a dialogue in which all interested parties – today, that means nearly everyone – can participate. These purposes underlie the present document.

We say again: the media do nothing by themselves; they are instruments, tools, used as people choose to use them. In reflecting upon the means of social communication, we must face honestly the 'most essential' question raised by technological progress: whether, as a result of it, the human person 'is becoming truly better, that is to say more mature spiritually, more aware of the dignity of his humanity, more responsible, more open to others, especially the neediest and the weakest, and readier to give and to aid all' (Pope John Paul II, *Redemptor hominis*, 15).

We take it for granted that the vast majority of people involved in social communication in any capacity are conscientious individuals who want to do the right thing. Public officials, policy-makers and corporate executives desire to respect and promote the public interest as they understand it. Readers and listeners and viewers want to use their time well for personal growth and development so that they can lead happier, more productive lives. Parents are anxious that what enters their homes through media be in their children's interests. Most professional communicators desire to use their talents to serve the human family and are troubled by the growing economic and ideological pressures to lower ethical standards present in many sectors of the media.

The contents of the countless choices made by all these people concerning the media are different from group to group and individual to individual, but the choices all have ethical weight and are subject to ethical evaluation. To choose rightly, those choosing need to 'know the principles of the moral order and apply them faithfully' (*Inter mirifica*, 4).

5. The Church brings several things to this conversation. She brings a long tradition of moral wisdom, rooted in divine revelation and human reflection (cf. Pope John Paul II, *Fides et ratio*, 36-48). Part of this is a substantial and growing body of social teaching, whose theological orientation is an important corrective to 'the "atheistic" solution, which deprives man of one of his basic dimensions, namely the spiritual one, and to permissive and consumerist solutions, which under various pretexts seek to convince man that he is free from every law and from God himself' (Pope John Paul II, *Centesimus annus*, 55). More than simply passing judgement, this tradition offers itself in service to the media. For example, 'the Church's culture of wisdom can save the media culture of information from becoming a meaningless accumulation of facts' (Pope John Paul II, Message for the 33rd World Communications Day, 1999).

The Church also brings something else to the conversation. Her special contribution to human affairs, including the world of social communication, is 'precisely her vision of the dignity of the person revealed in all its fullness in the mystery of the Incarnate Word' (*Centesimus annus*, 47). In the words of the Second Vatican Council, 'Christ the Lord, Christ the new Adam, in the very revelation of the mystery of the Father and of his love, fully reveals man to himself and brings to light his most high calling' (*Gaudium et spes*, 22).

Social Communication that Serves the Human Person

6. Following the Council's Pastoral Constitution on the Church in the Modern World, *Gaudium et spes* (cf. nos. 30-31), the Pastoral Instruction on Social Communications *Communio et progressio* makes it clear that the media are called to serve human dignity by helping people live well and function as persons in community. Media do this by encouraging men and women to be conscious of

their dignity, enter into the thoughts and feelings of others, cultivate a sense of mutual responsibility, and grow in personal freedom, in respect for others' freedom and in the capacity for dialogue.

Social communication has immense power to promote human happiness and fulfilment. Without pretending to do more than give an overview, we note here, as we have done elsewhere (cf. Pontifical Council for Social Communications, *Ethics in Advertising*, 4-8), some economic, political, cultural, educational and religious benefits.

7. *Economic.* The market is not a norm of morality or a source of moral value and market economics can be abused; but the market can serve the person (cf. *Centesimus annus*, 34), and media play an indispensable role in a market economy. Social communication supports business and commerce, helps spur economic growth, employment and prosperity, encourages improvements in the quality of existing goods and services and the development of new ones, fosters responsible competition that serves the public interest and enables people to make informed choices by telling them about the availability and features of products.

In short, today's complex national and international economic systems could not function without the media. Remove them and crucial economic structures would collapse, with great harm to countless people and to society.

8. *Political.* Social communication benefits society by facilitating informed citizen participation in the political process. The media draw people together for the pursuit of shared purposes and goals, thus helping to form and sustain authentic political communities.

Media are indispensable in today's democratic societies. They supply information about issues and events, office holders and candidates for office. They enable leaders to communicate quickly and directly with the public about urgent matters. They are important instruments of accountability, turning the spotlight on incompetence, corruption and abuses of trust, while also calling attention to instances of competence, public-spiritedness and devotion to duty.

9. *Cultural.* The means of social communication offer people access to literature, drama, music and art otherwise unavailable to them, and so promote human development in respect to knowledge and wisdom and beauty. We speak not only of presentations of classic works and the fruits of scholarship, but also of wholesome popular entertainment and useful information that draw families together, help people solve everyday problems, raise the spirits of the sick, shut-ins and the elderly, and relieve the tedium of life.

Media also make it possible for ethnic groups to cherish and celebrate their cultural traditions, share them with others and transmit them to new generations. In particular, they introduce children and young people to their cultural heritage. Communicators, like artists, serve the common good by preserving and enriching the cultural heritage of nations and peoples (cf. Pope John Paul II, *Letter to Artists*, 4).

10. *Educational.* The media are important tools of education in many contexts, from school to workplace, and at many stages in life. Preschoolers being introduced to the rudiments of reading and mathematics, young people seeking vocational training or degrees, elderly persons pursuing new learning in their latter years – these and many others have access via these means to a rich and growing panoply of educational resources.

Media are standard instructional tools in many classrooms. And beyond the classroom walls, the instruments of communication, including the Internet, conquer barriers of distance and isolation, bringing learning opportunities to villagers in remote areas, cloistered religious, the home-bound, prisoners and many others.

11. *Religious.* Many people's religious lives are greatly enriched through the media. They carry news and information about religious events, ideas and personalities; they serve as vehicles for evangelisation and catechesis. Day in and day out, they provide inspiration, encouragement and opportunities for worship to persons confined to their homes or to institutions.

Sometimes, too, media contribute to people's spiritual enrichment in extraordinary ways. For example, huge audiences around the world view and, in a sense, participate in important events in the life of the Church regularly telecast via satellite from Rome. And, over the years, media have brought the words and images of the Holy Father's pastoral visits to countless millions.

12. In all these settings – economic, political, cultural, educational, religious – as well as others, the media can be used to build and sustain human community. And indeed all communication ought to be open to community among persons.

'In order to become brothers and sisters, it is necessary to know one another. To do this, it is ... important to communicate more extensively and more deeply' (Congregation for Institutes of Consecrated Life and Societies of Apostolic Life, *Fraternal Life in Community*, 29). Communication that serves genuine community is 'more than the expression of ideas and the indication of emotion. At its most profound level, it is the giving of self in love' (*Communio et progressio*, 11).

Communication like this seeks the well being and fulfilment of community members in respect to the common good of all. But consultation and dialogue are needed to discern this common good. Therefore, it is imperative for the parties to social communication to engage in such dialogue and submit themselves to the truth about what is good. This is how the media can meet their obligation to 'witness to the truth about life, about human dignity, about the true meaning of our freedom and mutual interdependence' (Pope John Paul II, Message for the 33rd World Communications Day, 1999).

Social Communication that Violates the Good of the Person

13. The media also can be used to block community and injure the integral good of persons: by alienating people or marginalising and isolating them; drawing them into perverse communities organised around false, destructive values; fostering hostility and conflict, demonising others and creating a mentality of 'us' against 'them'; presenting what is base and degrading in a glamorous light, while ignoring or belittling what uplifts and ennobles; spreading misinformation and disinformation, fostering trivialisation and banality. Stereotyping – based on race and

ethnicity, sex and age and other factors, including religion – is distressingly common in media. Often, too, social communication overlooks what is genuinely new and important, including the good news of the Gospel, and concentrates on the fashionable or faddish. Abuses exist in each of the areas just mentioned.

14. *Economic*. The media sometimes are used to build and sustain economic systems that serve acquisitiveness and greed. Neoliberalism is a case in point: 'Based on a purely economic conception of man', it 'considers profit and the law of the market as its only parameters, to the detriment of the dignity of and the respect due to individuals and peoples' (Pope John Paul II, *Ecclesia in America*, 156). In such circumstances, means of communication that ought to benefit all are exploited for the advantage of the few.

The process of globalisation 'can create unusual opportunities for greater prosperity' (*Centesimus annus*, 58); but side by side with it, and even as part of it, some nations and peoples suffer exploitation and marginalisation, falling further and further behind in the struggle for development. These expanding pockets of privation in the midst of plenty are seedbeds of envy, resentment, tension and conflict. This underlines the need for 'effective international agencies which will oversee and direct the economy to the common good' (*Centesimus annus*, 58).

Faced with grave injustices, it is not enough for communicators simply to say that their job is to report things as they are. That undoubtedly is their job. But some instances of human suffering are largely ignored by media even as others are reported; and insofar as this reflects a decision by communicators, it reflects indefensible selectivity. Even more fundamentally, communication structures and policies and the allocation of technology are factors helping to make some people 'information rich' and others 'information poor' at a time when prosperity, and even survival, depend on information.

In such ways, then, media often contribute to the injustices and imbalances that give rise to suffering they report. 'It is necessary to break down the barriers and monopolies which leave so many countries on the margins of development, and to provide all individuals and nations with the basic conditions which will enable them to share in development' (*Centesimus annus*, 35). Communications and information technology, along with training in its use, is one such basic condition.

15. *Political.* Unscrupulous politicians use media for demagoguery and deception in support of unjust policies and oppressive regimes. They misrepresent opponents and systematically distort and suppress the truth by propaganda and 'spin'. Rather than drawing people together, media then serve to drive them apart, creating tensions and suspicions that set the stage for conflict.

Even in countries with democratic systems, it is all too common for political leaders to manipulate public opinion through the media instead of fostering informed participation in the political process. The conventions of democracy are observed, but techniques borrowed from advertising and public relations are deployed on behalf of policies that exploit particular groups and violate fundamental rights, including the right to life (cf. Pope John Paul II, *Evangulium vitae*, 70).

Often, too, the media popularise the ethical relativism and utilitarianism that underlie today's culture of death. They participate in the contemporary 'conspiracy against life' by 'lending credit to that culture which presents recourse to contraception, sterilisation, abortion and even euthanasia as a mark of progress and a victory of freedom, while depicting as enemies of freedom and progress those positions which are unreservedly pro-life' (*Evangulium vitae*, 17).

16. *Cultural.* Critics frequently decry the superficiality and bad taste of media, and although they are not obliged to be sombre and dull, they should not be tawdry and demeaning either. It is no excuse to say the media reflect popular standards; for they also powerfully influence popular standards and so have a serious duty to uplift, not degrade, them.

The problem takes various forms. Instead of explaining complex matters carefully and truthfully, news media avoid or oversimplify them. Entertainment media feature presentations of a corrupting, dehumanising kind, including exploitative treatments of sexuality and violence. It is grossly irresponsible to ignore or dismiss the fact that 'pornography and sadistic violence debase sexuality, corrode human relationships, exploit individuals – especially women and young people – undermine marriage and family life, foster anti-social behaviour and weaken the moral fibre of society itself' (Pontifical Council for Social Communications, *Pornography and Violence in the Communications Media: A Pastoral Response*, 10).

On the international level, cultural domination imposed through the means of social communication also is a serious, growing problem. Traditional cultural expressions are virtually excluded from access to popular media in some places and face extinction; meanwhile the values of affluent, secularised societies increasingly supplant the traditional values of societies less wealthy and powerful. In considering these matters, particular attention should go to providing children and young people with media presentations that put them in living contact with their cultural heritage.

Communication across cultural lines is desirable. Societies can and should learn from one another. But transcultural communication should not be at the expense of the less powerful. Today 'even the least-widespread cultures are no longer isolated. They benefit from an increase in contacts, but they also suffer from the pressures of a powerful trend toward uniformity' (*Toward a Pastoral Approach to Culture*, 33). That so much communication now flows in one direction only – from developed nations to the developing and the poor – raises serious ethical questions. Have the rich nothing to learn from the poor? Are the powerful deaf to the voices of the weak?

17. *Educational.* Instead of promoting learning, media can distract people and cause them to waste time. Children and young people are especially harmed in this way, but adults also suffer from exposure to banal, trashy presentations. Among the causes of this abuse of trust by communicators is greed that puts profits before persons.

Sometimes, too, media are used as tools of indoctrination, with the aim of controlling what people know and denying them access to information the authorities do not want them to have.

This is a perversion of genuine education, which seeks to expand people's knowledge and skills and help them pursue worthy purposes, not narrow their horizons and harness their energies in the service of ideology.

18. *Religious*. In the relationship between the means of social communication and religion there are temptations on both sides.

On the side of the media, these include ignoring or marginalising religious ideas and experience; treating religion with incomprehension, perhaps even contempt, as an object of curiosity that does not merit serious attention; promoting religious fads at the expense of traditional faith; treating legitimate religious groups with hostility; weighing religion and religious experience by secular standards of what is appropriate and favouring religious views that conform to secular tastes over those that do not; trying to imprison transcendence within the confines of rationalism and scepticism. Today's media often mirror the post-modern state of a human spirit 'locked within the confines of its own immanence without reference of any kind to the transcendent' (*Fides et ratio*, 81).

The temptations on the side of religion include taking an exclusively judgemental and negative view of media; failing to understand that reasonable standards of good media practice like objectivity and even-handedness may preclude special treatment for religion's institutional interests; presenting religious messages in an emotional, manipulative style, as if they were products competing in a glutted marketplace; using media as instruments for control and domination; practicing unnecessary secrecy and otherwise offending against truth; downplaying the Gospel's demand for conversion, repentance and amendment of life, while substituting a bland religiosity that asks little of people; encouraging fundamentalism, fanaticism and religious exclusivism that foment disdain and hostility toward others.

19. In short, the media can be used for good or for evil – it is a matter of choice. 'It can never be forgotten that communication through the media is not a utilitarian exercise intended simply to motivate, persuade or sell. Still less is it a vehicle for ideology. The media can at times reduce human beings to units of consumption

or competing interest groups, or manipulate viewers and readers and listeners as mere ciphers from whom some advantage is sought, whether product sales or political support; and these things destroy community. It is the task of communication to bring people together and enrich their lives, not isolate and exploit them. The means of social communication, properly used, can help to create and sustain a human community based on justice and charity; and, in so far as they do that, they will be signs of hope' (Pope John Paul II, Message for the 32nd World Communications Day, 1998).

Some Relevant Ethical Principles

20. Ethical principles and norms relevant in other fields also apply to social communication. Principles of social ethics like solidarity, subsidiarity, justice and equity and accountability in the use of public resources and the performance of roles of public trust are always applicable. Communication must always be truthful, since truth is essential to individual liberty and to authentic community among persons.

Ethics in social communication is concerned not just with what appears on cinema and television screens, on radio broadcasts, on the printed page and the Internet, but with a great deal else besides. The ethical dimension relates not just to the content of communication (the message) and the process of communication (how the communicating is done) but to fundamental structural and systemic issues, often involving large questions of policy bearing upon the distribution of sophisticated technology and product (who shall be information rich and who shall be information poor?). These questions point to other questions with economic and political implications for ownership and control. At least in open societies with market economies, the largest ethical question of all may be how to balance profit against service to the public interest understood according to an inclusive conception of the common good.

Even to reasonable people of good will it is not always immediately clear how to apply ethical principles and norms to particular cases; reflection, discussion and dialogue are needed. We offer what follows with the hope of encouraging such reflection and dialogue – among communication policy makers, professional communicators, ethicists and moralists, recipients of communication and others concerned.

21. In all three areas – message, process, structural and systemic issues – the fundamental ethical principle is this: the human person and the human community are the end and measure of the use of the media of social communication; communication should be by persons to persons for the integral development of persons.

Integral development requires a sufficiency of material goods and products, but it also requires attention to the 'inner dimension' (*Sollicitudo rei socialis*, 29; cf. 46). Everyone deserves the opportunity to grow and flourish in respect to the full range of physical, intellectual, emotional, moral and spiritual goods. Individuals have irreducible dignity and importance and may never be sacrificed to collective interests.

22. A second principle is complementary to the first: the good of persons cannot be realised apart from the common good of the communities to which they belong. This common good should be understood in inclusive terms, as the sum total of worthy shared purposes to whose pursuit community members jointly commit themselves and which the community exists to serve.

Thus, while social communication rightly looks to the needs and interests of particular groups, it should not do so in a way that sets one group against another – for example, in the name of class conflict, exaggerated nationalism, racial supremacy, ethnic cleansing and the like. The virtue of solidarity, 'a firm and persevering determination to commit oneself to the common good' (*Sollicitudo rei socialis*, 38), ought to govern all areas of social life – economic, political, cultural, religious.

Communicators and communication policy makers must serve the real needs and interests both of individuals and of groups, at all levels and of all kinds. There is a pressing need for equity at the international level, where the maldistribution of material goods between north and south is exacerbated by a maldistribution of communication resources and information technology upon which productivity and prosperity greatly depend. Similar problems also exist within wealthy countries, 'where the constant transformation of the methods of production and consumption devalues certain acquired skills and professional expertise' and 'those who fail to keep up with the times can easily be marginalised' (*Centesimus annus*, 33).

Clearly, then, there is a need for broad participation in making decisions not only about the messages and processes of social communication but also about systemic issues and the allocation of resources. The decision makers have a serious moral duty to recognise the needs and interests of those who are particularly vulnerable – the poor, the elderly and unborn, children and youth, the oppressed and marginalised, women and minorities, the sick and disabled – as well as families and religious groups. Today especially, the international community and international communications interests should take a generous and inclusive approach to nations and regions where what the means of social communication do – or fail to do – bears a share of the blame for the perpetuation of evils like poverty, illiteracy, political repression and violations of human rights, intergroup and interreligious conflicts and the suppression of indigenous cultures.

23. Even so, we continue to believe that 'the solution to problems arising from unregulated commercialisation and privatisation does not lie in state control of media but in more regulation according to criteria of public service and in greater public accountability. It should be noted in this connection that, although the legal and political frameworks within which media operate in some countries are currently changing strikingly for the better, elsewhere government intervention remains an instrument of oppression and exclusion' (*Aetatis novae*, 5).

The presumption should always be in favour of freedom of expression, for 'when people follow their natural inclination to exchange ideas and declare their opinions, they are not merely making use of a right. They are also performing a social duty' (*Communio et progressio*, 45). Still, considered from an ethical perspective, this presumption is not an absolute, indefeasible norm. There are obvious instances – for example, libel and slander, messages that seek to foster hatred and conflict among individuals and groups, obscenity and pornography, the morbid depiction of violence – where no right to communicate exists.

Plainly, too, free expression should always observe principles like truth, fairness and respect for privacy.

Professional communicators should be actively involved in developing and enforcing ethical codes of behaviour for their profession, in cooperation with public representatives. Religious bodies and other groups likewise deserve to be part of this continuing effort.

24. Another relevant principle, already mentioned, concerns public participation in making decisions about communications policy. At all levels, this participation should be organised, systematic and genuinely representative, not skewed in favour of particular groups. This principle applies even, and perhaps especially, where media are privately owned and operated for profit.

In the interests of public participation, communicators 'must seek to communicate with people, and not just speak to them. This involves learning about people's needs, being aware of their struggles and presenting all forms of communication with the sensitivity that human dignity requires' (Pope John Paul II, Address to Communications Specialists, Los Angeles, September 15, 1987).

Circulation, broadcast ratings and 'box office', along with market research, are sometimes said to be the best indicators of public sentiment – in fact, the only ones necessary for the law of the market to operate. No doubt the market's voice can be heard in these ways. But decisions about media content and policy should not be left only to the market and to economic factors – profits – since these cannot be counted on to safeguard either the public interest as a whole or, especially, the legitimate interests of minorities.

To some extent, this objection may be answered by the concept of the 'niche', according to which particular periodicals, programmes, stations and channels are directed to particular audiences. The approach is legitimate, up to a point. But diversification and specialisation – organising media to correspond to audiences broken down into ever-smaller units based largely on economic factors and patterns of consumption – should not be carried too far. Media of social communication must remain an 'Areopagus' (cf. *Redemptoris missio*, 37) – a forum for exchanging ideas and information, drawing individuals and groups together, fostering solidarity and peace. The Internet in particular raises concerns about some of the 'radically new consequences it brings: a loss of the intrinsic value of items of information, an undifferentiated uniformity in messages that are reduced to pure information, a lack of responsible feedback and a certain discouragement of interpersonal relationships' (*Toward a Pastoral Approach to Culture*, 9).

25. Professional communicators are not the only ones with ethical duties. Audiences – recipients – have obligations, too. Communicators attempting to meet their responsibilities deserve audiences conscientious about theirs.

The first duty of recipients of social communication is to be discerning and selective. They should inform themselves about media – their structures, mode of operation, contents – and make responsible choices, according to ethically sound criteria, about what to read or watch or listen to. Today everybody needs some form of continuing media education, whether by personal study or participation in an organised programme or both. More than just teaching about techniques, media education helps people form standards of good taste and truthful moral judgement, an aspect of conscience formation.

Through her schools and formation programmes the Church should provide media education of this kind (cf. *Aetatis novae*, 28; *Communio et progressio*, 107). Directed originally to institutes of consecrated life, the following words have a broader application: 'A community, aware of the influence of the media, should learn to use them for personal and community growth, with the evangelical clarity and inner freedom of those who have learned to know Christ (cf. *Gal* 4:17-23). The media propose, and often impose, a mentality and model of life in constant contrast with the Gospel. In this connection, in many areas one hears of the desire for deeper formation in receiving and using the media, both critically and fruitfully' (Congregation for Institutes of Consecrated Life and Societies of Apostolic Life, *Fraternal Life in Community*, 34).

Similarly, parents have a serious duty to help their children learn how to evaluate and use the media, by forming their consciences correctly and developing their critical faculties (cf. *Familiaris consortio*, 76). For their children's sake, as well as their own, parents must learn and practice the skills of discerning viewers and listeners and readers, acting as models of prudent use of media in the home. According to their age and circumstances, children and young people should be open to formation regarding media, resisting the easy path of uncritical passivity, peer pressure and commercial exploitation. Families – parents and children together – will find it helpful to come together in groups to study and discuss the problems and opportunities created by social communication.

26. Besides promoting media education, the institutions, agencies and programmes of the Church have other important responsibilities in regard to social communication. First and foremost, the Church's practice of communication should be exemplary, reflecting the highest standards of truthfulness, accountability, sensitivity to human rights and other relevant principles and norms. Beyond that, the Church's own media should be committed to communicating the fullness of the truth about the meaning of human life and history, especially as it is contained in God's revealed word and expressed by the teaching of the Magisterium. Pastors should encourage use of media to spread the Gospel (cf. *Code of Canon Law*, Canon 822.1).

Those who represent the Church must be honest and straightforward in their relations with journalists. Even though the questions they ask are 'sometimes embarrassing or disappointing, especially when they in no way correspond to the message we have to get across', one must bear in mind that 'these disconcerting questions are often asked by most of our contemporaries' (*Towards a Pastoral Approach to Culture*, 34). For the Church to speak credibly to people today, those who speak for her have to give credible, truthful answers to these seemingly awkward questions.

Catholics, like other citizens, have the right of free expression, including the right of access to the media for this purpose. The right of expression includes expressing opinions about the good of the Church, with due regard for the integrity of faith and morals, respect for the pastors and consideration for the common good and the dignity of persons (cf. Canon 212.3; Canon 227). No one, however, has a right to speak for the Church, or imply he or she does, unless properly designated; and personal opinions should not be presented as the Church's teaching (cf. Canon 227).

The Church would be well served if more of those who hold offices and perform functions in her name received communication training. This is true not only of seminarians, persons in formation in religious communities and young lay Catholics, but Church personnel generally. Provided the media are 'neutral, open and honest', they offer well-prepared Christians 'a frontline missionary role' and it is important that the latter be 'well-trained and supported'. Pastors also should offer their people guidance regarding media and their sometimes discordant and even destructive messages (cf. Canon 822.2, 3).

Similar considerations apply to internal communication in the Church. A two-way flow of information and views between pastors and faithful, freedom of expression sensitive to the well being of the community and to the role of the Magisterium in fostering it, and responsible public opinion all are important expressions of 'the fundamental right of dialogue and information within the Church' (*Aetatis novae*, 10; cf. *Communio et progressio*, 20).

The right of expression must be exercised with deference to revealed truth and the Church's teaching, and with respect for others' ecclesial rights (cf. Canon 212.1, 2, 3, Canon 220). Like other communities and institutions, the Church sometimes needs – in fact, is sometimes obliged – to practice secrecy and confidentiality. But this should not be for the sake of manipulation and control. Within the communion of faith, 'holders of office, who are invested with a sacred power, are, in fact, dedicated to promoting the interests of their brethren, so that all who belong to the People of God and are consequently endowed with true Christian dignity, may, through their free and well-ordered efforts toward a common good, attain to salvation' (*Lumen gentium*, 18). Right practice in communication is one of the ways of realising this vision.

Conclusion

27. As the third millennium of the Christian era begins, humankind is well along in creating a global network for the instantaneous transmission of information, ideas and value judgements in science, commerce, education, entertainment, politics, the arts, religion and every other field.

This network already is directly accessible to many people in their homes and schools and workplaces – indeed, wherever they may be. It is commonplace to view events, from sports to wars, happening in real time on the other side of the planet. People can tap directly into quantities of data beyond the reach of many scholars and students just a short time ago. An individual can ascend to heights of human genius and virtue, or plunge to the depths of human degradation, while sitting alone at a keyboard and screen. Communication technology constantly achieves new breakthroughs, with enormous potential for good and ill. As interactivity increases, the distinction between communicators and recipients blurs. Continuing research is needed into the impact, and especially the ethical implications, of new and emerging media.

28. But despite their immense power, the means of communication are, and will remain, only media – that is to say: instruments, tools, available for both good and evil uses. The choice is ours. The media do not call for a new ethic; they call for the application of established principles to new circumstances. And this is a task in which everyone has a role to play. Ethics in the media is not the business only of specialists, whether they be specialists in social communication or specialists in moral philosophy; rather, the reflection and dialogue that this document seeks to encourage and assist must be broad and inclusive.

29. Social communication can join people in communities of sympathy and shared interest. Will these communities be informed by justice, decency and respect for human rights; will they be committed to the common good? Or will they be selfish and inward-looking, committed to the benefit of particular groups – economic, racial, political, even religious – at others' expense? Will new technology serve all nations and peoples, while

respecting the cultural traditions of each; or will it be a tool to enrich the rich and empower the powerful? We have to choose.

The means of communication can also be used to separate and isolate. More and more, technology allows people to assemble packages of information and services uniquely designed for them. There are real advantages in that, but it raises an inescapable question: Will the audience of the future be a multitude of audiences of one? While the new technology can enhance individual autonomy, it has other, less desirable implications. Instead of being a global community, might the 'web' of the future turn out to be a vast, fragmented network of isolated individuals – human bees in their cells – interacting with data instead of with one another? What would become of solidarity – what would become of love – in a world like that?

In the best of circumstances, human communication has serious limitations, is more or less imperfect and in danger of failing. It is hard for people consistently to communicate honestly with one another, in a way that does no harm and serves the best interests of all. In the world of media, moreover, the inherent difficulties of communicating are often magnified by ideology, by the desire for profit and political control, by rivalries and conflicts between groups and by other social ills. Today's media vastly increase the outreach of social communication – its quantity, its speed; they do not make the reaching out of mind to mind and heart to heart any less fragile, less sensitive, less prone to fail.

30. As we have said, the special contributions which the Church brings to the discussion of these matters are a vision of human persons and their incomparable dignity and inviolable rights, and a vision of human community whose members are joined by the virtue of solidarity in pursuit of the common good of all. The need for these two visions is especially pressing 'at a time when we are faced with the patent inadequacy of perspectives in which the ephemeral is affirmed as a value and the possibility of discovering the real meaning of life is cast into doubt'; lacking them, 'many people stumble through life to the very edge of the abyss without knowing where they are going' (*Fides et ratio*, 6).

In the face of this crisis, the Church stands forth as an 'expert in humanity' whose expertise 'leads her necessarily to extend her religious mission to the various fields' of human endeavour (*Sollicitudo rei socialis*, 41; cf. Pope Paul VI, *Populorum progressio*, 13). She may not keep the truth about the human person and the human community to herself; she must share it freely, always aware that people can say no to the truth – and to her.

Attempting to foster and support high ethical standards in the use of the means of social communication, the Church seeks dialogue and collaboration with others: with public officials, who have a particular duty to protect and promote the common good of the political community; with men and women from the world of culture and the arts; with scholars and teachers engaged in forming the communicators and audiences of the future; with members of other churches and religious groups, who share her desire that media be used for the glory of God and the service of the human race (cf. Pontifical Council for Social Communications, *Criteria for Ecumenical and Inter-Religious Cooperation in Communications*); and especially with professional communicators – writers, editors, reporters, correspondents, performers, producers, technical personnel – together with owners, administrators and policy makers in this field.

31. Along with its limitations, human communication has in it something of God's creative activity. 'With loving regard, the divine Artist passes on to the human artist' – and, we might say, to the communicator as well – 'a spark of his own surpassing wisdom, calling him to share in his creative power'; in coming to understand this, artists and communicators 'come to a full understanding of themselves, their vocation and their mission' (*Letter to Artists*, 1).

The Christian communicator in particular has a prophetic task, a vocation: to speak out against the false gods and idols of the day – materialism, hedonism, consumerism, narrow nationalism, and the rest – holding up for all to see a body of moral truth based on human dignity and rights, the preferential option for the poor, the universal destination of goods, love of enemies and unconditional respect for all human life from conception to natural death; and seeking the more perfect realisation of the Kingdom in this world while remaining aware that, at the end of time, Jesus will restore all things and return them to the Father (cf. 1 Cor 15:24).

32. While these reflections are addressed to all persons of good will, not just Catholics, it is appropriate, in bringing them to a close, to speak of Jesus as a model for communicators. 'In these last days' God the Father 'has spoken to us by a Son' (Heb 1:2); and this Son communicates to us now and always the Father's love and the ultimate meaning of our lives.

'While he was on earth Christ revealed himself as the perfect communicator. Through his incarnation, he utterly identified himself with those who were to receive his communication, and he gave his message not only in words but in the whole manner of his life. He spoke from within, that is to say, from out of the press of his people. He preached the divine message without fear or compromise. He adjusted to his people's way of talking and to their patterns of thought. And he spoke out of the predicament of their time' (*Communio et progressio,* 11).

Throughout Jesus' public life crowds flocked to hear him preach and teach (cf. Mt 8:1, 18; Mk 2:2, 4:1; Lk 5:1, etc.), and he taught them 'as one who had authority' (Mt 7:29; cf. Mk 1:22; Lk 4:32). He told them about the Father and at the same time referred them to himself, explaining, 'I am the way, and the truth, and the life' (Jn 14:6) and 'he who has seen me has seen the Father' (Jn 14:9). He did not waste time on idle speech or on vindicating himself, not even when he was accused and condemned (cf. Mt 26:63, 27:12-14; Mk 15:5, 15:61). For his 'food' was to do the will of the Father who sent him (Jn 4:34), and all he said and did was spoken and done in reference to that.

Often Jesus' teaching took the form of parables and vivid stories expressing profound truths in simple, everyday terms. Not only his words but his deeds, especially his miracles, were acts of communication, pointing to his identity and manifesting the power of God (cf. *Evangelii nuntiandi*, 12). In his communications he showed respect for his listeners, sympathy for their situation and needs, compassion for their suffering (e.g., Lk 7:13), and resolute determination to tell them what they needed to hear, in a way that would command their attention and help them receive the message, without coercion or compromise, deception or manipulation. He invited others to open their minds and hearts to him, knowing this was how they would be drawn to him and his Father (e.g., Jn 3:1-15, 4:7-26).

Jesus taught that communication is a moral act: 'For out of the abundance of the heart the mouth speaks. The good man out of his good treasure brings forth good, and the evil man out of his evil treasure brings forth evil. I tell you, on the day of judgement men will render an account for every careless word they utter; for by your words you will be justified, and by your words you will be condemned' (Mt 12:34-37). He cautioned sternly against scandalising the 'little ones', and warned that for one who did, 'it would be better ... if a great millstone were hung round his neck and he were thrown into the sea' (Mk 9:42; cf. Mt 18:6, Lk 17:2). He was altogether candid, a man of whom it could be said that 'no guile was found on his lips'; and further: 'When he was reviled, he did not revile in return; when he suffered, he did not threaten; but he trusted to him who judges justly' (1 Pt 2:22-23). He insisted on candour and truthfulness in others, while condemning hypocrisy, dishonesty – any kind of communication that was bent and perverse: 'Let what you say be simply "Yes" or "No"; anything more than this comes from evil' (Mt 5:37).

33. Jesus is the model and the standard of our communicating. For those involved in social communication, whether as policy makers or professional communicators or recipients or in any other role, the conclusion is clear: 'Therefore, putting away falsehood, let every one speak the truth with his neighbour, for we are members one of another ... Let no evil talk come out of your mouths, but only such as is good for edifying, as fits the occasion, that it may impart grace to those who hear' (Eph 4:25, 29). Serving the human person, building up human community grounded in solidarity and justice and love, and speaking the truth about human life and its final fulfilment in God were, are, and will remain at the heart of ethics in the media.

Vatican City, 4 June 2000
World Communications Day, Jubilee of Journalists

✠ **John P. Foley**
President

✠ **Pierfranco Pastore**
Secretary

PONTIFICAL COUNCIL FOR SOCIAL COMMUNICATIONS

ETHICS IN INTERNET

28 FEBRUARY 2002

Introduction

1. 'Today's revolution in social communications involves a fundamental reshaping of the elements by which people comprehend the world about them, and verify and express what they comprehend. The constant availability of images and ideas, and their rapid transmission even from continent to continent, have profound consequences, both positive and negative, for the psychological, moral and social development of persons, the structure and functioning of societies, intercultural communications and the perception and transmission of values, world views, ideologies and religious beliefs'.[1]

The truth of these words has become clearer than ever during the past decade. Today it takes no great stretch of the imagination to envisage the earth as an interconnected globe humming with electronic transmissions – a chattering planet nestled in the provident silence of space. The ethical question is whether this is contributing to authentic human development and helping individuals and peoples to be true to their transcendent destiny.

And, of course, in many ways the answer is yes. The new media are powerful tools for education and cultural enrichment, for commercial activity and political participation, for intercultural dialogue and understanding; and, as we point out in the document that accompanies this one,[2] they also can serve the cause of religion. Yet this coin has another side. Media of communication that can be used for the good of persons and communities can be used to exploit, manipulate, dominate and corrupt.

2. The Internet is the latest and in many respects most powerful in a line of media – telegraph, telephone, radio, television – that for many people have progressively eliminated time and space as obstacles to communication during the last century and a half. It has enormous consequences for individuals, nations and the world.

In this document we wish to set out a Catholic view of the Internet, as a starting point for the Church's participation in dialogue with other sectors of society, especially other religious groups, concerning the development and use of this marvellous technological instrument. The Internet is being put to many good uses now, with the promise of many more, but much harm also can be done by its improper use. Which it will be, good or harm, is largely a matter of choice – a choice to whose making the Church brings two elements of great importance: her commitment to the dignity of the human person and her long tradition of moral wisdom.[3]

3. As with other media, the person and the community of persons are central to ethical evaluation of the Internet. In regard to the message communicated, the process of communicating, and structural and systemic issues in communication, 'the fundamental ethical principle is this: The human person and the human community are the end and measure of the use of the media of social communication; communication should be by persons to persons for the integral development of persons'.[4]

The common good – 'the sum total of social conditions which allow people, either as groups or as individuals, to reach their fulfilment more fully and more easily'[5] – provides a second basic principle for ethical evaluation of social communications. It should be understood inclusively, as the whole of those worthy purposes to which a community's members commit themselves together and which the community exists to realise and sustain. The good of individuals depends upon the common good of their communities.

The virtue disposing people to protect and promote the common good is solidarity. It is not a feeling of 'vague compassion or shallow distress' at other people's troubles, but 'a firm and persevering determination to commit oneself to the common good; that is to say to the good of all and of each individual, because we are all really responsible for all'.[6] Especially today solidarity has a clear, strong international dimension; it is correct to speak of, and obligatory to work for, the international common good.

4. The international common good, the virtue of solidarity, the revolution in communications media and information technology and the Internet are all relevant to the process of globalisation.

To a great extent, the new technology drives and supports globalisation, creating a situation in which 'commerce and communications are no longer bound by borders'.[7] This has immensely important consequences. Globalisation can increase wealth and foster development; it offers advantages like 'efficiency and increased production ... greater unity among peoples ... a better service to the human family'.[8] But the benefits have not been evenly shared up to now. Some individuals, commercial enterprises, and countries have grown enormously wealthy while others have fallen behind. Whole nations have been excluded almost entirely from the process, denied a place in the new world taking shape. 'Globalisation, which has profoundly transformed economic systems by creating unexpected possibilities of growth, has also resulted in many people being relegated to the side of the road: unemployment in the more developed countries and extreme poverty in too many countries of the southern hemisphere continue to hold millions of women and men back from progress and prosperity.'[9]

It is by no means clear that even societies that have entered into the globalisation process have done so entirely as a matter of free, informed choice. Instead, 'many people, especially the disadvantaged, experience this as something that has been forced upon them rather than as a process in which they can actively participate'.[10]

In many parts of the world, globalisation is spurring rapid, sweeping social change. This is not just an economic process but a cultural one, with both positive and negative aspects. 'Those who are subjected to it often see globalisation as a destructive flood threatening the social norms which had protected them and the cultural points of reference which had given them direction in life ... Changes in technology and work relationships are moving too quickly for cultures to respond.'[11]

5. One major consequence of the deregulation of recent years has been a shift of power from national states to transnational corporations. It is important that these corporations be encouraged and helped to use their power for the good of humanity; this points to a need for more communication and dialogue between them and concerned bodies like the Church.

Use of the new information technology and the Internet needs to be informed and guided by a resolute commitment to the practice of solidarity in the service of the common good, within and among nations. This technology can be a means for solving human problems, promoting the integral development of persons, creating a world governed by justice and peace and love. Now, even more than when the Pastoral Instruction on the Means of Social Communications *Communio et progressio* made the point more than thirty years ago, media have the ability to make every person everywhere 'a partner in the business of the human race'.[12]

This is an astonishing vision. The Internet can help make it real – for individuals, groups, nations and the human race – only if it is used in light of clear, sound ethical principles, especially the virtue of solidarity. To do so will be to everyone's advantage, for 'we know one thing today more than in the past: we will never be happy and at peace without one another, much less if some are against others'.[13] This will be an expression of that spirituality of communion which implies 'the ability to see what is positive in others, to welcome it and prize it as a gift from God', along with the ability to 'make room' for our brothers and sisters, bearing 'each other's burdens' (Gal 6:2) and resisting the 'selfish temptations which constantly beset us'.[14]

6. The spread of the Internet also raises a number of other ethical questions about matters like privacy, the security and confidentiality of data, copyright and intellectual property law, pornography, hate sites, the dissemination of rumour and character assassination under the guise of news, and much else. We shall speak briefly about some of these things below, while recognising that they call for continued analysis and discussion by

all concerned parties. Fundamentally, though, we do not view the Internet only as a source of problems; we see it as a source of benefits to the human race. But the benefits can be fully realised only if the problems are solved.

About the Internet

7. The Internet has a number of striking features. It is instantaneous, immediate, worldwide, decentralised, interactive, endlessly expandable in contents and outreach, flexible and adaptable to a remarkable degree. It is egalitarian, in the sense that anyone with the necessary equipment and modest technical skill can be an active presence in cyberspace, declare his or her message to the world, and demand a hearing. It allows individuals to indulge in anonymity, role-playing and fantasising and also to enter into community with others and engage in sharing. According to users' tastes, it lends itself equally well to active participation and to passive absorption into 'a narcissistic, self-referential world of stimuli with near-narcotic effects'.[15] It can be used to break down the isolation of individuals and groups or to deepen it.

8. The technological configuration underlying the Internet has a considerable bearing on its ethical aspects: people have tended to use it according to the way it was designed, and to design it to suit that kind of use. This 'new' system in fact dates back to the Cold War years of the 1960s, when it was intended to foil nuclear attack by creating a decentralised network of computers holding vital data. Decentralisation was the key to the scheme, since in this way, so it was reasoned, the loss of one or even many computers would not mean the loss of the data.

An idealistic vision of the free exchange of information and ideas has played a praiseworthy part in the development of the Internet. Yet its decentralised configuration and the similarly decentralised design of the World Wide Web of the late 1980s also proved to be congenial to a mindset opposed to anything smacking of legitimate regulation for public responsibility. An exaggerated individualism regarding the Internet thus emerged. Here, it was said, was a new realm, the marvellous land of cyberspace, where every sort of expression was allowed and the only law was total individual liberty to do as one pleased. Of course this meant that the only community whose rights and interests would be truly recognised in cyberspace was the community of radical libertarians. This way of thinking remains influential in some circles, supported by familiar libertarian arguments also used to defend pornography and violence in the media generally.[16]

Although radical individualists and entrepreneurs obviously are two very different groups, there is a convergence of interests between those who want the Internet to be a place for very nearly every kind of expression, no matter how vile and destructive, and those who want it to be a vehicle of untrammeled commercial activity on a neo-liberal model that 'considers profit and the law of the market as its only parameters, to the detriment of the dignity of and the respect due to individuals and peoples'.[17]

9. The explosion of information technology has increased the communication capabilities of some favoured individuals and groups many times over. The Internet can serve people in their responsible use of freedom and democracy, expand the range of choices available in diverse spheres of life, broaden educational and cultural horizons, break down divisions, promote human development in a multitude of ways. 'The free flow of images and speech on a global scale is transforming not only political and economic relations between peoples, but even our understanding of the world. It opens up a range of hitherto unthinkable possibilities'.[18] When based upon shared values rooted in the nature of the person, the intercultural dialogue made possible by the Internet and other media of social communication can be 'a privileged means for building the civilisation of love'.[19]

But that is not the whole story. 'Paradoxically, the very forces which can lead to better communication can also lead to increasing self-centeredness and alienation.'[20] The Internet can unite people, but it also can divide them, both as individuals and as mutually suspicious groups separated by ideology, politics, possessions, race and ethnicity, intergenerational differences and even religion. Already it has been used in aggressive ways, almost as a weapon of war, and people speak of the danger of 'cyber-terrorism'. It would be painfully ironic if this instrument of communication with so much potential for bringing people together reverted to its origins in the Cold War and became an arena of international conflict.

Some Areas of Concern

10. A number of concerns about the Internet are implicit in what has been said so far.

One of the most important of these involves what today is called the digital divide – a form of discrimination dividing the rich from the poor, both within and among nations, on the basis of access, or lack of access, to the new information technology. In this sense it is an updated version of an older gap between the 'information rich' and 'information poor'.

The expression 'digital divide' underlines the fact that individuals, groups and nations must have access to the new technology in order to share in the promised benefits of globalisation and development and not fall further behind. It is imperative 'that the gap between the beneficiaries of the new means of information and expression and those who do not have access to them ... not become another intractable source of inequity and discrimination'.[21] Ways need to be found to make the Internet accessible to less advantaged groups, either directly or at least by linking it with lower-cost traditional media. Cyberspace ought to be a resource of comprehensive information and services available without charge to all, and in a wide range of languages. Public institutions have a particular responsibility to establish and maintain sites of this kind.

As the new global economy takes shape, the Church is concerned 'that the winner in this process will be humanity as a whole' and not just 'a wealthy elite that controls science, technology and the planet's resources'; this is to say that the Church desires 'a globalisation which will be at the service of the whole person and of all people'.[22]

In this connection it should be borne in mind that the causes and consequences of the divide are not only economic but also technical, social and cultural. So, for example, another Internet 'divide' operates to the disadvantage of women, and it, too, needs to be closed.

11. We are particularly concerned about the cultural dimensions of what is now taking place. Precisely as powerful tools of the globalisation process, the new information technology and the Internet transmit and help instill a set of cultural values – ways of thinking about social relationships, family, religion, the human condition – whose novelty and glamour can challenge and overwhelm traditional cultures.

Intercultural dialogue and enrichment are of course highly desirable. Indeed, 'dialogue between cultures is especially needed today because of the impact of new communications technology on the lives of individuals and peoples'.[23] But this has to be a two-way street. Cultures have much to learn from one another, and merely imposing the world view, values and even language of one culture upon another is not dialogue but cultural imperialism.

Cultural domination is an especially serious problem when a dominant culture carries false values inimical to the true good of individuals and groups. As matters stand, the Internet, along with the other media of social communication, is transmitting the value-laden message of western secular culture to people and societies in many cases ill-prepared to evaluate and cope with it. Many serious problems result – for example, in regard to marriage and family life, which are experiencing 'a radical and widespread crisis'[24] in many parts of the world.

Cultural sensitivity and respect for other people's values and beliefs are imperative in these circumstances. Intercultural dialogue that 'protects the distinctiveness of cultures as historical and creative expressions of the underlying unity of the human family, and ... sustained understanding and communion between them'[25] is needed to build and maintain the sense of international solidarity.

12. The question of freedom of expression on the Internet is similarly complex and gives rise to another set of concerns.

We strongly support freedom of expression and the free exchange of ideas. Freedom to seek and know the truth is a fundamental human right[26] and freedom of expression is a cornerstone of democracy. 'Man, provided he respects the moral order and the common interest, is entitled to seek after truth, express and make known his opinions ... he ought to be truthfully informed about matters of public interest'.[27] And public opinion, 'an essential expression of human nature organised in society', absolutely requires 'freedom to express ideas and attitudes'.[28]

In light of these requirements of the common good, we deplore attempts by public authorities to block access to information – on the Internet or in other media of social communication – because they find it threatening or embarrassing to them, to manipulate the public by propaganda and disinformation, or to impede legitimate freedom of expression and opinion. Authoritarian regimes are by far the worst offenders in this regard; but the problem also exists in liberal democracies, where access to media for political expression often depends on wealth, and politicians and their advisors violate truthfulness and fairness by misrepresenting opponents and shrinking issues to sound-bite dimensions.

13. In this new environment, journalism is undergoing profound changes. The combination of new technologies and globalisation has 'increased the powers of the media, but has also made them more liable to ideological and commercial pressures',[29] and this is true of journalism as well.

The Internet is a highly effective instrument for bringing news and information rapidly to people. But the economic competitiveness and round-the-clock nature of Internet journalism also contribute to sensationalism and rumour-mongering, to a merging of news, advertising and entertainment and to an apparent decline in serious reporting and commentary. Honest journalism is essential to the common good of nations and the international community. Problems now visible in the practice of journalism on the Internet call for speedy correcting by journalists themselves.

The sheer overwhelming quantity of information on the Internet, much of it unevaluated as to accuracy and relevance, is a problem for many. But we also are concerned lest people make use of the medium's technological capacity for customising information simply to raise electronic barriers against unfamiliar ideas. That would be an unhealthy development in a pluralistic world where people need to grow in mutual understanding. While Internet users have a duty to be selective and self-disciplined, that should not be carried to the extreme of walling themselves off from others. The medium's implications for psychological development and health likewise need continued study, including the possibility that prolonged immersion in the virtual world of cyberspace may be damaging to some. Although there are many advantages in the capacity technology gives people to 'assemble packages of information and services uniquely designed for them', this also 'raises an inescapable question: Will the audience of the future be a multitude of audiences of one? ... What would become of solidarity – what would become of love – in a world like that?'[30]

14. Standing alongside issues that have to do with freedom of expression, the integrity and accuracy of news, and the sharing of ideas and information, is another set of concerns generated by libertarianism. The ideology of radical libertarianism is both mistaken and harmful – not least, to legitimate free expression in the service of truth. The error lies in exalting freedom 'to such an extent that it becomes an absolute, which would then be the source of values ... In this way the inescapable claims of truth disappear, yielding their place to a criterion of sincerity, authenticity and "being at peace with oneself".'[31] There is no room for authentic community, the common good and solidarity in this way of thinking.

Recommendations and Conclusion

15. As we have seen, the virtue of solidarity is the measure of the Internet's service of the common good. It is the common good that supplies the context for considering the ethical question: 'Are the media being used for good or evil?'[32]

Many individuals and groups share responsibility in this matter – for example, the transnational corporations of which we spoke above. All users of the Internet are obliged to use it in an informed, disciplined way, for morally good purposes; parents should guide and supervise children's use.[33] Schools and other educational institutions and programmes for children and adults should provide training in discerning use of the Internet as part of a comprehensive media education including not just training in technical skills – 'computer literacy' and the like – but a capacity for informed, discerning evaluation of content. Those whose decisions and actions contribute to shaping the structure and contents of the Internet have an especially serious duty to practice solidarity in the service of the common good.

16. Prior censorship by government should be avoided; 'censorship ... should only be used in the very last extremity.'[34] But the Internet is no more exempt than other media from reasonable laws against hate speech, libel, fraud, child pornography and pornography in general, and other offenses. Criminal behaviour in other contexts is criminal behaviour in cyberspace, and the civil authorities have a duty and a right to enforce such laws. New regulations also may be needed to deal with special 'Internet' crimes like the dissemination of computer viruses, the theft of personal data stored on hard disks, and the like.

Regulation of the Internet is desirable, and in principle industry self-regulation is best. 'The solution to problems arising from unregulated commercialisation and privatisation does not lie in state control of media but in more regulation according to criteria of public service and in greater public accountability.'[35] Industry codes of ethics can play a useful role, provided they are seriously intended, involve representatives of the public in their formulation and enforcement and, along with giving encouragement to responsible communicators, carry appropriate penalties for violations, including public censure.[36] Circumstances sometimes may require state intervention: for example, by setting up media advisory boards representing the range of opinion in the community.[37]

17. The Internet's transnational, boundary-bridging character and its role in globalisation require international cooperation in setting standards and establishing mechanisms to promote and protect the international common good.[38] In regard to media technology, as in regard to much else, 'there is a pressing need for equity at the international level'.[39] Determined action in the private and public sectors is needed to close and eventually eliminate the digital divide.

Many difficult Internet-related questions call for international consensus: for example, how to guarantee the privacy of law-abiding individuals and groups without keeping law enforcement and security officials from exercising surveillance over criminals and terrorists; how to protect copyright and intellectual property rights without limiting access to material in the public domain – and how to define the 'public domain' itself; how to establish and maintain broad-based Internet repositories of information freely available to all Internet users in a variety of languages; how to protect women's rights in regard to Internet access and other aspects of the new information technology. In particular, the question of how to close the digital divide between the information rich and the information poor requires urgent attention in its technical, educational and cultural aspects.

There is today a 'growing sense of international solidarity' that offers the United Nations system in particular 'a unique opportunity to contribute to the globalisation of solidarity by serving as a meeting place for states and civil society and as a convergence of the varied interests and needs ... Cooperation between international agencies and non-governmental organisations will help to ensure that the interests of states – legitimate though they may be – and of the different groups within them, will not be invoked or defended at the expense of the interests or rights of other peoples, especially the less fortunate'.[40] In this connection we hope that the World Summit of the Information Society scheduled to take place in 2003 will make a positive contribution to the discussion of these matters.

18. As we pointed out above, a companion document to this one called *The Church and Internet* speaks specifically about the Church's use of the Internet and the Internet's role in the life of the Church. Here we wish only to emphasise that the Catholic Church, along with other religious bodies, should have a visible, active presence on the Internet and be a partner in the public dialogue about its development. 'The Church does not presume to dictate these decisions and choices, but it does seek to be of help by indicating ethical and moral criteria which are relevant to the process – criteria which are to be found in both human and Christian values.'[41]

The Internet can make an enormously valuable contribution to human life. It can foster prosperity and peace, intellectual and aesthetic growth, mutual understanding among peoples and nations on a global scale.

It also can help men and women in their age-old search for self-understanding. In every age, including our own, people ask the same fundamental questions: 'Who am I? Where have I come from and where am I going? Why is there evil? What is there after this life?' [42] The Church cannot impose answers, but she can – and must – proclaim to the world the answers she has received; and today, as always, she offers the one ultimately satisfying answer to the deepest questions of life – Jesus Christ, who 'fully reveals man to himself and brings to light his most high calling'.[43] Like today's world itself, the world of media, including the Internet, has been brought by Christ, inchoately yet truly, within the boundaries of the Kingdom of God and placed in service to the word of salvation. Yet 'far from diminishing our concern to develop this earth, the expectancy of a new earth should spur us on, for it is here that the body of a new human family grows, foreshadowing in some way the age which is to come'.[44]

Vatican City, 22 February 2002
Feast of the Chair of St Peter the Apostle

✠ **John P. Foley**
President

✠ **Pierfranco Pastore**
Secretary

Notes

1. Pontifical Council for Social Communications, Pastoral Instruction *Aetatis novae* on Social Communications on the twentieth anniversary of *Communio et progressio*, n. 4.
2. Pontifical Council for Social Communications, *The Church and Internet*.
3. Cf. Pontifical Council for Social Communications, *Ethics in Communications*, n. 5.
4. Ibid., n. 21.
5. Vatican Council II, *Gaudium et spes*, n. 26; cf. *Catechism of the Catholic Church*, n. 1906.

6. John Paul II, *Sollicitudo rei socialis*, n. 38.
7. John Paul II, Address to the Pontifical Academy of Social Sciences, n. 2, April 27, 2001.
8. John Paul II, Post-Synodal Apostolic Exhortation *Ecclesia in America*, n. 20.
9. John Paul II, Address to the Diplomatic Corps Accredited to the Holy See, n. 3, January 10, 2000.
10. Address to the Pontifical Academy of Social Sciences, n. 2.
11. Ibid., n. 3.
12. Pontifical Commission for Social Communications, Pastoral Instruction on the Means of Social Communication, *Communio et progressio*, n. 19.
13. Address to the Diplomatic Corps, n. 4.
14. John Paul II, Apostolic Letter *Novo millennio ineunte*, n. 43.
15. *Ethics in Communications*, n. 2.
16. Pontifical Council for Social Communications, *Pornography and Violence in the Communications Media: A Pastoral Response*, n. 20.
17. *Ecclesia in America*, n. 56.
18. Message for the Celebration of the World Day of Peace 2001, n. 11.
19. Ibid., n. 16.
20. John Paul II, Message for the 33rd World Communications Day, n. 4, January 24, 1999.
21. John Paul II, Message for the 31st World Day of Communications, 1997.
22. Address to the Pontifical Academy of Social Sciences, n. 5.
23. Ibid., n. 11.
24. *Novo millennio ineunte*, n. 47.
25. Message for the World Day of Peace 2001, n. 10.
26. John Paul II, *Centesimus annus*, n. 47.
27. *Gaudium et spes*, n. 59.
28. *Communio et progressio*, n. 25, 26.
29. John Paul II, Address to the Jubilee of Journalists, n. 2, June 4, 2000.
30. *Ethics in Communications*, n. 29.
31. John Paul II, *Veritatis splendor*, n. 32.
32. *Ethics in Communications*, n. 1.
33. Cf. John Paul II, Post-Synodal Apostolic Exhortation *Familiaris consortio*, n. 76.
34. *Communio et progressio*, n. 86.
35. *Aetatis Novae*, n. 5.
36. Cf. *Communio et progressio*, n. 79.
37. Ibid., n. 88.

38. Cf. Address to the Pontifical Academy of Social Sciences, n. 2.
39. *Ethics in Communications*, n. 22.
40. John Paul II, Address to the UN Secretary General and to the Administrative Committee on Coordination of the United Nations, n. 2, 3, April 7, 2000.
41. *Aetatis novae*, n. 12.
42. John Paul II, Encyclical Letter *Fides et ratio*, n. 1.
43. *Gaudium et spes*, n. 22.
44. Ibid., n. 39.

PONTIFICAL COUNCIL FOR SOCIAL COMMUNICATIONS

THE CHURCH AND INTERNET

28 FEBRUARY 2002

Introduction

1. The Church's interest in the Internet is a particular expression of her longstanding interest in the media of social communication. Seeing the media as an outcome of the historical scientific process by which humankind 'advances further and further in the discovery of the resources and values contained in the whole of creation',[1] the Church often has declared her conviction that they are, in the words of the Second Vatican Council, 'marvellous technical inventions'[2] that already do much to meet human needs and may yet do even more.

Thus the Church has taken a fundamentally positive approach to the media.[3] Even when condemning serious abuses, documents of this Pontifical Council for Social Communications have been at pains to make it clear that 'a merely censorious attitude on the part of the Church ... is neither sufficient nor appropriate'.[4]

Quoting Pope Pius XII's 1957 encyclical letter *Miranda prorsus*, the Pastoral Instruction on the Means of Social Communication Communio et progressio, published in 1971, underlined that point: 'The Church sees these media as "gifts of God" which, in accordance with his providential design, unite men in brotherhood and so help them to cooperate with his plan for their salvation.'[5] This remains our view, and it is the view we take of the Internet.

2. As the Church understands it, the history of human communication is something like a long journey, bringing humanity 'from the pride-driven project of Babel and the collapse

into confusion and mutual incomprehension to which it gave rise (cf. Gen 11:1-9), to Pentecost and the gift of tongues: a restoration of communication, centred on Jesus, through the action of the Holy Spirit'.[6] In the life, death and resurrection of Christ, 'communication among men found its highest ideal and supreme example in God who had become man and brother'.[7]

The modern media of social communication are cultural factors that play a role in this story. As the Second Vatican Council remarks, 'although we must be careful to distinguish earthly progress clearly from the increase of the Kingdom of Christ', nevertheless 'such progress is of vital concern to the Kingdom of God, insofar as it can contribute to the better ordering of human society'.[8] Considering the media of social communication in this light, we see that they 'contribute greatly to the enlargement and enrichment of men's minds and to the propagation and consolidation of the Kingdom of God'.[9]

Today this applies in a special way to the Internet, which is helping bring about revolutionary changes in commerce, education, politics, journalism, the relationship of nation to nation and culture to culture – changes not just in how people communicate but in how they understand their lives. In a companion document, *Ethics in Internet*, we discuss these matters in their ethical dimension.[10] Here we consider the Internet's implications for religion and especially for the Catholic Church.

3. The Church has a two-fold aim in regard to the media. One aspect is to encourage their right development and right use for the sake of human development, justice and peace – for the upbuilding of society at the local, national and community levels in light of the common good and in a spirit of solidarity. Considering the great importance of social communications, the Church seeks 'honest and respectful dialogue with those responsible for the communications media' – a dialogue that relates primarily to the shaping of media policy.[11] 'On the Church's side this dialogue involves efforts to understand the media – their purposes, procedures, forms and genres, internal structures and modalities – and to offer support and encouragement to those involved in media work. On the basis of this sympathetic understanding and support, it becomes possible

to offer meaningful proposals for removing obstacles to human progress and the proclamation of the Gospel.'[12]

But the Church's concern also relates to communication in and by the Church herself. Such communication is more than just an exercise in technique, for it 'finds its starting point in the communion of love among the divine Persons and their communication with us', and in the realisation that Trinitarian communication 'reaches out to humankind: The Son is the Word, eternally "spoken" by the Father; and in and through Jesus Christ, Son and Word made flesh, God communicates himself and his salvation to women and men'.[13]

God continues to communicate with humanity through the Church, the bearer and custodian of his revelation, to whose living teaching office alone he has entrusted the task of authentically interpreting his word.[14] Moreover, the Church herself is a *communio*, a communion of persons and eucharistic communities arising from and mirroring the communion of the Trinity;[15] communication therefore is of the essence of the Church. This, more than any other reason, is why 'the Church's practice of communication should be exemplary, reflecting the highest standards of truthfulness, accountability, sensitivity to human rights and other relevant principles and norms'.[16]

4. Three decades ago *Communio et progressio* pointed out that 'modern media offer new ways of confronting people with the message of the Gospel'.[17] Pope Paul VI said the Church 'would feel guilty before the Lord' if it failed to use the media for evangelisation.[18] Pope John Paul II has called the media 'the first Areopagus of the modern age', and declared that 'it is not enough to use the media simply to spread the Christian message and the Church's authentic teaching. It is also necessary to integrate that message into the "new culture" created by modern communications'.[19] Doing that is all the more important today, since not only do the media now strongly influence what people think about life but also to a great extent 'human experience itself is an experience of media'.[20]

All this applies to the Internet. And even though the world of social communications 'may at times seem at odds with the Christian message, it also offers unique opportunities for proclaiming the saving truth of Christ to the whole human family. Consider ... the positive capacities of the Internet to carry religious information and teaching beyond all barriers and frontiers. Such a wide audience would have been beyond the wildest imaginings of those who preached the Gospel before us ... Catholics should not be afraid to throw open the doors of social communications to Christ, so that his Good News may be heard from the housetops of the world'.[21]

Opportunities and Challenges

5. 'Communication in and by the Church is essentially communication of the Good News of Jesus Christ. It is the proclamation of the Gospel as a prophetic, liberating word to the men and women of our times; it is testimony, in the face of radical secularisation, to divine truth and to the transcendent destiny of the human person; it is witness given in solidarity with all believers against conflict and division, to justice and communion among peoples, nations and cultures.'[22]

Since announcing the Good News to people formed by a media culture requires taking carefully into account the special characteristics of the media themselves, the Church now needs to understand the Internet. This is necessary in order to communicate effectively with people – especially young people – who are steeped in the experience of this new technology, and also in order to use it well.

The media offer important benefits and advantages from a religious perspective: 'They carry news and information about religious events, ideas and personalities; they serve as vehicles for evangelisation and catechesis. Day in and day out, they provide inspiration, encouragement and opportunities for worship to persons confined to their homes or to institutions.'[23] But over and above these, there are also benefits more or less peculiar to the Internet. It offers people direct and immediate access to important religious and spiritual resources – great libraries and museums and places of worship, the teaching documents of the Magisterium, the writings of the Fathers and Doctors of the Church and the religious wisdom of the ages. It has a remarkable capacity to overcome distance and isolation, bringing people into contact with like-minded persons of good will who join in virtual communities of faith to encourage and support one another. The Church can perform an important service to Catholics and non-Catholics alike by the selection and transmission of useful data in this medium.

The Internet is relevant to many activities and programmes of the Church – evangelisation, including both re-evangelisation and new evangelisation and the traditional missionary work *ad gentes*, catechesis and other kinds of education, news and information, apologetics, governance and administration and some forms of pastoral counselling and spiritual direction. Although the virtual reality of cyberspace cannot substitute for real interpersonal community, the incarnational reality of the sacraments and the liturgy, or the immediate and direct proclamation of the Gospel, it can complement them, attract people to a fuller experience of the life of faith and enrich the religious lives of users. It also provides the Church with a means for communicating with particular groups – young people and young adults, the elderly and home-bound, persons living in remote areas, the members of other religious bodies – who otherwise may be difficult to reach.

A growing number of parishes, dioceses, religious congregations and church-related institutions, programmes and organisations of all kinds now make effective use of the Internet for these and other purposes. Creative projects under Church sponsorship exist in some places on the national and regional levels. The Holy See has been active in this area for several years and is continuing to expand and develop its Internet presence. Church-related groups that have not yet taken steps to enter cyberspace are encouraged to look into the possibility of doing so at an early date. We strongly recommend the exchange of ideas and information about the Internet among those with experience in the field and those who are newcomers.

6. The Church also needs to understand and use the Internet as a tool of internal communications. This requires keeping clearly in view its special character as a direct, immediate, interactive and participatory medium.

Already, the two-way interactivity of the Internet is blurring the old distinction between those who communicate and those who receive what is communicated,[24] and creating a situation in which, potentially at least, everyone can do both. This is not the one-way, top-down communication of the past. As more and more people become familiar with this characteristic of the Internet in other areas of their lives, they can be expected also to look for it in regard to religion and the Church.

The technology is new, but the idea is not. Vatican Council II said members of the Church should disclose to their pastors 'their needs and desires with that liberty and confidence which befits children of God and brothers of Christ'; in fact, according to knowledge, competence, or position, the faithful are not only able but sometimes obliged 'to manifest their opinion on those things which pertain to the good of the Church'.[25] *Communio et progressio* remarked that as a 'living body' the Church 'needs public opinion in order to sustain a giving and taking among her members'.[26] Although truths of faith 'do not leave room for arbitrary interpretations', the pastoral instruction noted 'an enormous area where members of the Church can express their views'.[27]

Similar ideas are expressed in the Code of Canon Law[28] as well as in more recent documents of the Pontifical Council for Social Communications.[29] *Aetatis novae* calls two-way communication and public opinion 'one of the ways of realising in a concrete manner the Church's character as *communio*'.[30] *Ethics in Communications* says: 'A two-way flow of information and views between pastors and faithful, freedom of expression sensitive to the well being of the community and to the role of the Magisterium in fostering it, and responsible public opinion are all important expressions of "the fundamental right of dialogue and information within the Church".'[31] The Internet provides an effective technological means of realising this vision.

Here, then, is an instrument that can be put creatively to use for various aspects of administration and governance. Along with opening up channels for the expression of public opinion, we have in mind such things as consulting experts, preparing meetings and practising collaboration in and among particular churches and religious institutes on local, national and international levels.

7. Education and training are another area of opportunity and need. 'Today everybody needs some form of continuing media education, whether by personal study or participation in an organised programme or both. More than just teaching about techniques, media education helps people form standards of good taste and truthful moral judgement, an aspect of conscience formation. Through her schools and formation programmes the Church should provide media education of this kind.'[32]

Education and training regarding the Internet ought to be part of comprehensive programmes of media education available to members of the Church. As much as possible, pastoral planning for social communications should make provision for this training in the formation of seminarians, priests, religious and lay pastoral personnel as well as teachers, parents and students.[33]

Young people in particular need to be taught 'not only to be good Christians when they are recipients but also to be active in using all the aids to communication that lie within the media ... So, young people will be true citizens of that age of social communications which has already begun'[34] – an age in which media are seen to be 'part of a still unfolding culture whose full implications are as yet imperfectly understood'.[35] Teaching about the Internet and the new technology thus involves much more than teaching techniques; young people need to learn how to function well in the world of cyberspace, make discerning judgements according to sound moral criteria about what they find there, and use the new technology for their integral development and the benefit of others.

8. The Internet also presents some special problems for the Church, over and above those of a general nature discussed in *Ethics in Internet*, the document accompanying this one.[36] While emphasising what is positive about the Internet, it is important to be clear about what is not.

At a very deep level, 'the world of the media can sometimes seem indifferent and even hostile to Christian faith and morality. This is partly because media culture is so deeply imbued with a typically postmodern sense that the only absolute truth is that there are no absolute truths or that, if there were, they would be inaccessible to human reason and therefore irrelevant'.[37]

Among the specific problems presented by the Internet is the presence of hate sites devoted to defaming and attacking religious and ethnic groups. Some of these target the Catholic Church. Like pornography and violence in the media, Internet hate sites are 'reflections of the dark side of a human nature marred by sin'.[38] And while respect for free expression may require tolerating even voices of hatred up to a point, industry self-regulation – and, where required, intervention by public authority – should establish and enforce reasonable limits to what can be said.

The proliferation of web sites calling themselves Catholic creates a problem of a different sort. As we have said, church-related groups should be creatively present on the Internet; and well-motivated, well-informed individuals and unofficial groups acting on their own initiative are entitled to be there as well. But it is confusing, to say the least, not to distinguish eccentric doctrinal interpretations, idiosyncratic devotional practices and ideological advocacy bearing a 'Catholic' label from the authentic positions of the Church. We suggest an approach to this issue below.

9. Certain other matters still require much reflection. Regarding these, we urge continued research and study, including 'the development of an anthropology and a theology of communication'[39] – now, with specific reference to the Internet. Along with study and research, of course, positive pastoral planning for the use of the Internet can and should go forward.[40]

One area for research concerns the suggestion that the wide range of choices regarding consumer products and services available on the Internet may have a spillover effect in regard to religion and encourage a 'consumer' approach to matters of faith. Data suggest that some visitors to religious web sites may be on a sort of shopping spree, picking and choosing elements of customised religious packages to suit their personal tastes. The 'tendency on the part of some Catholics to be selective in their adherence' to the Church's teaching is a recognised problem in other contexts;[41] more information is needed about whether and to what extent the problem is exacerbated by the Internet.

Similarly, as noted above, the virtual reality of cyberspace has some worrisome implications for religion as well as for other areas of life. Virtual reality is no substitute for the Real Presence of Christ in the Eucharist, the sacramental reality of the other sacraments and shared worship in a flesh-and-blood human community. There are no sacraments on the Internet; and even the religious experiences possible there by the grace of God are insufficient apart from real-world interaction with other persons of faith. Here is another aspect of the Internet that calls for study and reflection. At the same time, pastoral planning should consider how to lead people from cyberspace to true community and how, through teaching and catechesis, the Internet might subsequently be used to sustain and enrich them in their Christian commitment.

Recommendations and Conclusion

10. Religious people, as concerned members of the larger Internet audience who also have legitimate particular interests of their own, wish to be part of the process that guides the future development of this new medium. It goes without saying that this will sometimes require them to adjust their own thinking and practice.

It is important, too, that people at all levels of the Church use the Internet creatively to meet their responsibilities and help fulfil the Church's mission. Hanging back timidly from fear of technology or for some other reason is not acceptable, in view of the very many positive possibilities of the Internet. 'Methods of facilitating communication and dialogue among her own members can strengthen the bonds of unity between them. Immediate access to information makes it possible for [the Church] to deepen her dialogue with the contemporary world ... The Church can more readily inform the world of her beliefs and explain the reasons for her stance on any given issue or event. She can hear more clearly the voice of public opinion and enter into a continuous discussion with the world around her, thus involving herself more immediately in the common search for solutions to humanity's many pressing problems.'[42]

11. In concluding these reflections, therefore, we offer words of encouragement to several groups in particular – Church leaders, pastoral personnel, educators, parents and especially young people.

To Church leaders. People in leadership positions in all sectors of the Church need to understand the media, apply this understanding in formulating pastoral plans for social communications[43] together with concrete policies and programmes in this area and make appropriate use of media. Where necessary, they should receive media education themselves; in fact, 'the Church would be well served if more of those who hold offices and perform functions in her name received communication training'.[44]

This applies to the Internet as well as to the older media. Church leaders are obliged to use 'the full potential of the "computer age" to serve the human and transcendent vocation of every person, and thus to give glory to the Father from whom all good things come'.[45] They ought to employ this remarkable technology in many different aspects of the Church's mission, while also exploring opportunities for ecumenical and interreligious cooperation in its use.

A special aspect of the Internet, as we have seen, concerns the sometimes confusing proliferation of unofficial web sites labelled 'Catholic'. A system of voluntary certification at the local and national levels under the supervision of representatives of the Magisterium might be helpful in regard to material of a specifically doctrinal or catechetical nature. The idea is not to impose censorship but to offer Internet users a reliable guide to what expresses the authentic position of the Church.

To pastoral personnel. Priests, deacons, religious and lay pastoral workers should have media education to increase their understanding of the impact of social communications on individuals and society and help them acquire a manner of communicating that speaks to the sensibilities and interests of people in a media culture. Today this clearly includes training regarding the Internet, including how to use it in their work. They can also profit from websites offering theological updating and pastoral suggestions.

As for Church personnel directly involved in media, it hardly needs saying that they must have professional training. But they also need doctrinal and spiritual formation, since 'in order to witness to Christ it is necessary to encounter him oneself and foster a personal relationship with him through prayer, the

Eucharist and sacramental reconciliation, reading and reflection on God's word, the study of Christian doctrine and service to others'.[46]

To educators and catechists. The Pastoral Instruction *Communio et progressio* spoke of the 'urgent duty' of Catholic schools to train communicators and recipients of social communications in relevant Christian principles.[47] The same message has been repeated many times. In the age of the Internet, with its enormous outreach and impact, the need is more urgent than ever.

Catholic universities, colleges, schools and educational programmes at all levels should provide courses for various groups – 'seminarians, priests, religious brothers and sisters and lay leaders ... teachers, parents and students'[48] – as well as more advanced training in communications technology, management, ethics and policy issues for individuals preparing for professional media work or decision-making roles, including those who work in social communications for the Church. Furthermore, we commend the issues and questions mentioned above to the attention of scholars and researchers in relevant disciplines in Catholic institutions of higher learning.

To parents. For the sake of their children, as well as for their own sakes, parents must 'learn and practice the skills of discerning viewers and listeners and readers, acting as models of prudent use of media in the home'.[49] As far as the Internet is concerned, children and young people are often more familiar with it than their parents are, but parents still are seriously obliged to guide and supervise their children in its use.[50] If this means learning more about the Internet than they have up to now, that will be all to good.

Parental supervision should include making sure that filtering technology is used in computers available to children when that is financially and technically feasible, in order to protect them as much as possible from pornography, sexual predators and other threats. Unsupervised exposure to the Internet should not be allowed. Parents and children should dialogue together about what is seen and experienced in cyberspace; sharing with other families who have the same values and concerns will also be helpful. The fundamental parental duty here is to help children become discriminating, responsible Internet users and not addicts of the Internet, neglecting contact with their peers and with nature itself.

To children and young people. The Internet is a door opening on a glamorous and exciting world with a powerful formative influence; but not everything on the other side of the door is safe and wholesome and true. 'Children and young people should be open to formation regarding media, resisting the easy path of uncritical passivity, peer pressure and commercial exploitation.'[51] The young owe it to themselves – and to their parents and families and friends, their pastors and teachers, and ultimately to God – to use the Internet well.

The Internet places in the grasp of young people at an unusually early age an immense capacity for doing good and doing harm, to themselves and others. It can enrich their lives beyond the dreams of earlier generations and empower them to enrich others' lives in turn. It also can plunge them into consumerism, pornographic and violent fantasy and pathological isolation.

Young people, as has often been said, are the future of society and the Church. Good use of the Internet can help prepare them for their responsibilities in both. But this will not happen automatically. The Internet is not merely a medium of entertainment and consumer gratification. It is a tool for accomplishing useful work, and the young must learn to see it and use it as such. In cyberspace, at least as much as anywhere else, they may be called on to go against the tide, practice counter-culturalism, even suffer persecution for the sake of what is true and good.

12. *To all persons of good will.* Finally, then, we would suggest some virtues that need to be cultivated by everyone who wants to make good use of the Internet; their exercise should be based upon and guided by a realistic appraisal of its contents.

Prudence is necessary in order to see clearly the implications – the potential for good and evil – in this new medium and to respond creatively to its challenges and opportunities.

Justice is needed, especially justice in working to close the digital divide – the gap between the information–rich and the information–poor in today's world.[52] This requires a commitment to the international common good, no less than the 'globalisation of solidarity'.[53]

Fortitude, courage, is necessary. This means standing up for truth in the face of religious and moral relativism, for altruism and generosity in the face of individualistic consumerism, for decency in the face of sensuality and sin.

And temperance is needed – a self-disciplined approach to this remarkable technological instrument, the Internet, so as to use it wisely and only for good.

Reflecting on the Internet, as upon all the other media of social communications, we recall that Christ is 'the perfect communicator'[54] – the norm and model of the Church's approach to communication, as well as the content that the Church is obliged to communicate. 'May Catholics involved in the world of social communications preach the truth of Jesus ever more boldly from the housetops, so that all men and women may hear about the love which is the heart of God's self-communication in Jesus Christ, the same yesterday, and today, and for ever.'[55]

Vatican City, 22 February 2002
Feast of the Chair of St Peter the Apostle

✠ **John P. Foley**
President

✠ **Pierfranco Pastore**
Secretary

Notes

1. John Paul II, encyclical letter *Laborem exercens*, n. 25; cf. Vatican Council II, Pastoral Constitution on the Church in the Modern World *Gaudium et spes*, n. 34.
2. Vatican Council II, Decree on the Means of Social Communication *Inter mirifica*, n. 1.
3. For example, *Inter mirifica*; the Messages of Pope Paul VI and Pope John Paul II on the occasion of the World Communication Days; Pontifical Council for Social Communications, Pastoral Instruction *Communio et progressio*, *Pornography and Violence in the*

Communications Media: A Pastoral Response, Pastoral Instruction *Aetatis novae*, *Ethics in Advertising*, *Ethics in Communications*.

4. *Pornography and Violence in the Communications Media*, n. 30.
5. *Communio et progressio*, n. 2.
6. John Paul II, Message for the 34th World Communications Day, June 4, 2000.
7. *Communio et progressio*, n. 10.
8. Vatican Council II, Pastoral Constitution on the Church in the Modern World *Gaudium et spes*, 39.
9. *Inter Mirifica*, 2.
10. Pontifical Council for Social Communications, *Ethics in Internet*.
11. *Aetatis novae*, 8.
12. Ibid.
13. *Ethics in Communications*, n. 3.
14. Cf. Vatican Council II, Dogmatic Constitution on Divine Revelation *Dei verbum*, n. 10.
15. *Aetatis novae*, n. 10.
16. *Ethics in Communications*, n. 26.
17. *Communio et progressio*, 128.
18. Apostolic Exhortation *Evangelii nuntiandi*, n. 45.
19. Encyclical *Redemptoris missio*, n. 37.
20. *Aetatis novae*, n. 2.
21. John Paul II, Message for the 35th World Communications Day, n. 3, May 27, 2001.
22. *Aetatis novae*, n. 9.
23. *Ethics in Communications*, n. 11.
24. Cf. *Communio et progressio*, n. 15.
25. Dogmatic Constitution on the Church *Lumen Gentium*, n. 37.
26. *Communio et progressio*, n. 116.
27. Ibid., n. 117.
28. Cf. Canon 212.2, 212.3.
29. Cf. *Aetatis novae*, n. 10; *Ethics in Communications*, n. 26.
30. *Aetatis novae*, n. 10.
31. *Ethics in Communications*, n. 26.
32. Ibid., n. 25.
33. *Aetatis novae*, n. 28.
34. *Communio et progressio*, n. 107.
35. John Paul II, Message for the 24th World Communications Day, 1990.
36. Cf. *Ethics in Internet*.
37. John Paul II, Message for the 35th World Communications Day, n. 3.
38. *Pornography and Violence in the Communications Media*, n. 7.

39. *Aetatis novae*, 8.
40. Cf. John Paul II, Apostolic Letter *Novo millennio Ineunte*, n. 39.
41. Cf. John Paul II, Address to the Bishops of the United States, n. 5, Los Angeles, September 16, 1987.
42. John Paul II, Message for the 24th World Communications Day, 1990.
43. Cf. *Aetatis novae*, nn. 23-33.
44. *Ethics in Communications*, n. 26.
45. Message for the 24th World Communications Day, 1999.
46. Message for the 34th World Communications Day, 2000.
47. *Communio et progressio*, n. 107.
48. *Aetatis novae*, n. 28.
49. *Ethics in Communications*, n. 25.
50. Cf. John Paul II, Post-Synodal Apostolic Exhortation *Familiaris Consortio*, n. 76.
51. *Ethics in Communications*, n. 25.
52. Cf. *Ethics in Internet*, nn. 10, 17.
53. John Paul II, Address to the UN Secretary General and to the Administrative Committee on Coordination of the United Nations, n. 2, April 7, 2000.
54. *Communio et progressio*, n. 11.
55. Message for the 35th World Communications Day, n. 4.

APOSTOLIC LETTER
OF THE HOLY FATHER
JOHN PAUL II
THE RAPID DEVELOPMENT

TO THOSE RESPONSIBLE FOR COMMUNICATIONS

24 JANUARY 2005

1. The rapid development of technology in the area of the media is surely one of the signs of progress in today's society. In view of these innovations in continuous evolution, the words found in the Decree of the Second Vatican Ecumenical Council, *Inter mirifica*, promulgated by my venerable predecessor, the servant of God Paul VI, December 4, 1963, appear even more pertinent: 'Man's genius has with God's help produced marvellous technical inventions from creation, especially in our times. The Church, our mother, is particularly interested in those which directly touch man's spirit and which have opened up new avenues of easy communication of all kinds of news, of ideas and orientations.'[1]

Fruitful Progress in the Wake of the Decree *Inter mirifica*

2. More than forty years after the publication of that document, it appears appropriate to reflect on the 'challenges' which the communications media constitute for the Church, which Paul VI said 'would feel guilty before the Lord if she did not utilise these powerful means'.[2] In fact, the Church is not only called upon to use the mass media to spread the Gospel but, today more than ever, to integrate the message of salvation into the 'new culture' that these powerful means of communication create and amplify. It tells us that the use of the techniques and the technologies of contemporary communications is an integral part of its mission in the third millennium.

Moved by this awareness, the Christian community has taken significant steps in the use of the means of communication for religious information, for evangelization and catechesis, for the formation of pastoral workers in this area and for the education to a mature responsibility of the users and the recipients of the various communications media.

3. Many challenges face the new evangelization in a world rich with communicative potential like our own. Because of this, I wanted to underline in the encyclical *Redemptoris missio* that the first Areopagus of modern times is the world of communications, which is capable of unifying humanity and transforming it into – as it is commonly referred to – 'a global village'. The communications media have acquired such importance as to be the principal means of guidance and inspiration for many people in their personal, familial and social behaviour. We are dealing with a complex problem, because the culture itself, prescinding from its content, arises from the very existence of new ways to communicate with hitherto unknown techniques and vocabulary.

Ours is an age of global communication in which countless moments of human existence are either spent with, or at least confronted by, the different processes of the mass media. I limit myself to mentioning the formation of personality and conscience, the interpretation and structuring of affective relationships, the coming together of the educative and formative phases, the elaboration and diffusion of cultural phenomena and the development of social, political and economic life.

The mass media can and must promote justice and solidarity according to an organic and correct vision of human development, by reporting events accurately and truthfully, analysing situations and problems completely and providing a forum for different opinions. An authentically ethical approach to using the powerful communication media must be situated within the context of a mature exercise of freedom and responsibility, founded upon the supreme criteria of truth and justice.

Gospel Reflection and Missionary Commitment

4. The world of mass media also has need of Christ's redemption. To analyse with the eyes of faith the processes and value of communications, the deeper appreciation of sacred scripture can undoubtedly help as a 'great code' of

communication of a message which is not ephemeral, but fundamental for its saving value.

Salvation history recounts and documents the communication of God with man, a communication which uses all forms and ways of communicating. The human being is created in the image and likeness of God in order to embrace divine revelation and to enter into loving dialogue with him. Because of sin, this capacity for dialogue at both the personal and social level has been altered and humanity has had to suffer, and will continue to suffer, the bitter experience of incomprehension and separation. God, however, did not abandon the human race, but sent his own son (Cf. Mk 12:1-11). In the word made flesh communication itself takes on its most profound saving meaning: thus, in the Holy Spirit, the human being is given the capacity to receive salvation and to proclaim and give witness to it before the world.

5. The communication between God and humanity has thus reached its perfection in the Word made flesh. The act of love by which God reveals himself, united to the response of faith by humanity, generates a fruitful dialogue. Precisely for this reason, making our own in a certain sense the request of the disciples, 'teach us to pray' (Lk 11:1), we can ask the Lord to help us to understand how to communicate with God and with other human beings through the marvellous communications media. In light of so decisive and definitive a communication, the media provide a providential opportunity to reach people everywhere, overcoming barriers of time, of space and of language; presenting the content of faith in the most varied ways imaginable; and offering to all who search the possibility of entering into dialogue with the mystery of God, revealed fully in Christ Jesus.

The incarnate word has left us an example of how to communicate with the Father and with humanity, whether in moments of silence and recollection, or in preaching in every place and in every way. He explains the scriptures, expresses himself in parables, dialogues within the intimacy of the home, speaks in the squares, along the streets, on the shores of the lake and on the mountaintops. The personal encounter with him does not leave one indifferent, but stimulates imitation: 'What I say to you in the darkness, speak in the light; what you hear whispered, proclaim on the housetops' (Mt 10:27).

There is, however, a culminating moment in which communication becomes full communion: the Eucharistic encounter. By recognising Jesus in the 'breaking of the bread,' (cf. Lk 24:30-31), believers feel themselves urged on to announce his death and resurrection, and to become joyful and courageous witnesses of his kingdom (cf. Lk 24:35).

6. Thanks to the redemption, the communicative capacity of believers is healed and renewed. The encounter with Christ makes them new creatures and permits them to become part of that people which he, dying on the cross, has won through his blood, and introduces them into the intimate life of the Trinity, which is continuous and circular communication of perfect and infinite love among the Father, the Son and the Holy Spirit.

Communication permeates the essential dimensions of the Church which is called to announce to all the joyful message of salvation. For this reason, the Church takes advantage of the opportunities offered by the communications media as pathways providentially given by God to intensify communion and to render more penetrating the proclamation of His word.[3] The media permit the manifestation of the universal character of the people of God, favouring a more intense and immediate exchange among local Churches and nourishing mutual awareness and cooperation.

We give thanks to God for the presence of these powerful media which, if used by believers with the genius of faith and in docility to the light of the Holy Spirit, can facilitate the communication of the Gospel and render the bonds of communion among ecclesial communities more effective.

A Change of Mentality and Pastoral Renewal

7. In the communications media the Church finds a precious aid for spreading the Gospel and religious values, for promoting dialogue, ecumenical and inter-religious cooperation and also for defending those solid principles which are indispensable for building a society which respects the dignity of the human person and is attentive to the common good. The Church willingly

employs these media to furnish information about itself and to expand the boundaries of evangelization, of catechesis and of formation, considering their use as a response to the command of the Lord: 'Go into the whole world and proclaim the gospel to every creature' (Mk 16:15).

This is certainly not an easy mission in an age such as ours, in which there exists the conviction that the time of certainties is irretrievably past. Many people, in fact, believe that humanity must learn to live in a climate governed by an absence of meaning, by the provisional and by the fleeting.[4] In this context, the communications media can be used 'to proclaim the Gospel or to reduce it to silence within men's hearts'.[5] This poses a serious challenge for believers, especially for parents, families and all those responsible for the formation of children and young people. Those individuals in the Church community particularly gifted with talent to work in the media should be encouraged with pastoral prudence and wisdom, so that they may become professionals capable of dialoguing with the vast world of the mass media.

8. The appreciation of the media is not reserved only to those already adept in the field, but to the entire Church community. If, as has already been noted, the communications media take into account different aspects of the expression of faith, Christians must take into account the media culture in which they live: from the liturgy, the fullest and fundamental expression of communication with God and with one another, to catechesis, which cannot prescind from the fact of being directed to people immersed in the language and the culture of the day.

The current phenomenon of communications impels the Church towards a sort of pastoral and cultural revision, so as to deal adequately with the times in which we live. Pastors, above all, must assume this responsibility. Everything possible must be done so that the Gospel might permeate society, stimulating people to listen to and embrace its message.[6] Consecrated persons belonging to institutions having the charism of using the mass media have a particular responsibility in this regard. Spiritually and professionally formed towards this end, these institutions, 'should willingly lend their help, wherever pastorally appropriate

[...] in order to offset the inappropriate use of the media and to promote higher quality programmes, the contents of which will be respectful of the moral law and rich in human and Christian values'.[7]

9. Such is the importance of the mass media that fifteen years ago I considered it inopportune to leave their use completely up to the initiatives of individuals or small groups, and suggested that they be decisively inserted into pastoral programmes.[8] New technologies, in particular, create further opportunities for communication understood as a service to the pastoral government and organisation of the different tasks of the Christian community. One clear example today is how the internet not only provides resources for more information, but habituates persons to interactive communication.[9] Many Christians are already creatively using this instrument, exploring its potential to assist in the tasks of evangelization and education, as well as of internal communication, administration and governance. However, alongside the internet, other new means of communication, as well as traditional ones, should be used. Daily and weekly newspapers, publications of all types and Catholic television and radio still remain highly useful means within a complete panorama of Church communications.

While the content being communicated must obviously be adapted to the needs of different groups, the goal must always be to make people aware of the ethical and moral dimension of the information.[10] In the same way, it is important to assure that media professionals receive the necessary formation and pastoral attention to confront the particular tensions and ethical dilemmas that arise in their daily work. Often these men and women 'sincerely desire to know and practice what is ethically and morally just,' and look to the Church for guidance and support.[11]

The Mass Media, the Crossroads of the Great Social Questions

10. The Church, which in light of the message of salvation entrusted to it by the Lord is also a teacher of humanity, recognises the duty to offer its own contribution for a better understanding of outlooks and responsibilities connected with

current developments in communications. Especially because these influence the consciences of individuals, form their mentality and determine their view of things, it is important to stress in a forceful and clear way that the mass media constitute a patrimony to safeguard and promote. The communications media must enter into the framework of organically structured rights and duties, be it from the point of view of formation and ethical responsibility, or from reference to laws and institutional codes.

The positive development of the media at the service of the common good is a responsibility of each and every one.[12] Because of the close connections the media have with economics, politics and culture, there is required a management system capable of safeguarding the centrality and dignity of the person, the primacy of the family as the basic unit of society and the proper relationship among them.

11. We are faced with three fundamental options: formation, participation and dialogue.

In the first place, a vast work of formation is needed to assure that the mass media be known and used intelligently and appropriately. The new vocabulary they introduce into society modifies both learning processes and the quality of human relations, so that, without proper formation, these media run the risk of manipulating and heavily conditioning, rather than serving people. This is especially true for young people, who show a natural propensity towards technological innovations and as such are in even greater need of education in the responsible and critical use of the media.

In the second place, I would like to recall our attention to the subject of media access and of co-responsible participation in their administration. If the communications media are a good destined for all humanity, then ever-new means must be found – including recourse to opportune legislative measures – to make possible a true participation in their management by all. The culture of co-responsibility must be nurtured.

Finally, there cannot be forgotten the great possibilities of mass media in promoting dialogue, becoming vehicles for reciprocal knowledge, of solidarity and of peace. They become a powerful resource for good if used to foster understanding between peoples; a destructive 'weapon' if used to foster injustice and conflicts. My venerable predecessor, Blessed John XXIII, already prophetically warned humanity of such potential risks in the Encyclical, *Pacem in terris*.[13]

12. The reflection upon the role 'of public opinion in the Church,' and 'of the Church in public opinion' aroused great interest. In a meeting with the editors of Catholic publications, my venerable predecessor, Pius XII, stated that something would be missing from the life of the Church were it not for public opinion. This same idea has since been repeated on other occasions,[14] and in *The Code of Canon Law* there is recognised, under certain conditions, the right to the expression of one's own opinion.[15] While it is true that the truths of the faith are not open to arbitrary interpretations, and that respect for the rights of others places intrinsic limits upon the expression of one's judgements, it is no less true that there is still room among Catholics for an exchange of opinions in a dialogue which is respectful of justice and prudence.

Communication both within the Church community and between the Church and the world at large requires openness and a new approach towards facing questions regarding the world of media. This communication must tend towards a constructive dialogue, so as to promote a correctly-informed and discerning public opinion within the Christian community. The Church, like other institutions and groups, has the need and the right to make its activities known. However, when circumstances require, it must be able to guarantee an adequate confidentiality, without thereby prejudicing a timely and sufficient communication about Church events. This is one of the areas in which collaboration between the lay faithful and pastors is most needed, as the council appropriately emphasised, 'A great many wonderful things are to be hoped for from this familiar dialogue between the laity and their spiritual leaders: in the laity a strengthened sense of personal responsibility; a renewed enthusiasm; a more ready application of their talents to the projects of their spiritual leaders. The latter, on the other hand, aided by the experience of the laity, can more clearly and more incisively come to decisions regarding both spiritual and temporal matters. In this way, the whole Church, strengthened by each one of its members, may more effectively fulfil its mission for the life of the world.'[16]

To Communicate with the Power of the Holy Spirit

13. The great challenge of our time for believers and for all people of good will is that of maintaining truthful and free communication which will help consolidate integral progress in the world. Everyone should know how to foster an attentive discernment and constant vigilance, developing a healthy critical capacity regarding the persuasive force of the communications media.

Also in this field, believers in Christ know that they can count upon the help of the Holy Spirit. Such help is all the more necessary when one considers how greatly the obstacles intrinsic to communication can be increased by ideologies, by the desire for profit or for power and by rivalries and conflicts between individuals and groups, and also because of human weakness and social troubles. The modern technologies increase to a remarkable extent the speed, quantity and accessibility of communication, but they above all do not favour that delicate exchange which takes place between mind and mind, between heart and heart and which should characterise any communication at the service of solidarity and love.

Throughout the history of salvation, Christ presents himself to us as the 'communicator' of the Father: 'God, in these last days, has spoken to us through his Son' (Heb 1:2). The eternal word made flesh, in communicating himself, always shows respect for those who listen, teaches understanding of their situation and needs, is moved to compassion for their suffering and to a resolute determination to say to them only what they need to hear without imposition or compromise, deceit or manipulation. Jesus teaches that communication is a moral act, 'A good person brings forth good out of a store of goodness, but an evil person brings forth evil out of a store of evil. I tell you, on the Day of Judgement people will render an account for every careless word they speak. By your words you will be acquitted, and by your words you will be condemned' (Mt 12: 35-37).

14. The apostle Paul has a clear message for those engaged in communications (politicians, professional communicators,

spectators), 'Therefore, putting away falsehood, speak the truth, each one to his neighbour, for we are members one of another ... No foul language should come out of your mouths, but only such as is good for needed edification, that it may impart grace to those who hear' (Eph 4:25; 29).

To those working in communication, especially to believers involved in this important field of society, I extend the invitation which, from the beginning of my ministry as Pastor of the Universal Church, I have wished to express to the entire world 'Do not be afraid!'

Do not be afraid of new technologies! These rank 'among the marvellous things' – *Inter mirifica* – which God has placed at our disposal to discover, to use and to make known the truth, also the truth about our dignity and about our destiny as his children, heirs of his eternal kingdom.

Do not be afraid of being opposed by the world! Jesus has assured us, 'I have conquered the world!' (Jn 16:33)

Do not be afraid even of your own weakness and inadequacy! The Divine Master has said, 'I am with you always, until the end of the world' (Mt 28:20). Communicate the message of Christ's hope, grace and love, keeping always alive, in this passing world, the eternal perspective of heaven, a perspective which no communications medium can ever directly communicate, 'What eye has not seen, and ear has not heard, and what has not entered the human heart, what God has prepared for those who love him' (1 Cor 2:9).

To Mary, who gave us the word of life, and who kept his unchanging words in her heart, do I entrust the journey of the Church in today's world. May the Blessed Virgin help us to communicate by every means the beauty and joy of life in Christ our Saviour.

To all I give my apostolic blessing!

From the Vatican, 24 January 2005, the Feast of St Francis de Sales, Patron Saint of Journalists

IOANNES PAULUS II

Notes

1. No. 1.
2. Apostolic Exhortation *Evangelio nuntiandi* (8 December 1975): AAS 68 (1976), 45.

3. Cf. John Paul II, Apostolic Exhortation *Christifideles laici* (30 December 1988), 18–24: AAS 81 (1989), 421–435; cf. Pontifical Council for Social Communications, Pastoral Instructive *Aetatis novae* (22 February 1992), 10: AAS 84 (1992), 454–455.
4. Cf. John Paul II, Encyclical Letter *Fides et ratio* (14 September 1998), 91: AAS 91 (1999), 76–77.
5. cf. Pontifical Council for Social Communications, Pastoral Instructive *Aetatis novae* (22 February 1992), 4: AAS 84 (1992), 450.
6. Cf. John Paul II, Post-Synodal Apostolic Exhortation, *Pastores Gregis*, 30: *L'Osservatore Romano*, 17 October 2003, p. 6.
7. John Paul II, Post-Synodal Apostolic Exhortation, *Vita Consecrata* (March 25 th , 1996), 99: AAS 88 (1996), 476.
8. Cf. John Paul II, Encyclical Letter, *Redemptoris missio* (7 December 1990), 37: AAS 83 (1991), 282–286.
9. Cf. Pontifical Council for Social Communications, *The Church and Internet* (22 February 2002), 6: Vatican City, 2002, p. 13–15.
10. Cf. Second Vatican Ecumenical Council, *Inter mirifica*, 15–16; Pontifical Council for Social Communications, Pastoral Instructional *Communio et progressio* (23 May 1971), 107: AAS 63 (1971), 631–632; Pontifical Council for Social Communications, Pastoral Instructional *Aetatis novae* (22 February 1992), 18: AAS 84 (1992), 460.
11. Cf. Ibid., 19: l.c.
12. Cf. The *Catechism of the Catholic Church*, num. 2494.
13. Cf. John Paul II, Message for the 37th World Communications Day (24 January 2003): *L'Osservatore Romano*, 25 January 2003, p. 6.
14. Cf. Second Vatican Ecumenical Council, *Lumen gentium*, 37; Pontifical Council for Social Communications, Pastoral Instruction *Communio et progressio* (23 May 1971), 114–117: AAS 63 (1971), 634–635.
15. Can. 212, §3: According to the knowledge, competence and prestige which they possess, they have the right and even at times the duty to manifest to the sacred pastors their opinion on matters which pertain to the good of the Church and to make their opinion known to the rest of the Christian faithful, without prejudice to the integrity of faith and morals, with reverence toward their pastors and attentive to common advantage and the dignity of persons.
16. Second Vatican Ecumenical Council, *Lumen gentium*, 37.

Unofficial translation of the Pontifical Council